The Dark Web Decoded: Understanding Cyber Threats and Mastering Online Safety

A Comprehensive Guide from Beginner to Expert on Understanding, Navigating, and Securing the Dark Web

Andrew N. Gonzalez

Preface

Welcome to *The Dark Web Decoded: Understanding Cyber Threats and Mastering Online Safety*. Whether you're just beginning to explore the world of the dark web or you're already a seasoned cybersecurity professional, this book is designed to guide you through the complexities of navigating and securing your digital presence in this often misunderstood and enigmatic corner of the internet.

The dark web has been a subject of intrigue and concern for many. On one hand, it's a space used by individuals seeking privacy and anonymity—journalists, activists, whistleblowers, and those living under oppressive regimes. On the other hand, it's also a haven for cybercriminals, hosting illicit activities ranging from the sale of stolen data to illegal substances and even human trafficking. This duality of purpose makes the dark web both fascinating and dangerous, which is why understanding it thoroughly is crucial in today's interconnected world.

Why This Book?

As a cybersecurity professional with years of experience in the field, I've seen the growing importance of understanding the dark web—not only from the perspective of investigating cybercrime but also from the standpoint of **online safety**. Our personal and professional lives are increasingly intertwined with the digital world, and as much as we depend on the internet for convenience, it's also a place where we're vulnerable to various threats. **Cybercrime** is evolving, and the dark web is central to many of these emerging threats.

However, it's not all doom and gloom. While there are significant risks, there are also solutions and strategies that can help us protect ourselves, our businesses, and our organizations. This book aims to **decode** the dark web, break down the complex concepts associated with it, and equip you with the knowledge to both understand and mitigate the risks it poses.

In the following chapters, you will learn:

- The **basics of the dark web**—what it is, how it works, and how it differs from the surface web and deep web.
- How to **navigate the dark web safely**, using the right tools and maintaining privacy while avoiding the risks of cyber threats.
- How to **identify and protect yourself from common cyber threats** such as malware, ransomware, phishing, and scams, which are prevalent on dark web marketplaces.
- The **ethical and legal considerations** when investigating or engaging with the dark web, and how to operate within the boundaries of the law.
- How **businesses** and **individuals** can implement proactive security measures to defend against dark web threats.

A Word on the Approach

This book is structured to be practical and engaging, guiding you step-by-step through each critical aspect of the dark web and cybersecurity. While I provide technical insights where appropriate, my goal is to keep things **relatable** and **accessible**, regardless of your level of expertise.

You'll find practical tips, real-world case studies, and expert opinions sprinkled throughout the chapters, designed to make complex ideas easier to grasp. For those of you who are more hands-on learners, there are also references to tools and resources that you can start using immediately to enhance your understanding and improve your security posture.

Why You Should Care About Cybersecurity

It's easy to think that cybercrime is something that happens to other people, or that it's a concern for **big corporations** and **government agencies**. But in reality, **every one of us** is at risk. Whether you're an individual browsing the internet or a small business owner, you're exposed to cyber threats daily. The dark web isn't just a far-off, distant issue; it's closer than you think, and understanding its dangers is crucial in safeguarding your digital life.

As you move through this book, I hope you'll feel empowered to take charge of your online safety and security. Cybersecurity isn't something that should only concern professionals—it's a **mindset** that anyone using the internet should adopt. After all, **we all have something worth protecting**.

Looking Ahead

By the end of this book, you'll have a solid foundation in both understanding the **dark web** and implementing the necessary safety measures to protect yourself online. This book is just the beginning of your journey into **cybersecurity**. As technology continues to evolve, so too must our approach to staying safe in an increasingly connected world.

I encourage you to continue learning and adapting as the threat landscape shifts. Cybersecurity isn't a one-time fix; it's an ongoing process, and the more you engage with it, the more capable you'll be at defending yourself and others from digital threats.

Let's get started on this journey to decode the dark web and master online safety!

Table of Contents

Part 1: Introduction to the Dark Web

Chapter 1: What is the Dark Web?

The internet is a vast, ever-expanding network that connects billions of people worldwide, allowing us to search for information, connect with others, shop, and so much more. But did you know that only a small portion of this digital space is visible to most users? The rest, hidden beneath the surface, forms part of what we call the **deep web** and **dark web**. In this chapter, we'll explore what the dark web really is, how it differs from the surface web and deep web, and address some of the most common misconceptions about this hidden part of the internet.

1.1: Definition and Structure of the Dark Web

The **dark web** is often misunderstood. Many people associate it exclusively with illegal activity, but it is so much more than that. In this section, we will break down the structure of the dark web, how it operates, and its distinct place in the overall digital ecosystem.

Let's begin with the basics: understanding **what** the dark web is and **how** it functions in a way that differs from the regular internet we access every day.

What is the Dark Web?

At its core, the dark web is a part of the **internet that is intentionally hidden** from the general public. It is a subset of the **deep web**, which itself comprises all the web content not indexed by standard search engines like Google. Unlike the deep web, however, the dark web is specifically designed to offer **anonymity and privacy**, making it more difficult to trace users and their activities.

Here's an analogy to simplify it:

Think of the **surface web** as the tip of an iceberg—public and accessible. The **deep web** is like the part of the iceberg submerged beneath the water, filled with content that's not visible to the average user, such as password-protected accounts or private databases. Now, the **dark web** is like the deep, hidden, and shadowy portion of the iceberg—the part that is intentionally difficult to access and often used to host websites that require extra privacy.

How Does the Dark Web Work?

The key to the dark web is its **anonymity**. Unlike the surface web, which relies on standard browsers (like Chrome or Safari) to access websites, the dark web requires **specialized software** to ensure privacy and secure communication.

The most common tool used to access the dark web is **Tor (The Onion Router)**. Let's break down how Tor works:

1. **Layered Encryption**: When you access a website through Tor, your data passes through a network of volunteer-operated servers. Each server adds an extra layer of encryption, much like the layers of an onion (hence the name **"Onion Routing"**). As the data is routed through multiple layers, it becomes increasingly difficult to trace back to the source.
2. **Tor Network**: The Tor network is a decentralized network of thousands of nodes (servers) that relay your internet traffic. Each time your data is passed from node to node, it is decrypted one layer at a time, with each node only knowing the previous and next stop. This multi-layer encryption ensures that even if one node is compromised, the entire connection remains secure.
3. **.onion Websites**: Websites hosted on the dark web use **.onion** domain names instead of the usual .com or .org. These .onion sites are not indexed by traditional search engines like Google. Instead, they can only be accessed via the Tor browser. The anonymity provided by the Tor network ensures that both the user and the website are difficult to trace.

Structure of the Dark Web

To understand the **structure** of the dark web, it's important to think of it in layers. Let's break it down:

1. **Layer 1: The Surface Web**
   o   This is the visible part of the internet, easily accessible using any standard browser. Websites like Google, Facebook, Amazon, and Wikipedia fall under this category.
2. **Layer 2: The Deep Web**
   o   This is the part of the internet that is hidden from traditional search engines. It includes things like private email accounts, online banking, academic databases, and encrypted communication systems. Although it is not indexed by search engines, it is mostly harmless and contains much of the internet's essential infrastructure.
3. **Layer 3: The Dark Web**
   o   The dark web sits at the bottom of this hierarchy, intentionally hidden and requiring specialized tools to access. It is not indexed by search engines, and sites on the dark web use the .onion extension, which is not recognized by traditional browsers. The content here can range from forums and blogs dedicated to anonymity and privacy, to illicit activities such as black markets or hacking forums.

How to Access the Dark Web: A Practical Guide

While accessing the dark web is easy, it requires specific steps and precautions. Here's a **step-by-step guide** on how to set up and use the Tor browser to access dark web websites securely:

1. **Go to the official Tor website** (*https://www.torproject.org/*) and download the Tor Browser for your operating system (Windows, macOS, or Linux).
2. Once downloaded, follow the installation instructions. It's similar to installing any other software on your computer.

Step 2: Set Up the Tor Browser

1. After installation, open the Tor browser. You will be prompted with two options: "Connect" or "Configure."
2. If you are in a region where Tor is blocked, you might need to use the "Configure" option to set up additional security measures like bridges or pluggable transports.
3. Click "Connect" to launch the browser.

Step 3: Browse the Dark Web

1. Once connected, you can start browsing .onion websites.
2. To find .onion sites, you can use **dark web search engines** like DuckDuckGo, NotEvil, or Ahmia, which index .onion domains.
3. For example, to visit a site, type its **.onion address** directly into the Tor browser's address bar (e.g., *http://3g2upl4pq6kufc4m.onion*).

Visual Aid: Structure of the Dark Web

Below is a simple illustration to help visualize the structure of the dark web:

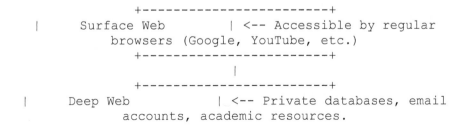

```
            +------------------------+
   |     Surface Web       | <-- Accessible by regular
           browsers (Google, YouTube, etc.)
            +------------------------+
                       |
            +------------------------+
   |     Deep Web           | <-- Private databases, email
            accounts, academic resources.
```

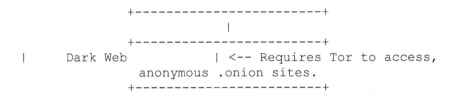

```
                    +------------------------+
                              |
                    +------------------------+
     |       Dark Web         | <-- Requires Tor to access,
                       anonymous .onion sites.
                    +------------------------+
```

Case Study: Secure Communications in Oppressive

Regimes

In many countries where internet usage is highly censored or monitored, the dark web provides a **safe space** for individuals to communicate anonymously. Let's look at the **case of journalists** in countries with heavy surveillance.

Case Study: Journalists in Syria

- In war-torn regions like Syria, journalists face severe risks when reporting on government activities. Many use the dark web, particularly Tor, to communicate with sources, share reports, and even access information without fear of surveillance.
- The **Anonymous Sudan group** even used the dark web to publish reports and documents that were censored in their home countries, allowing for an unfiltered flow of information.

Real-World Applications and Use Cases

While the dark web is often portrayed negatively, it has significant **legitimate uses**. Here are some examples of how it is used in the real world:

1. **Whistleblowing**: Platforms like **SecureDrop** allow whistleblowers to submit documents and communicate securely with journalists without revealing their identity.

2. **Free Speech**: In countries with restricted access to free speech, the dark web offers a platform for individuals to express dissenting views anonymously. Websites dedicated to political discourse or human rights advocacy thrive in these regions.
3. **Privacy-Focused Communication**: Individuals who prioritize their privacy, such as activists or political dissidents, turn to the dark web for encrypted communication.

The dark web may seem like a mysterious and dangerous part of the internet, but it is a tool with a dual purpose: **anonymity and privacy**. Its structure—built on layers of encryption and a decentralized network—makes it an essential resource for those seeking online security and protection from surveillance. However, as with any powerful tool, it requires responsibility and awareness.

1.2: Difference Between the Dark Web, Deep Web, and Surface Web

To understand the internet's structure, it's crucial to know that what we commonly access—the websites, blogs, and social media platforms—make up only a small fraction of the vast digital space that exists online. This space is divided into three major categories: the **Surface Web**, the **Deep Web**, and the **Dark Web**.

Each part of the web serves a different purpose and operates under different levels of visibility and accessibility. In this section, we'll dissect the key differences between these three layers, their functions, and provide practical examples and visual aids to enhance your understanding.

---

1. Surface Web: The Visible Internet

The **Surface Web** is the most familiar part of the internet. It is what we interact with every day when we open our browsers and search for something on Google or log into social media platforms like Facebook or Twitter.

What is the Surface Web?

The Surface Web refers to all the websites that are indexed by traditional search engines such as Google, Bing, and Yahoo. These are the sites that you can access by typing their domain names or clicking on search engine links. Essentially, the **Surface Web** is what most of us consider "the internet."

Characteristics of the Surface Web:

- **Indexed by Search Engines**: Websites here are indexed by traditional search engines and can be easily found using a Google search or other search engines.
- **Public Accessibility**: Anyone with internet access can browse these sites.
- **Common Sites**: Social media platforms (Facebook, Instagram), e-commerce sites (Amazon, eBay), news outlets (CNN, BBC), and forums (Reddit, StackOverflow).

Example:

When you search "how to make pasta" on Google, the search results page consists of links to recipe websites, food blogs, and cooking tutorials—all accessible with a click.

2. Deep Web: The Hidden Internet

The **Deep Web** represents a vast portion of the internet that is not indexed by standard search engines. It is much larger than the Surface Web and consists of websites and databases that require specific access credentials, often behind paywalls or protected by passwords. While the Deep Web is sometimes confused with the Dark Web, they are very different.

The Deep Web is a collection of content that is **invisible to traditional search engines**. This can include personal email accounts, private cloud storage, subscription-based databases, or intranet systems of companies.

Characteristics of the Deep Web:

- **Not Indexed by Search Engines**: Websites in the Deep Web don't show up in search results because they require special access (such as passwords, user IDs, or encryption).
- **Personal and Private**: Much of the Deep Web contains personal information, protected content, and secure communications.
- **Examples**:
    - **Email Accounts**: Gmail, Outlook, and Yahoo email inboxes are part of the Deep Web.
    - **Private Databases**: Corporate databases, medical records, and academic research repositories.
    - **Cloud Storage**: Google Drive, Dropbox, and iCloud files are part of the Deep Web as they require authentication.
    - **Password-Protected Websites**: Any website that requires login credentials to access, such as banking accounts or private forums.

Practical Example:

If you log into your personal Google account and access Gmail or Google Drive, those pages are part of the Deep Web. They're private and can't be found through regular search engines.

---

3. Dark Web: The Hidden and Anonymized Internet

The **Dark Web** is a specific subset of the Deep Web, and it's designed to allow users to operate anonymously, without the fear of surveillance. Unlike the Deep Web, the Dark Web is intentionally hidden and requires special software (such as the **Tor browser**) to access.

What is the Dark Web?

The Dark Web is intentionally hidden from search engines and is used by individuals seeking **complete anonymity**. Sites on the Dark Web typically use the **.onion** extension, making them untraceable by traditional browsers like Chrome or Firefox.

Characteristics of the Dark Web:

- **Anonymity and Encryption**: The Dark Web is designed to protect the identities of both users and websites. It uses **onion routing**, which encrypts the data multiple times as it passes through various nodes.
- **.onion Domain Names**: Websites on the Dark Web use the `.onion` extension, which can only be accessed through specialized software like Tor.
- **Illegal and Legal Activities**: While much of the Dark Web is associated with illegal activities (such as illegal markets, hacking, and other illicit services), it also hosts legitimate uses such as anonymous communication, privacy protection, and free speech.

Examples of Dark Web Usage:

- **Whistleblowing Platforms**: Websites like **SecureDrop** allow whistleblowers to anonymously share sensitive information with journalists.
- **Cryptocurrency Markets**: The Dark Web is home to cryptocurrency-based markets like Silk Road (now defunct), where illicit goods were once bought and sold.
- **Dark Web Forums**: Forums dedicated to discussions about hacking, privacy protection, and cybercrime.

Practical Example:

To access the Dark Web, you would typically need the **Tor browser**. After downloading and installing Tor, you can visit .onion sites, which could include anything from encrypted communication tools to hidden marketplaces.

Visual Aid: Breakdown of the Three Web Layers

Below is a flowchart that visually represents the differences between the Surface Web, Deep Web, and Dark Web. This will help you understand their relative positions and how they interconnect:

```
              +---------------------------+
|            Surface Web          |        <-- Easily accessible
             via regular browsers (Google, Facebook)
              +---------------------------+
                            |
              +---------------------------+
|             Deep Web            |        <-- Requires login
         credentials, protected databases (email, cloud)
              +---------------------------+
                            |
              +---------------------------+
|             Dark Web            |        <-- Hidden, requires
             Tor or similar browsers, .onion websites
              +---------------------------+
```

4. Practical Implementations: Accessing Each Layer

Let's look at practical examples of how to access and navigate each layer of the web:

1. Surface Web:

Simply open any web browser (Google Chrome, Safari, Firefox) and use a search engine like Google to find websites. For example:

- Search: "Best Italian Pasta Recipes"
- Access: Websites like **AllRecipes.com**, **BBC Good Food**, or **YouTube**.

2. Deep Web:

The Deep Web requires authentication to access. Here's how to navigate:

- **Example 1**: Log into your **email** account (Gmail, Outlook).
- **Example 2**: Access your **cloud storage** (Google Drive, Dropbox).
- **Example 3**: Visit a **private academic database** (like JSTOR or PubMed) via your university credentials.

3. Dark Web:

To access the Dark Web, you need to:

1. **Download the Tor Browser** from *TorProject.org.*
2. **Install and Configure Tor** for secure browsing.
3. **Browse .onion sites** such as *DuckDuckGo's Tor version* to start your journey.

Case Study: Tor and Its Role in Privacy

To help contextualize the Dark Web, let's look at a **real-world application** of the Tor browser and its benefits in promoting privacy:

Case Study: Political Dissidents in Authoritarian Countries

- In countries where the internet is heavily censored (like China or Iran), the **Tor network** has become a lifeline for individuals seeking to **express dissent** without being tracked by the government. Dissidents use the Tor network to bypass firewalls and censorship, accessing information and communicating anonymously.

Understanding the **Surface Web**, **Deep Web**, and **Dark Web** is crucial for anyone seeking to understand the full scope of the internet's ecosystem. While the Surface Web is what we use every day, the Deep Web is vast and contains much of the internet's private data. The Dark Web, though often misunderstood, plays a vital role in maintaining privacy and anonymity for those who need it most, though it also houses risks.

1.3: Common Misconceptions About the Dark Web

The **dark web** is often misunderstood, and many myths and misconceptions surround it. These myths can lead to a distorted view of this hidden part of the internet, often associating it only with criminal activities and nefarious deeds. In this section, we will explore and debunk some of the most common misconceptions about the dark web. By the end, you'll have a clearer understanding of what the dark web is, how it works, and why it's not as dangerous or mysterious as it's often portrayed.

Misconception 1: "The Dark Web is Only for Illegal Activities"

One of the most persistent myths about the dark web is that it's a lawless zone filled with illegal activity. While it's true that some illegal activities do occur on the dark web, this is only a small fraction of its use.

Why This is a Misconception:

- **Privacy and Anonymity**: The dark web is primarily used by individuals who need anonymity for various legitimate reasons, such as journalists, activists, and dissidents in authoritarian countries. For example, journalists often use the dark web to communicate securely with whistleblowers without exposing their identities to surveillance.
- **Whistleblowing**: Platforms like **SecureDrop** allow whistleblowers to anonymously share documents with journalists, providing a vital tool for transparency in cases of corruption or government malpractice.
- **Free Speech**: In countries with heavy censorship, the dark web offers a safe space for individuals to express dissenting opinions or

participate in political discussions without fear of government retaliation.

Case Study: Dissidents in Iran
In countries like Iran, where internet access is heavily monitored, activists use the dark web to communicate and organize anonymously. The **Tor network** provides a secure channel for bypassing censorship and surveillance. Without the dark web, many of these activists would be silenced by oppressive regimes.

Misconception 2: "The Dark Web is Impossible to Access"

Another misconception is that accessing the dark web is incredibly complicated and requires extensive technical knowledge. While it does require specialized tools, the process is not as difficult as many people think.

Why This is a Misconception:

- **Using Tor**: The most common way to access the dark web is by using the **Tor browser**, which is based on the principle of onion routing. Tor is easy to download and install, and there are step-by-step guides available to help you get started.

Steps to Access the Dark Web:

1. Download the **Tor Browser** from the official Tor Project website.
2. Install and run the browser.
3. Use it just like any other browser, but visit websites that end in **.onion** (the dark web equivalent of traditional websites).
4. Be cautious of security risks and always follow best practices for online privacy.

While using Tor and accessing the dark web may require a little setup, it's not much different from downloading and using a new app or tool.

Visual Aid: Simple Steps to Access the Dark Web

Here's a simple flowchart to visualize how you can safely access the dark web:

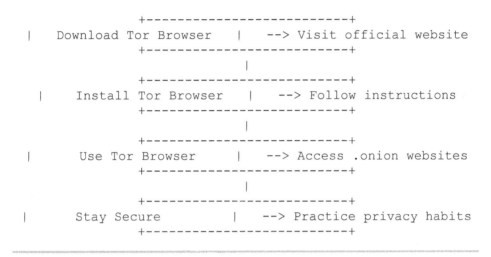

```
        +--------------------------+
    |   Download Tor Browser   |    --> Visit official website
        +--------------------------+
                     |
        +--------------------------+
    |     Install Tor Browser  |    --> Follow instructions
        +--------------------------+
                     |
        +--------------------------+
    |    Use Tor Browser       |    --> Access .onion websites
        +--------------------------+
                     |
        +--------------------------+
    |    Stay Secure           |    --> Practice privacy habits
        +--------------------------+
```

Misconception 3: "The Dark Web is Only Dangerous"

The dark web is often painted as an inherently dangerous place, where malware, viruses, and cybercriminals lurk at every corner. While the dark web does pose certain risks, just like any part of the internet, it is **not inherently dangerous** if used properly.

Why This is a Misconception:

- **Risks Are Manageable**: With the proper precautions, you can navigate the dark web securely. This includes using **VPNs**, ensuring that the Tor browser is up to date, and being cautious about the websites you visit.
- **Security Best Practices**: Just like on the surface web, staying safe on the dark web involves basic cybersecurity measures, such as using strong passwords, enabling two-factor authentication, and avoiding suspicious links.

For example, if you're exploring the dark web to access anonymous communication platforms or encrypted news sources, as long as you follow security protocols, the experience can be **safe and enriching**.

Real-World Example:

Case Study: Researchers Using the Dark Web for Secure Communication
Researchers who work with sensitive data often use the dark web to communicate securely with colleagues and organizations. These researchers understand the risks, but they implement strong security protocols to mitigate them. In this context, the dark web becomes a safe tool to protect information from hackers and government surveillance.

Misconception 4: "The Dark Web is Completely Anonymous, and No One Can Track You"

While the dark web provides a much higher level of anonymity than the surface web, it's not completely foolproof. The idea that users can be entirely **untraceable** on the dark web is a dangerous myth.

Why This is a Misconception:

- **Onion Routing Is Not Perfect**: Tor provides strong anonymity by routing your traffic through multiple nodes and encrypting it at each stage, but advanced methods can still potentially trace users, especially if additional tracking techniques or vulnerabilities are exploited.
- **Human Error**: Even if you're using Tor, certain behaviors—like logging into personal accounts, revealing identifiable information, or not using a VPN—can compromise your anonymity.

Experts in cybersecurity regularly warn that while Tor provides significant privacy protections, users must take extra precautions to stay safe.

Case Study: The Silk Road Takedown
In 2013, **Ross Ulbricht**, the creator of the Silk Road (a dark web marketplace), was arrested despite the site's use of Tor for anonymity. Investigators were able to track Ulbricht's activities due to a combination of mistakes, including his use of personal identifiers and flaws in the site's code. This illustrates that complete anonymity on the dark web requires **vigilance and multiple layers of security**.

Misconception 5: "The Dark Web is Full of Malware and Scams"

It's true that there are some websites on the dark web that are designed to spread malware or scam visitors. However, this is not the case for every website on the dark web. Just like the surface web, the dark web hosts a wide variety of sites, some legitimate and some malicious.

Why This is a Misconception:

- **Not All Sites Are Malicious**: There are plenty of **legitimate and ethical** sites on the dark web, including secure communication platforms, privacy-enhancing tools, and forums for sensitive topics. It's just that, like any digital space, there are bad actors.
- **Avoiding Malware**: As long as you stick to reputable websites, use updated antivirus software, and refrain from clicking on suspicious links, you can minimize the risk of encountering malware.

Practical Example:

Case Study: The Rise of Secure Communication Platforms
Many privacy-conscious individuals and organizations use the dark web to communicate securely. Platforms like **SecureDrop** and **Signal** are used for confidential exchanges. These services are trusted and legitimate, offering encrypted communication without any malicious intent.

The dark web is a misunderstood space, and it's often framed in an overly negative light. While there are some risks associated with it, the reality is that the dark web is not inherently dangerous or illegal. It serves as a powerful tool for those who require **anonymity** and **privacy**, including journalists, activists, and individuals living under oppressive regimes.

The most important takeaway here is that while navigating the dark web, like any other part of the internet, requires **vigilance** and **security awareness**, it is by no means the dangerous, lawless zone it's often made out to be. By understanding these common misconceptions, we can approach the dark web with a more informed and balanced perspective, utilizing its strengths while minimizing its risks.

Chapter 2: The History and Evolution of the Dark Web

The dark web is often seen as a mysterious and dangerous place, but its origins and evolution tell a much more complex story. While today it is widely associated with cybercrime, it was initially created for a very different purpose: to provide a platform for **privacy and anonymity** in an increasingly interconnected world. In this chapter, we'll explore the **origins** of the dark web, its early uses, and how it has evolved over time—especially as it has become a breeding ground for cybercrime. By the end, you'll gain a deeper understanding of how the dark web came to be, and how its transformation mirrors the growing concerns over privacy and security in the digital age.

2.1: Origins and Purpose of the Dark Web

The **dark web** is a unique and often misunderstood part of the internet. It's the hidden, encrypted layer beneath the surface web that can only be accessed using specific tools like the **Tor browser**. The **origins** of the dark web are tied to **privacy**, **anonymity**, and **censorship resistance**, rather than illegal activities as many might think. Understanding its origins and the purpose for which it was created provides essential context for the rest of this book. In this section, we'll break down how the dark web came into existence, its original objectives, and the role it plays in the digital landscape today.

The Genesis of the Dark Web: From Military to Public Use

The dark web has its roots in a military project known as **Tor**, short for **The Onion Router**. Its development began in the mid-1990s, and its primary goal was to help protect government communications from being intercepted.

The Military Beginnings:

In the early days of the internet, military and intelligence agencies were struggling with the challenge of securing online communications. With the rapid spread of the internet, **surveillance** and **data interception** became real concerns. The **U.S. Naval Research Laboratory (NRL)** initiated the creation of **onion routing**, a technique that uses layers of encryption to anonymize internet traffic. The basic idea was to create a communication network that could not be easily intercepted or traced back to its source.

The **Tor network** was designed to make online communication secure and anonymous by routing internet traffic through multiple encrypted layers, much like the layers of an onion. This routing method allows users to browse the web without revealing their **IP address** or **physical location**, making it ideal for use by military personnel, intelligence agents, and diplomats who needed to keep their activities confidential.

Key Goals of Tor (Early Days):

- **Anonymity**: Hide the identity and location of the user.
- **Privacy**: Prevent surveillance of internet activities.
- **Security**: Protect sensitive information from being intercepted.

At this stage, **Tor was not intended for public use**; it was a highly specialized tool for government and military personnel. However, as the project developed, its potential for civilian use became evident.

The Shift to Public Use: From Military Tool to Privacy Advocate

In 2002, the **Tor Project**, a non-profit organization, was founded to further develop the Tor network and make it available to the public. The project was spearheaded by a team of privacy advocates, developers, and researchers, including key figures from the original U.S. Naval Research Laboratory group.

Why Was Tor Released to the Public?

By the early 2000s, the internet had grown exponentially, and concerns about **privacy** and **data security** were becoming more prominent. With the rise of personal data being collected by companies, governments, and hackers, many individuals began seeking ways to protect their online activities. The Tor Project's mission shifted to a more **public service** role, with the goal of offering a secure and anonymous browsing option for anyone who was concerned about privacy.

Tor became an essential tool for individuals living in **authoritarian regimes**, **whistleblowers**, and **journalists** who required a way to communicate **securely** and **anonymously**. Tor enabled users to **bypass censorship**, access blocked websites, and communicate without fear of being tracked.

The release of Tor marked the beginning of the dark web's transformation from a **military tool** to a **public privacy tool**. It allowed civilians to use encryption and anonymity for **personal safety**, **freedom of speech**, and **access to information** that might be otherwise restricted.

Tor and the Birth of the Dark Web: A Safe Haven for Privacy and Free Speech

With Tor's capabilities of ensuring privacy and anonymity, the **dark web**—a part of the internet that could only be accessed through **Tor** or other anonymizing tools—began to emerge as a platform for **free speech** and **uncensored information**.

The Dark Web's Purpose:

The dark web was not intended to be a **criminal underworld**, but rather a space where people could speak freely without fear of surveillance. Here are some of the primary reasons why people began using the dark web:

1. **Bypassing Censorship**: In many countries with strict internet controls, the dark web offered a means to access information freely, avoiding government-imposed censorship and surveillance. This was especially vital for individuals living in regimes that suppressed political expression or restricted access to information.
2. **Secure Communication**: The dark web allowed for **secure communications**, particularly for journalists and activists working in dangerous or oppressive environments. For example, journalists could safely communicate with sources without revealing their identity or location.
3. **Whistleblowing**: The dark web provided an anonymous platform for whistleblowers to disclose sensitive information, such as government or corporate misconduct, without fear of retaliation. Websites like **SecureDrop** allowed whistleblowers to send documents and communicate with journalists securely.
4. **Privacy Advocacy**: The dark web became a place for privacy advocates to gather and discuss the implications of online surveillance, helping users understand how to protect their digital identities.

Real-World Example: WikiLeaks

The rise of WikiLeaks and its impact on global politics is a clear example of how the dark web facilitated secure, anonymous communication. **WikiLeaks** provided a platform for whistleblowers to release classified government and corporate information, using encryption and Tor to protect their identities. Over the years, WikiLeaks has exposed numerous high-profile scandals, from government surveillance programs to corporate corruption, thanks to the anonymity provided by the dark web.

The Evolution of the Dark Web: From Privacy Tool to a Mixed Ecosystem

Over time, the dark web's initial purpose—**privacy** and **free speech**—became increasingly complicated as more people began using it for illegal activities. The dark web's anonymity and encryption features provided a safe haven for **cybercriminals**, **hackers**, and **illegal marketplaces**.

Rise of Cybercrime:

One of the most significant shifts in the evolution of the dark web occurred in the early 2010s with the rise of **black market platforms**. The first major dark web marketplace, **Silk Road**, was launched in 2011 and allowed users to anonymously buy and sell illegal goods, particularly drugs. Silk Road's success highlighted the dark web's potential for illicit trade, and it was followed by numerous other marketplaces, many of which facilitated the illegal exchange of **drugs**, **weapons**, **stolen data**, and **hacking services**.

While **Silk Road** was eventually shut down by the FBI in 2013, its **legacy** continued, and other marketplaces followed. The ability to use **Bitcoin** and other cryptocurrencies made transactions on these sites harder to trace, attracting more criminals.

Security and Law Enforcement Challenges:

As cybercrime flourished, law enforcement agencies began to focus on infiltrating the dark web. High-profile takedowns, such as the arrest of **Ross Ulbricht** (the founder of Silk Road), highlighted the risks of using the dark web for illegal activities. However, due to the sophisticated encryption and the decentralized nature of dark web marketplaces, it remains a challenge for law enforcement to fully eradicate such activities.

Visual Aid: The Evolution of the Dark Web

Here's a simple timeline that helps visualize the evolution of the dark web from a privacy tool to the more complex digital ecosystem we see today:

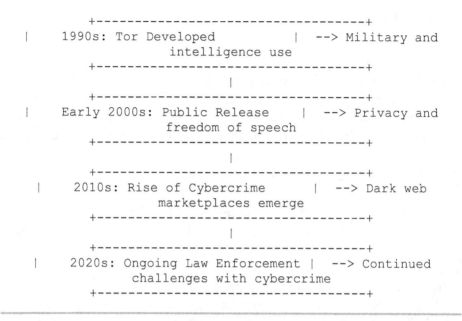

```
        +-----------------------------------+
|       1990s: Tor Developed        |  --> Military and
                    intelligence use
        +-----------------------------------+
                          |
        +-----------------------------------+
|     Early 2000s: Public Release   |  --> Privacy and
                    freedom of speech
        +-----------------------------------+
                          |
        +-----------------------------------+
|      2010s: Rise of Cybercrime    |  --> Dark web
                    marketplaces emerge
        +-----------------------------------+
                          |
        +-----------------------------------+
|    2020s: Ongoing Law Enforcement |  --> Continued
                  challenges with cybercrime
        +-----------------------------------+
```

The **dark web** started as a tool for **privacy**, **anonymity**, and **free speech**, designed to protect sensitive communications and information in an increasingly surveilled world. However, its evolution into a space where **cybercrime** thrives has complicated its legacy. While it remains a critical tool for privacy advocates, journalists, and political dissidents, it also presents challenges for law enforcement and cybersecurity.

2.2: Early Uses: Privacy and Anonymity in the Digital Age

In the early days of the internet, privacy and anonymity were not as major concerns as they are today. People were simply excited about the new possibilities the web offered—shopping online, communicating with people across the globe, and accessing information at the touch of a button. However, as the digital age progressed, **privacy** and **anonymity** started to become more critical issues, especially as online surveillance, data mining, and censorship increased. The **dark web**, specifically through tools like **Tor** (The Onion Router), quickly became the go-to solution for those who wanted to maintain their **privacy** while navigating the increasingly surveilled and data-harvesting digital landscape.

In this section, we'll explore how **privacy** and **anonymity** came to the forefront in the digital age, the early use cases of these technologies, and how the **dark web** offered a platform for individuals to protect their personal data, communicate freely, and bypass censorship.

The Rise of Privacy Concerns in the Digital Age

As the internet evolved, so did the collection of data about users. In the early days of the internet, users could engage with websites without much concern about how much information was being gathered about them. But as e-commerce grew, along with the rise of social media, it became clear that **companies, governments, and hackers** could gather and analyze massive amounts of personal data.

The Shift from Public to Private Data

In the early 2000s, **data collection** became more systematic, as search engines like **Google** and social media platforms like **Facebook** started gathering data on users' activities. The internet had become a data mine, where personal preferences, habits, and interests were being tracked, often without users fully understanding the extent of this surveillance.

In this climate, the concept of **online privacy** began to surface as a major concern. As people became more aware of the **surveillance** and **tracking** occurring online, the desire for anonymity grew.

- **Privacy Concerns**: Users became concerned about their **digital footprint**, especially as identity theft, targeted advertising, and corporate surveillance became more widespread.
- **Tracking and Surveillance**: Governments and intelligence agencies, like the NSA, were collecting massive amounts of data on users' online behaviors, raising concerns about the **erosion of civil liberties**.

The Development of Anonymity Tools: Enter Tor

In response to these growing concerns, the Tor network was developed as a tool for individuals to **browse the internet anonymously**. Tor uses a method known as **onion routing**, which layers encryption over data, making it incredibly difficult for anyone to trace the origin of the information being exchanged.

What Is Tor?

- **Tor (The Onion Router)**: Tor is a network that uses a series of volunteer-operated servers (called nodes) to route internet traffic. When you use Tor, your traffic is encrypted and passed through multiple nodes before reaching its destination, ensuring that no one node knows both the origin and destination of the data. This provides strong **anonymity** and **privacy** by obscuring the identity of the user and their location.

How Tor Works:

1. **Onion Routing**: When you send data using Tor, it's encrypted multiple times, like the layers of an onion. Each layer is removed as the data moves through each node, ultimately reaching its final destination.
2. **Distributed Network**: The Tor network relies on thousands of volunteer-operated nodes distributed around the world, making it difficult to trace the path of the data. Each node only knows the previous and next nodes, ensuring that no one node has access to the full route.

By using Tor, users could browse the internet without leaving a trace, making it harder for corporations, hackers, or even governments to monitor their activities.

Early Uses of Tor and the Dark Web: Privacy and Freedom

Tor was initially designed for government and military use. However, as it became available to the public, it quickly found a broad range of uses among individuals concerned about their **privacy** and **anonymity**. Let's break down how Tor and the early dark web became essential tools for **privacy advocates**, **journalists**, and **political dissidents**.

1. Political Dissidents and Activists

In countries with **restrictive governments** or **censorship**, Tor provided a way for individuals to bypass government-imposed restrictions on the internet. Political activists and dissidents used Tor to organize, communicate, and access information without fear of surveillance or retaliation.

- **Example**: In countries like **China**, where the government censors access to information, Tor became a lifeline for citizens looking to access the full internet or communicate securely without fear of government monitoring.
- **Case Study**: **Censorship in Iran**: During the 2009 Iranian elections, Iranian citizens used Tor to bypass internet censorship and communicate securely with the outside world. The use of Tor enabled them to share information about protests and human rights violations, despite the government's attempts to monitor and shut down access to social media and news sites.

2. Journalists and Whistleblowers

One of the most significant uses of the dark web, particularly Tor, is for **journalists** and **whistleblowers** who need to communicate securely without revealing their identity or the identity of their sources. The **dark web** provided a **safe haven** where individuals could leak sensitive documents or report on corruption without fear of being tracked or arrested.

- **SecureDrop**: A platform created by **The Guardian** and other media outlets, **SecureDrop** allows whistleblowers to send documents anonymously. SecureDrop uses Tor to protect the identity of the whistleblower, ensuring that sensitive information can be shared securely with journalists.
- **Example**: The **WikiLeaks** platform, which became famous for publishing classified government information, relies on tools like Tor to allow whistleblowers to share documents anonymously.

3. Privacy-Conscious Individuals

Beyond activists and journalists, everyday users began adopting Tor as a way to protect their **personal privacy** and **digital identity**. With the rise of **data mining** and **targeted advertising**, people sought out ways to prevent companies from collecting and profiting from their data.

Tor allowed individuals to:

- **Browse anonymously**: Prevent online tracking by advertisers and prevent websites from collecting personal data.
- **Avoid profiling**: Avoid the use of personal browsing data to create detailed digital profiles that could be sold or used without the individual's consent.

4. Circumventing Censorship and Geo-Restrictions

In addition to privacy, Tor allowed users to bypass **geo-restrictions** on content. For example, people in countries where certain services (like Netflix, Hulu, or news sites) were blocked could use Tor to access these websites without being detected.

- **Example**: In countries where certain websites were restricted, Tor became a tool for users to **circumvent censorship** and access a **free internet**.

Real-World Example: WikiLeaks and the Role of Tor

A prime example of the early use of Tor and the dark web for **privacy** and **free speech** is **WikiLeaks**. This organization gained worldwide attention for its publication of sensitive government documents. **Julian Assange**, the founder of WikiLeaks, used Tor to enable whistleblowers to anonymously submit classified information.

- **How WikiLeaks Used Tor**: WikiLeaks provided an encrypted platform for whistleblowers to send documents without revealing their identities. This was crucial for the organization's ability to protect the safety of sources and reporters.
- **Why Tor Was Essential**: The use of Tor ensured that WikiLeaks could continue its operations without being shut down by governments or corporate entities that were targeted by the leaks. Tor offered the **anonymity** and **secure communication** required to manage this sensitive work.

Visual Aid: The Anatomy of a Tor Connection

Here's a basic flowchart to visualize how Tor works and its benefits for privacy:

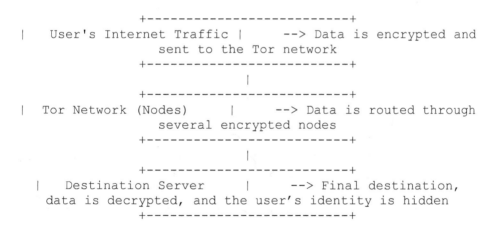

```
            +---------------------------+
|   User's Internet Traffic |     --> Data is encrypted and
            sent to the Tor network
            +---------------------------+
                         |
            +---------------------------+
|   Tor Network (Nodes)       |     --> Data is routed through
            several encrypted nodes
            +---------------------------+
                         |
            +---------------------------+
|    Destination Server       |     --> Final destination,
    data is decrypted, and the user's identity is hidden
            +---------------------------+
```

This flow ensures that the user's **IP address** and **location** are hidden, making it virtually impossible to trace the activity back to the user.

The early use of Tor and the dark web was driven by a desire for **privacy**, **anonymity**, and **freedom of speech**. These tools provided individuals with the ability to communicate and share information without fear of surveillance or censorship. While the dark web would later become associated with cybercrime and illicit activity, its origins were rooted in **privacy protection** and a **commitment to freedom**.

2.3: The Growth of Cybercrime on the Dark Web

The **dark web** was originally designed to offer anonymity, security, and freedom of speech, but over the years, it has also become a haven for **cybercriminals**. With its inherent features of **privacy** and **anonymity**, the dark web has provided a secure platform for illegal activities, ranging from **black market trading** to **hacking services** and **fraudulent schemes**. The growth of cybercrime on the dark web has raised significant concerns for law enforcement, cybersecurity experts, and the public alike.

In this section, we will explore how the dark web evolved from a privacy tool to a **hub for cybercrime**, the types of criminal activities that thrive on this hidden part of the internet, and how law enforcement and cybersecurity professionals are fighting back.

The Dark Web's Role in Cybercrime

While the dark web was initially created for secure communications and free speech, its **anonymity** and **lack of regulation** made it an attractive space for **illegal activities**. Over time, as Tor and other similar networks gained popularity, a wide range of illicit transactions started taking place.

Why Is the Dark Web Attractive to Cybercriminals?

1. **Anonymity and Encryption**: The Tor network and similar tools provide high levels of encryption, making it difficult to trace users

or activities. This makes the dark web an appealing platform for criminals who need to hide their identity.

2. **Decentralized Nature**: The dark web is decentralized, meaning it lacks any central governing body. Without centralized oversight, criminals have more freedom to operate without fear of being easily shut down.

3. **Cryptocurrency**: The rise of **cryptocurrencies** like **Bitcoin**, **Monero**, and **Ethereum** has further fueled cybercrime on the dark web. These digital currencies are often used for illegal transactions because they are harder to trace than traditional methods of payment.

Key Features of Cybercrime on the Dark Web

- **Black Marketplaces**: These websites serve as platforms where illegal goods and services are bought and sold.
- **Hacking Services**: The dark web has become a marketplace for **hacking tools** and **cyberattack services**.
- **Stolen Data**: Criminals often trade **stolen personal data**, including credit card information, identities, and bank account details.
- **Malware and Ransomware**: The dark web is a hub for **malware developers** and **ransomware operators**, offering tools and services to those looking to commit cybercrimes.

Types of Cybercrime on the Dark Web

Cybercriminals use the dark web for a wide range of illegal activities. Here, we will explore some of the most common types of cybercrime that thrive in the shadows of the dark web.

1. Black Market Trading: Drugs, Weapons, and More

One of the most well-known uses of the dark web is the sale of illegal goods. Websites such as **Silk Road**, which was founded in 2011, enabled users to purchase **drugs**, **weapons**, and other illicit items anonymously.

- **Drugs**: The dark web is notorious for facilitating the anonymous trade of illegal drugs. Buyers and sellers can connect, negotiate, and make transactions with little fear of being caught.
- **Weapons**: In addition to drugs, weapons such as firearms and explosives have been sold through dark web marketplaces. While these transactions are often hidden behind encryption and cryptocurrency payments, the risks are high, and law enforcement agencies have been cracking down on these markets.

Real-World Example: Silk Road

The **Silk Road** was one of the first and most famous dark web marketplaces that enabled the anonymous purchase and sale of illegal goods, particularly drugs. It was shut down by the FBI in 2013, and its founder, **Ross Ulbricht**, was arrested. The shutdown of Silk Road marked the first significant crack in dark web cybercrime, but it also led to the emergence of new marketplaces like **AlphaBay** and **Dream Market**.

---

2. Hacking Services and Exploits

The dark web has become a thriving market for **cybercriminals** who want to buy or sell **hacking tools** and **cyberattack services**.

- **Exploit Kits**: These are tools that allow hackers to exploit vulnerabilities in software and networks. Many of these kits are sold on the dark web to low-level criminals who may not have the expertise to develop their own attacks.
- **DDoS (Distributed Denial-of-Service) Services**: Cybercriminals can buy or rent **DDoS** services on the dark web. These services flood a target website with traffic, causing it to crash. This can be used for **extortion**, as hackers demand payment to stop the attack.
- **RATs (Remote Access Trojans)**: Hackers can also buy or sell RATs, which are malicious programs that give attackers control over victims' computers.

Real-World Example: Hacking Forums

Dark web forums like **The Hub** and **DarkNetMarketplace** serve as platforms where hackers can buy and sell **zero-day vulnerabilities** and hacking software. These tools allow criminals to target financial institutions, governments, and individuals, often resulting in severe financial losses.

---

3. Stolen Data and Identity Theft

The dark web is a major source of **stolen data**, which is often sold to other criminals or used in various forms of fraud.

- **Credit Card Fraud**: Hackers and data thieves can steal **credit card numbers**, **bank account details**, and **social security numbers** and sell them on dark web marketplaces.
- **Personal Identification Information**: Stolen **identities** are sold in bulk, with buyers using this data for **fraudulent activities** such as opening fake bank accounts or applying for loans in someone else's name.

Real-World Example: The 2017 Equifax Data Breach

In 2017, the **Equifax** data breach exposed the personal data of over 140 million individuals, including **names**, **addresses**, **social security numbers**, and **credit card information**. This information ended up being traded on dark web marketplaces, leading to a surge in identity theft and financial fraud.

---

4. Malware and Ransomware

The dark web is also home to a large number of **malware developers** and **ransomware operators**.

- **Malware**: The dark web is a place where cybercriminals can buy and sell malware programs that can be used to infiltrate computers, steal information, and launch attacks.
- **Ransomware**: Cybercriminals use the dark web to sell **ransomware-as-a-service**. This service enables anyone to buy ransomware to launch attacks on organizations or individuals, with the criminal operator receiving a share of the ransom.

The **WannaCry** ransomware attack in 2017 encrypted hundreds of thousands of computers around the world, demanding payment in Bitcoin to unlock the files. The ransomware was based on an exploit leaked from the **NSA**, and its operators used the dark web to facilitate the attack and collect payments.

Visual Aid: A Flowchart of Cybercrime Activities on the Dark Web

Here's a simplified flowchart to illustrate how cybercrime works on the dark web:

```
                    +------------------------------+
                    |    Cybercrime on Dark Web    |
                    +------------------------------+
                                  |
                                  v
 +-----------------------------+      +--------------------
                     -------+
 |  Black Market Trading       | --> | Hacking Services &
                   Exploits |
 | (Drugs, Weapons, etc.)      |      | (DDoS, RATs, Exploit
                     Kits)  |
 +-----------------------------+      +--------------------
                     -------+
                                  |
                                  v
 +-----------------------------+      +--------------------
                     -------+
 |  Stolen Data & Identity     | --> | Malware & Ransomware
                              |
 | (Credit Cards, Personal     |      | (RATs, Ransomware as
                    a         |
      | Info, Financial Fraud)      |      | Service)
                              |
 +-----------------------------+      +--------------------
                     -------+
```

The Impact of Cybercrime on the Dark Web

The **growth of cybercrime** on the dark web has had serious implications for both the online world and the real world. The anonymity provided by the dark web has made it harder for law enforcement to track down criminals, making it a **challenging environment** for **cybersecurity professionals**.

- **Financial Losses**: Cybercrime activities on the dark web, such as **identity theft**, **financial fraud**, and **ransomware**, have caused billions of dollars in losses worldwide.
- **Reputational Damage**: Businesses targeted by cybercriminals often face reputational damage, especially if sensitive customer information is compromised.
- **Legal and Regulatory Challenges**: Law enforcement agencies are struggling to keep up with the rapidly evolving tactics used by cybercriminals on the dark web.

Law Enforcement's Efforts to Combat Cybercrime

Law enforcement agencies around the world have made significant strides in tackling cybercrime on the dark web. High-profile operations like the **Silk Road takedown** and the **shutdown of AlphaBay** have shown that the dark web is not beyond the reach of law enforcement. However, the decentralized nature of the dark web, coupled with the use of **cryptocurrencies** and **anonymizing tools** like Tor, makes it a difficult battleground.

Tools for Fighting Cybercrime on the Dark Web

- **Undercover Operations**: Law enforcement agencies infiltrate dark web marketplaces and forums to gather intelligence and identify criminal activity.
- **Blockchain Analysis**: Tools like **Chainalysis** are used to trace cryptocurrency transactions on the dark web, making it easier to track down cybercriminals.

- **Collaboration**: International collaboration between law enforcement agencies, such as **Europol**, is crucial in the fight against cybercrime on the dark web.

The dark web's growth as a hub for cybercrime has raised significant challenges for law enforcement, cybersecurity professionals, and the public. From **black market trading** and **stolen data** to **hacking services** and **malware**, the dark web is a breeding ground for illegal activity. While the dark web was originally designed to provide privacy and freedom of speech, it has become a double-edged sword, serving both legitimate users and cybercriminals.

As cybercrime continues to thrive on the dark web, it's essential for **law enforcement** and **cybersecurity experts** to develop new strategies and tools to fight back. Understanding the evolution and mechanics of dark web cybercrime will help us better prepare for the challenges ahead, while also preserving the important **privacy** and **freedom of expression** that the dark web continues to offer.

Part 2: Beginner Level – Understanding the Dark Web and Common Myths

Chapter 3: Dispelling the Myths of the Dark Web

The **dark web** is often portrayed as a shadowy corner of the internet filled with crime, secrecy, and danger. However, many of the ideas we associate with the dark web are based on **myths** that don't tell the full story. In this chapter, we will explore and debunk some of the most common myths about the dark web, shedding light on its legitimate uses and explaining why **anonymity** is crucial for a growing number of users.

3.1: Common Myths and Their Truths

The **dark web** has a reputation that is often misunderstood, and much of the fear and mystery surrounding it stems from **myths** that exaggerate or misrepresent its nature. From being a space entirely dominated by illegal activity to being impossible to access, these misconceptions only scratch the surface of the truth. In this section, we'll explore the most common myths about the dark web and debunk them with the real facts.

By understanding these myths and their truths, you'll gain a clearer, more accurate understanding of what the dark web actually is and how it functions.

Myth 1: "The Dark Web is Only Used for Illegal Activities"

One of the most pervasive myths about the dark web is that it's a lawless place where **illegal activities** happen behind closed doors. This is the myth that paints the entire space with the same brush—associating it exclusively with **cybercrime** such as **drug trafficking**, **human trafficking**, **illegal marketplaces**, and **hacking services**.

The Truth:

While the dark web certainly has its share of criminal activity, it is **not limited** to this. The dark web was originally designed to protect users' **privacy** and **anonymity**, offering a way for people to communicate securely in environments where their safety or freedom might be compromised. It's important to understand that **privacy** and **anonymity** are fundamental aspects of the dark web, and these principles benefit more than just criminals.

Legitimate Uses of the Dark Web:

- **Whistleblowing**: Whistleblowers, who expose sensitive governmental or corporate corruption, use platforms like **SecureDrop** to send documents to journalists anonymously and securely. This ensures they can share crucial information without the fear of retaliation.
- **Journalism**: Journalists in oppressive regimes use the dark web to communicate with sources securely, ensuring that they can conduct investigative work without risking their safety or the safety of their informants.
- **Activism and Free Speech**: The dark web provides a platform for **human rights activists** and **political dissidents** to organize, share information, and communicate freely, without fearing government surveillance or censorship.
- **Secure Communication**: The dark web provides **secure channels** for individuals who wish to protect their identities from surveillance. It enables **encrypted communications**, ensuring that sensitive information remains private.

Real-World Example: WikiLeaks

WikiLeaks, the organization that exposed government and corporate secrets, uses the dark web as a platform for whistleblowers to anonymously submit documents. While some may associate WikiLeaks with controversial information, its use of the dark web as a safe space for **free speech** and **transparency** underscores the legitimate, privacy-driven purposes of the dark web.

Myth 2: "The Dark Web is Impossible to Access"

Another myth that's often spread is that the dark web is an exclusive, difficult-to-reach part of the internet that requires advanced technical knowledge to access. People imagine it as a hidden labyrinth that only hackers or cybercriminals can navigate.

The Truth:

Accessing the dark web is actually **fairly simple**, thanks to tools like the **Tor browser**. While it does require special software, it is not beyond the reach of everyday internet users. The **Tor browser** allows anyone to access **.onion websites**, which are the domain extensions used exclusively by the dark web.

How to Access the Dark Web (Step-by-Step):

1. **Download the Tor Browser**: Visit the official Tor Project website to download the browser. It's available for **Windows, macOS**, and **Linux**.
2. **Install the Browser**: After downloading the Tor browser, follow the simple installation instructions to set it up on your system.
3. **Connect to the Tor Network**: Once installed, open the Tor browser and click "Connect" to join the Tor network. This network encrypts your internet traffic and routes it through multiple layers of nodes, masking your identity.
4. **Browse .onion Websites**: After connecting, you can access dark web websites that end in **.onion**, such as **DuckDuckGo's dark web version** *(http://3g2upl4pq6kufc4m.onion)* or other privacy-focused search engines like **Ahmia**.

Important Tip: Although accessing the dark web is simple, it's crucial to use security practices, like enabling a **VPN**, avoiding risky websites, and ensuring that your system is up-to-date with the latest security patches.

Myth 3: "The Dark Web is Always Dangerous"

Another common myth is that the dark web is inherently **dangerous**. Many believe that it's a **hotbed of malware**, **viruses**, and **scams** that put users at constant risk of exposure. While risks do exist on the dark web, they are similar to the risks you face on the surface web.

The Truth:

Just like the surface web, the dark web has its **good and bad** parts. There are plenty of **reliable and secure** services and websites operating on the dark web, but there are also websites run by **malicious actors** trying to exploit naive users.

The key to staying safe on the dark web is exercising caution and following basic cybersecurity best practices.

Safety Tips for Navigating the Dark Web:

- **Use Strong Security**: Always use a **VPN** (Virtual Private Network) alongside the **Tor browser** to further protect your identity and encrypt your internet traffic.
- **Avoid Suspicious Links**: Just as you would avoid clicking on questionable links on the surface web, be cautious on the dark web. Don't download files from untrusted sources, and be wary of engaging with unknown websites.
- **Keep Software Up-to-Date**: Ensure that your operating system, antivirus software, and Tor browser are regularly updated to defend against known vulnerabilities.

Real-World Example: The Silk Road Takedown

While the **Silk Road** marketplace was shut down by the FBI in 2013 for facilitating the sale of illegal goods, it's important to note that not every dark web marketplace is tied to criminal activity. The Silk Road's closure sent a message about law enforcement's ability to infiltrate illicit markets, but it also led to **new, legitimate platforms** emerging in its place— marketplaces where users can exchange goods or services in a **secure** and **anonymous** way.

Myth 4: "The Dark Web Is Completely Anonymous, and No One Can Track You"

Many believe that the **anonymity** provided by the dark web is absolute, offering complete protection from anyone trying to track your activities online. After all, Tor is designed to anonymize users' internet traffic, so surely you cannot be tracked, right?

The Truth:

While Tor provides a **high level of anonymity**, it's **not foolproof**. Advanced techniques, human error, and vulnerabilities in the network can still lead to **de-anonymization**.

Why Complete Anonymity Is Challenging:

- **Vulnerabilities in Tor**: Tor is not invincible. There have been occasions where vulnerabilities in Tor were exploited to track users. For example, law enforcement agencies have employed **traffic correlation attacks** to break through Tor's encryption.
- **Human Error**: Even when using Tor, users can still make mistakes that compromise their anonymity. For example, logging into personal accounts (like Gmail or Facebook) while using the Tor network can expose your real identity. Avoiding any personal or identifiable information is crucial to maintaining anonymity.
- **Sophisticated Tracking Techniques**: Some law enforcement agencies have developed techniques to trace Tor traffic, especially when users engage in **criminal activities**. However, regular internet users who take precautions, like using **VPNs**, will remain more protected.

Practical Example:

The **Silk Road** case offers an example of how human error and network vulnerabilities led to the identification of the dark web marketplace's founder, **Ross Ulbricht**. While Silk Road itself used Tor to ensure anonymity, Ulbricht's failure to fully cover his tracks and the exploitation of weaknesses in the system led to his eventual arrest. This demonstrates that even on the dark web, complete anonymity is never guaranteed.

Myth 5: "You Can Only Find Dangerous or Illegal Content on the Dark Web"

While the dark web is often associated with criminal behavior and dangerous content, it's also home to a wide variety of **legitimate** and **useful** resources that promote privacy, freedom of speech, and access to uncensored information.

The Truth:

The dark web is a space where individuals can access services that prioritize **privacy** and **security**, and often those services are not available on the surface web. There are **discussion forums**, **news sources**, and **tools** that allow people to communicate securely, conduct research, and engage in activities that support their **freedom of expression** and **privacy**.

Useful Resources on the Dark Web:

- **SecureDrop**: A platform that allows whistleblowers to communicate anonymously with journalists and share sensitive information without risking their identity.
- **Privacy-Focused Search Engines**: Websites like **DuckDuckGo** or **Ahmia** allow users to search the dark web without leaving a trace or revealing their identity.
- **Encrypted Email Services**: Secure email services like **ProtonMail** and **Tutanota** provide encrypted email communication, ensuring that messages remain private and secure.

The myths surrounding the dark web—such as it being exclusively for illegal activities or being impossible to access—are rooted in misunderstanding and exaggeration. The reality is that the dark web is a complex, multifaceted space with both **good and bad** actors. While it does host illegal activity, it also serves a critical role in protecting privacy, enabling free speech, and supporting whistleblowing and activism.

3.2: Legitimate Uses of the Dark Web

The **dark web** is often shrouded in a cloud of mystery and suspicion. While many people associate it with illicit activities like cybercrime and illegal markets, it's crucial to recognize that the dark web serves legitimate purposes for many individuals and organizations. In fact, it plays a key role in **privacy**, **free speech**, and **secure communication**, especially for those who are at risk of surveillance or censorship.

In this section, we will explore the **legitimate uses** of the dark web in **journalism**, **activism**, **whistleblowing**, and **secure communication**. By the end of this chapter, you'll gain a clearer understanding of how the dark web contributes to protecting freedom and privacy, offering real-world examples and practical applications that highlight its positive impact.

1. Journalism: Secure Communication and Whistleblowing

One of the most important and **legitimate uses** of the dark web is in **journalism**, especially for reporters working in countries with oppressive governments or those investigating sensitive issues. The anonymity and encryption provided by tools like **Tor** make it possible for journalists to protect their sources, safeguard their communication, and access information that would otherwise be censored.

Whistleblowing and Secure Submissions

Journalists rely on the dark web to **protect the identity** of their sources and ensure that sensitive information can be shared safely. **Whistleblowers**, often people who have access to classified or confidential information, can submit their documents anonymously to trusted journalists without fear of retribution.

- **SecureDrop**: SecureDrop is one of the most well-known tools used by journalists and news organizations to protect the identity of whistleblowers. It provides a secure platform for individuals to submit documents and communicate with reporters while maintaining their anonymity. The platform operates via the Tor network, ensuring that neither the whistleblower nor the journalist can be traced.
- **Case Study: Edward Snowden**: Edward Snowden, the former NSA contractor who leaked classified information about government surveillance programs, used secure platforms like **Tor** and **SecureDrop** to communicate with journalists and reveal this sensitive information. His use of the dark web protected him from detection and ensured that the information could be shared with the public.

How Does It Work?

1. **Whistleblower Access**: A whistleblower accesses the SecureDrop platform via the Tor browser. They can upload documents securely and send messages to a journalist without revealing their identity.
2. **Journalist's Side**: Journalists use the same platform to read and download documents from whistleblowers. They can reply to messages or request more information, all while remaining anonymous.

---

2. Activism: Free Speech in Repressive Regimes

The dark web has become an essential platform for **activists** working in countries where freedom of expression is severely restricted. In many regions, governments control access to information and monitor citizens' communications. The dark web provides a space where individuals can speak freely, organize movements, and protest government censorship without the threat of surveillance or retaliation.

- **Circumventing Censorship**: In countries where internet censorship is a daily reality (like **China**, **Iran**, and **Saudi Arabia**), the dark web allows individuals to access **uncensored information** and communicate with others without government interference.
- **Organizing Protests**: Activists use the dark web to organize movements, arrange protests, and share messages that may be suppressed by the mainstream media or blocked by government authorities.
- **Anonymous Social Media**: Many activists use the dark web to create **anonymous social media accounts** to bypass censorship and avoid being traced by their government.

Real-World Example: Arab Spring

During the **Arab Spring** protests in 2011, activists in countries like **Tunisia**, **Egypt**, and **Libya** used Tor and other dark web tools to circumvent government censorship and communicate with the outside world. They used these platforms to spread the word about protests, coordinate demonstrations, and share video footage of government crackdowns. The dark web helped ensure that these voices could not be silenced by oppressive regimes.

---

3. Secure Communication: Privacy for Everyone

In an age where privacy is becoming increasingly rare, many individuals and organizations turn to the dark web for **secure communication**. Whether it's sending encrypted messages, conducting private transactions, or browsing anonymously, the dark web offers a refuge from surveillance and data collection.

Why Privacy Matters

As governments and corporations collect vast amounts of data about users, the need for privacy has never been more critical. The dark web provides tools that allow individuals to communicate, browse, and make transactions without leaving a digital footprint.

- **Encrypted Communication**: Services like **ProtonMail** (a secure email provider) and **Signal** (an encrypted messaging app) allow users to send messages or emails securely, ensuring that their communications remain private.
- **Anonymous Browsing**: The Tor browser allows users to browse the internet without revealing their **IP address** or **physical location**, providing a level of **privacy** that is becoming increasingly difficult to achieve on the surface web.
- **Cryptocurrency Transactions**: The dark web is also home to cryptocurrency services that allow individuals to make anonymous payments. This ensures that users can purchase services or products without revealing their financial details.

How Does Secure Communication Work?

- **Encryption**: Services like ProtonMail and Signal use encryption to scramble messages so that only the intended recipient can decrypt them. This ensures that even if a third party intercepts the message, they will not be able to read it.
- **Anonymity**: The Tor browser ensures that users' browsing activities cannot be traced back to them. By routing traffic through multiple nodes, Tor makes it incredibly difficult to track the user's location or identity.

---

4. Academic Research: Accessing Uncensored

Knowledge

For **academics**, the dark web offers access to research and information that might be otherwise inaccessible due to **censorship** or **government control**. In some countries, access to educational materials, scientific journals, or historical records is restricted or tightly monitored. The dark web allows individuals to bypass these restrictions and access **uncensored knowledge**.

- **Access to Banned Information**: In countries with strict censorship laws, the dark web provides an outlet for individuals to access **academic papers**, **scientific articles**, and other resources that may be restricted by the government.
- **Safe Sharing of Research**: Scholars and researchers can use encrypted channels on the dark web to share their findings without the risk of intellectual property theft or government interference.

Example:

- **Academics in Repressive Countries**: Scholars in countries with government-controlled internet access, such as **China** or **Russia**, use Tor to bypass restrictions and access **research papers**, **libraries**, and **publications** from institutions around the world.

Visual Aid: The Use of the Dark Web for Secure

Communication and Free Speech

Here's a simple diagram illustrating how the dark web facilitates secure communication and free speech:

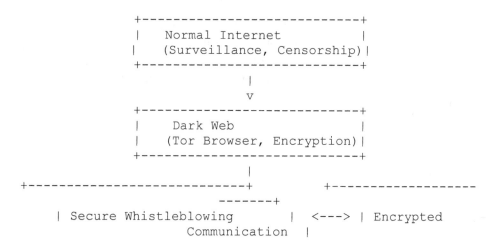

```
        +-----------------------------+
        |    Normal Internet          |
        |  (Surveillance, Censorship) |
        +-----------------------------+
                      |
                      v
        +-----------------------------+
        |    Dark Web                 |
        |  (Tor Browser, Encryption)  |
        +-----------------------------+
                      |
+---------------------------------+          +-------------------
                         -------+
 | Secure Whistleblowing         | <---> | Encrypted
                Communication    |
```

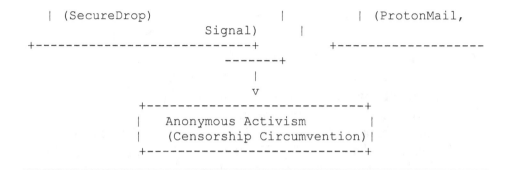

```
|  (SecureDrop)                  |              |  (ProtonMail,
                    Signal)      |              +-------------------
+-----------------------------+              +-------------------
                    -------+
                    |
                    v
       +-----------------------------+
       |  Anonymous Activism         |
       |  (Censorship Circumvention) |
       +-----------------------------+
```

While the **dark web** is often associated with **cybercrime**, its **legitimate uses** are invaluable for **privacy, freedom of speech, activism**, and **secure communication**. The dark web allows people to **speak freely** without fear of censorship or surveillance, providing them with the tools to engage in political activism, share whistleblowing information, and communicate securely.

Whistleblowers, journalists, and **activists** all rely on the dark web to protect their identity and ensure their message reaches its intended audience. In a world where **privacy** is becoming increasingly scarce, the dark web provides a vital platform for individuals to communicate securely and without fear of retribution.

3.3: Why Anonymity is Important Online

In today's hyper-connected world, the question of **online anonymity** is more critical than ever. From **identity theft** and **corporate surveillance** to **government monitoring** and **data profiling**, the need to protect your personal information and activities on the internet is essential for maintaining **privacy, security**, and **freedom**. In this section, we'll explore the **importance of anonymity online**, its benefits, and why it matters not just for **cybersecurity** professionals or activists, but for everyone who engages in digital spaces.

The Digital Footprint: Why Anonymity Matters

Every time you interact with the internet, you leave behind a **digital footprint**. This can include everything from the websites you visit and the messages you send, to the apps you use and the devices you connect with.

What's at Risk?

1. **Personal Data**: Personal information such as your **name, address, email, phone number**, and even your **behavioral patterns** are constantly collected by websites, apps, and online services.
2. **Financial Information**: Credit card details, bank account numbers, and online payment information can also be intercepted if proper security measures aren't taken.
3. **Location Tracking**: With the rise of location-based services, your **physical location** can be tracked through your phone, apps, or even your IP address.

Even if you're not engaged in anything illegal or controversial, the lack of anonymity exposes you to risks like **identity theft, targeted advertising**, or **unwanted surveillance**.

Why Anonymity?

Anonymity online means that your **identity** and **activities** are not easily traced or identified by other parties. It's about **protecting** your personal information and ensuring that you have control over how much of it is visible to the world. With **anonymity**, you can reduce the risk of **exploitation** and safeguard your privacy.

---

1. Protecting Privacy from Surveillance

In recent years, **government surveillance** has become a significant concern. Government agencies, such as the **NSA** (National Security Agency) in the U.S. or similar bodies in other countries, have the capability to monitor and track citizens' online activities on a massive scale.

In 2013, **Edward Snowden**, a former NSA contractor, exposed the extent of government surveillance programs. These programs were collecting vast amounts of data on **phone calls**, **email communications**, and **internet browsing habits** of ordinary citizens—without their knowledge or consent.

Snowden's revelations led to public outcry about the lack of privacy online and the power governments hold over their citizens' personal data. This case underscores why **anonymity** is important for protecting **personal freedom** and preventing overreach by governments or other entities.

Practical Implementation: Using Encryption for Privacy

One way to protect your online privacy is by using **encryption tools**. For example:

- **Signal** and **WhatsApp** provide end-to-end encryption for text messages and voice calls, ensuring that only the sender and receiver can read or listen to the messages.
- **ProtonMail**, a secure email service, encrypts email communication, making it unreadable to anyone except the intended recipient.

By using encrypted communication tools, users can ensure that their online conversations and transactions are **private** and protected from prying eyes.

---

2. Preventing Identity Theft and Financial Fraud

Without anonymity, your **personal information** can easily be exposed, making you vulnerable to identity theft. Hackers and cybercriminals can steal sensitive data such as **credit card numbers**, **social security numbers**, and **login credentials** through various means, including phishing attacks, data breaches, and malware.

In 2017, **Equifax**, one of the largest credit reporting agencies, experienced a massive data breach that exposed the **personal information** of 147 million Americans. This data included names, addresses, birth dates, and **social security numbers**—all of which are critical for identity theft.

Once this information was stolen, cybercriminals used it to open fake accounts, apply for loans, and commit fraud. The breach highlighted the importance of **protecting personal data** and maintaining anonymity to prevent **financial fraud** and **identity theft**.

Practical Implementation: Using Strong Passwords and Two-Factor Authentication

- **Strong passwords**: Use a combination of letters, numbers, and symbols to create strong passwords that are hard for hackers to guess.
- **Two-Factor Authentication (2FA)**: Enable 2FA on your accounts. This adds an extra layer of security, requiring a code sent to your phone or email in addition to your password.
- **Password Managers**: Use a password manager (e.g., **LastPass**, **1Password**) to generate and store unique, complex passwords for every website you use.

By employing these **security measures**, you can reduce the chances of your **identity** and **financial information** being compromised.

---

3. Avoiding Targeted Advertising and Data Profiling

Every time you visit a website or use an app, your behavior is tracked and analyzed to create a **digital profile**. This profile includes your interests, buying habits, and even your personal beliefs or preferences.

While targeted ads can sometimes be useful (showing you products you're interested in), they also raise privacy concerns. The sheer amount of personal data collected can be invasive, and many people feel uncomfortable with the idea of their online behavior being watched and analyzed.

For example, if you're browsing websites about travel, you may soon see ads for flights and hotels. While this may seem harmless, it's based on the collection of **personal data** and patterns that reveal intimate details about your life. Without anonymity, this data can be exploited for **commercial purposes**, leading to **privacy violations** and potentially **unwanted manipulation**.

Practical Implementation: Using Privacy Tools

- **Ad Blockers**: Use **ad blockers** like **uBlock Origin** or **AdGuard** to prevent targeted ads from appearing on websites. This also helps speed up browsing.
- **Privacy-Focused Search Engines**: Use search engines like **DuckDuckGo** or **StartPage**, which don't track your searches or build a profile of you.
- **VPNs**: A **VPN** (Virtual Private Network) can help mask your IP address, preventing websites from tracking your location and online behavior.

By using these tools, you can maintain your **online anonymity** and prevent your data from being harvested for **commercial** or **malicious** purposes.

---

4. Enabling Freedom of Speech in Repressive Environments

In many parts of the world, **free speech** is not a guaranteed right. Activists, journalists, and political dissidents are often at risk of persecution for expressing dissenting opinions or sharing information critical of the government. The dark web, through tools like **Tor**, provides a **safe space** for these individuals to express themselves without the fear of government surveillance or retaliation.

Real-World Example: Political Dissidents in Authoritarian Countries

In **China**, where internet access is heavily censored, activists use **Tor** to access restricted information and communicate securely. The government actively monitors online activity, and those who speak out against the regime face imprisonment or worse. By using Tor, these individuals can avoid detection and ensure that their communications remain private.

Practical Implementation: Using Tor for Anonymity

- **Tor Browser**: The Tor browser anonymizes your internet traffic, making it harder for your government or hackers to trace your activities.
- **VPNs**: Combine **Tor** with a VPN for an added layer of security. The VPN will mask your real IP address, while Tor ensures that your internet traffic is encrypted and routed through multiple nodes to preserve your anonymity.

By ensuring **online anonymity**, individuals in repressive regimes can **express their opinions**, **share information**, and **organize** without fearing retribution.

Visual Aid: How Anonymity Protects Privacy and Freedom

Here's a simple diagram showing how anonymity and privacy tools help protect individuals online:

```
+----------------------------+
```

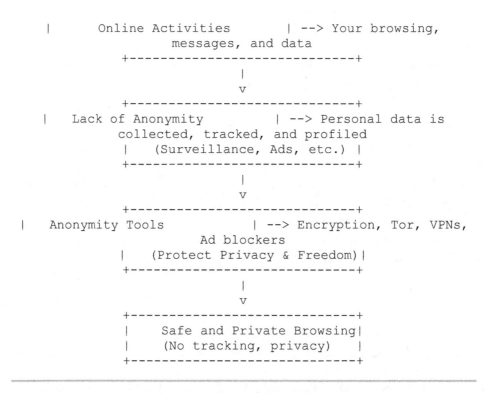

```
|      Online Activities       | --> Your browsing,
               messages, and data
     +-----------------------------+
                    |
                    v
     +-----------------------------+
|    Lack of Anonymity         | --> Personal data is
          collected, tracked, and profiled
          |   (Surveillance, Ads, etc.) |
     +-----------------------------+
                    |
                    v
     +-----------------------------+
|    Anonymity Tools           | --> Encryption, Tor, VPNs,
                    Ad blockers
          |   (Protect Privacy & Freedom)|
     +-----------------------------+
                    |
                    v
     +-----------------------------+
     |    Safe and Private Browsing|
     |    (No tracking, privacy)   |
     +-----------------------------+
```

The internet has become a critical part of our daily lives, but with this connectivity comes the risk of losing **privacy** and **control over personal data**. Maintaining **anonymity** online is essential for protecting **freedom of expression**, **privacy**, and **security**. Whether you're trying to **avoid surveillance**, **prevent identity theft**, or simply **protect your freedom of speech**, anonymity provides a crucial layer of protection.

By using tools like **Tor**, **VPNs**, and **encrypted communication**, you can take control of your online presence and ensure that your **personal information** remains safe from prying eyes. The need for anonymity online is only going to grow as we move further into the digital age, and it's up to us to understand its importance and take the necessary steps to protect ourselves.

Chapter 4: How to Access the Dark Web Safely

Navigating the **dark web** safely is essential if you want to protect your **privacy**, **security**, and avoid any potential threats. While the dark web offers incredible opportunities for secure communication, **anonymous browsing**, and accessing restricted information, it also comes with risks— just like any other part of the internet. This chapter will guide you through the **basic steps** to access the dark web securely and discuss the tools and practices you need to ensure your activities remain safe.

We'll start by introducing **Tor** and other **dark web browsers**, then move on to setting up a **secure browsing environment** using **VPNs** and **encryption**, and finally, discuss some **enhanced security tools** to keep your browsing activities private and protected.

4.1: Introduction to Tor and Other Dark Web Browsers

Navigating the dark web securely begins with understanding the **browsers** designed to access it. The most popular and widely used browser is **Tor** (The Onion Router), but there are also other tools that offer similar functionality. This chapter will walk you through **Tor**, its capabilities, and alternative dark web browsers. You'll also understand the **importance** of anonymity and security when accessing the dark web, and how these tools achieve that.

What is Tor?

Tor is a free, open-source software that allows you to browse the internet anonymously. The name **"Tor"** stands for **The Onion Router**, which is a reference to how it encrypts and routes your internet traffic through multiple layers—like the layers of an onion.

How Tor Works

Tor's **primary purpose** is to ensure **anonymity** by routing your traffic through a decentralized network of nodes (volunteer-operated relays) across the world. When you use Tor, your data is encrypted multiple times, and each relay on the network only decrypts one layer of encryption before passing the data to the next relay. This process ensures that no single node knows both your **origin** and your **destination**.

- **Multi-layer encryption**: Each node decrypts only one layer of encryption, making it difficult to trace your data back to you.
- **Routing through multiple relays**: Your data travels through a series of nodes before reaching its destination, enhancing your anonymity.

The end result is that Tor helps mask your **IP address**, **location**, and online activities, making it **extremely difficult** for anyone to trace your browsing back to you.

Why Use Tor?

Tor's **primary advantage** is its ability to provide users with **online anonymity**. It's not just for the dark web—it can be used for any internet browsing activity where privacy is important. Here's why Tor is a widely trusted tool:

1. Bypass Censorship

Tor allows users to access websites that are **blocked** or **censored** in certain countries. This is especially useful for users in regions where **internet censorship** is rampant, like **China**, **Iran**, or **Turkey**.

2. Protect Personal Data

Tor helps **secure personal information** by preventing websites from tracking your **IP address**. For example, when you access a website using Tor, the website cannot see your real **IP address**; instead, it sees the IP address of the **last Tor relay** your data passed through.

3. Secure Communication

For individuals and organizations that need secure communication, Tor can be used to communicate anonymously over **email**, **messaging apps**, and more. It's also commonly used by **journalists**, **whistleblowers**, and **activists** working in **repressive environments**.

4. Avoid Tracking

Tor helps you avoid being tracked by advertisers, governments, and even hackers. With **cookies** and **tracking mechanisms** blocked, Tor ensures that websites can't track your online behavior.

Installing and Using Tor

Using **Tor** for secure browsing is relatively straightforward. Let's go through the basic steps to install and configure it.

Step 1: Downloading Tor

1. Visit the official **Tor Project website**: https://www.torproject.org
2. Select the appropriate version for your operating system (**Windows, macOS**, or **Linux**).
3. Download and **install** the Tor Browser.

Step 2: Setting Up Tor

Once you've installed the browser, you'll need to **configure** it:

- Launch the Tor Browser.

- If you're in a region where Tor is **blocked**, you'll need to configure your connection by selecting the **"Configure"** option and using **bridges** or **pluggable transports** to bypass censorship.
- If no such restrictions are present, click **"Connect"** to join the Tor network.

Step 3: Browsing with Tor

Once connected, Tor Browser works just like any regular browser. You can visit websites, search for information, and navigate the web—but with the benefit of **anonymity** and **security**. Just remember that **.onion** websites, which are specific to the dark web, can only be accessed through Tor.

Alternatives to Tor: Other Dark Web Browsers

While Tor is by far the most popular tool for accessing the dark web, there are alternative tools designed to provide similar levels of **anonymity** and **privacy**. Let's look at a couple of the most well-known alternatives.

1. I2P (Invisible Internet Project)

I2P is another **anonymity network** that enables users to browse the internet securely and privately. I2P is similar to Tor but with a few key differences:

- **Peer-to-Peer Network**: While Tor relies on relays to route traffic, I2P uses a **peer-to-peer** network, where nodes (called **routers**) communicate directly with each other.
- **Focus on Hidden Services**: I2P is particularly focused on hosting **anonymous websites** (also called **eepsites**) and **anonymous file sharing**.
- **Not as popular as Tor**: While I2P offers strong anonymity, it's not as widely used as Tor, and its user base is relatively smaller.

Use Case: I2P is often used by individuals who need to host anonymous websites or communicate securely over **peer-to-peer networks**, like **file sharing**.

2. Freenet

Freenet is another tool designed for secure and anonymous communication, but with a few key differences:

- **Decentralized Storage**: Freenet allows users to **store files** and **publish content** in a completely **decentralized** manner. This means that there is no central server or authority controlling the data.
- **Focus on Censorship Resistance**: The goal of Freenet is to provide **resistance** to censorship, enabling users to share information freely without the risk of being blocked by governments or other authorities.

Use Case: Freenet is primarily used for **censorship-resistant publishing** and is popular among people who want to publish **anonymous content** or share information that might be blocked in their country.

Comparison of Tor, I2P, and Freenet

Here's a simple comparison of the three major tools used to access the dark web:

Feature	Tor	I2P	Freenet
Focus	Anonymity for browsing	Anonymous P2P networks & hidden services	Censorship-resistant publishing
Network Type	Centralized (relays)	Peer-to-peer	Decentralized (nodes)
Speed	Moderate (depends on network)	Faster for P2P activities	Slower (due to decentralized storage)

Feature	Tor	I2P	Freenet
Use Cases	General browsing, dark web access	File sharing, hidden services	Anonymous publishing, file sharing
Popularity	Most popular	Less popular	Niche, focused on content sharing

Using Tor for Dark Web Access

Once you have **Tor** installed and configured, you're ready to start accessing **.onion** websites—the specific domain used for dark web sites.

Step 1: Accessing .onion Sites

1. **Enter the URL**: In the Tor browser's address bar, you can type the **.onion** address of a website you wish to visit. These addresses end with **.onion** and are only accessible through Tor.
2. **Search via Dark Web Search Engines**: If you don't have a specific .onion website in mind, you can use dark web search engines like **Ahmia, DuckDuckGo (onion version)**, or **NotEvil** to find resources on the dark web.
3. **Browse Securely**: While browsing the dark web, be cautious of malicious websites and avoid downloading any files from untrusted sources.

Step 2: Staying Safe While Using Tor

- **Don't log into personal accounts**: Avoid logging into personal accounts such as Gmail, Facebook, or your banking account, as this can expose your identity.
- **Be cautious of links**: Dark web sites can sometimes contain harmful content like malware or phishing schemes. Always double-check the websites you visit and ensure they are trustworthy.

- **Use additional security**: While Tor offers strong encryption, consider using a **VPN** alongside Tor for added protection and to prevent potential tracking of your online activities.

Visual Aid: How Tor Works – Layered Encryption

Here's a simplified diagram illustrating how **Tor's layered encryption** works:

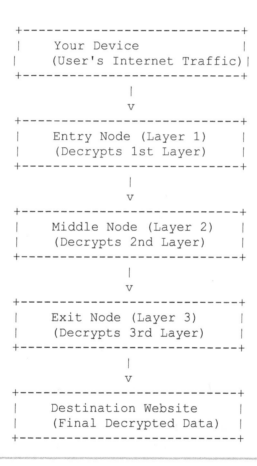

```
        +-------------------------------+
        |      Your Device              |
        |    (User's Internet Traffic)  |
        +-------------------------------+
                        |
                        v
        +-------------------------------+
        |    Entry Node (Layer 1)       |
        |    (Decrypts 1st Layer)       |
        +-------------------------------+
                        |
                        v
        +-------------------------------+
        |    Middle Node (Layer 2)      |
        |    (Decrypts 2nd Layer)       |
        +-------------------------------+
                        |
                        v
        +-------------------------------+
        |    Exit Node (Layer 3)        |
        |    (Decrypts 3rd Layer)       |
        +-------------------------------+
                        |
                        v
        +-------------------------------+
        |    Destination Website        |
        |    (Final Decrypted Data)     |
        +-------------------------------+
```

Tor is the most popular and widely used browser for accessing the dark web, offering users strong **anonymity**, **privacy**, and **security**. Whether you're browsing for **research**, **free speech**, or **secure communication**,

Tor provides a reliable tool for navigating the internet without revealing your identity.

However, other browsers like **I2P** and **Freenet** also offer valuable alternatives depending on your needs. Whether you're looking for **decentralized communication** or **censorship-resistant publishing**, these tools can further enhance your privacy and security.

4.2: Setting Up Secure Browsing (Tor, VPNs, and Encryption)

Navigating the **dark web** securely requires more than just using the Tor browser. To ensure that your **privacy** and **anonymity** are fully protected, you need to combine several security layers. These include using **VPNs** (Virtual Private Networks), **encryption** methods, and safe browsing practices to shield your identity and activities from prying eyes.

In this section, we'll guide you step-by-step on how to **set up secure browsing** using **Tor**, a **VPN**, and **encryption tools**. We'll also explain why each of these tools is important for maintaining your **digital privacy** and protecting your data. The goal is to help you create a **secure browsing environment** that minimizes risks while accessing the dark web or simply browsing online.

Why Is Secure Browsing Important?

In the age of **surveillance**, **data breaches**, and **cyberattacks**, your online activities are constantly being tracked. **Governments**, **corporations**, and even **hackers** can gather personal data, track your movements, and expose you to various online threats.

Secure browsing protects you from:

1. **Data interception**: Ensures your communication and data are not intercepted by hackers or malicious entities.
2. **Location tracking**: Hides your IP address and physical location to prevent others from identifying you.
3. **Identity theft**: Protects personal data, including your browsing habits, emails, and financial details.

By using **Tor**, **VPNs**, and **encryption**, you can mask your identity, secure your data, and minimize exposure to digital threats. Let's dive into how to configure each tool for maximum protection.

Step 1: Setting Up Tor Browser

Tor is the first and most important tool for accessing the dark web. It provides **anonymity** by encrypting your internet traffic and routing it through multiple relays (nodes), making it difficult to trace your activity back to you.

How to Install and Use Tor Browser:

1. **Download Tor Browser**:
   Visit the official Tor Project website: *https://www.torproject.org/.*
   Avoid downloading it from third-party sources to reduce the risk of malware.
2. **Installation**:
   Choose the correct version for your operating system (**Windows, macOS, Linux**), then follow the installation prompts. The installation process is straightforward, and the browser is designed to be simple and easy to use.
3. **Configure Tor**:
   When you open Tor for the first time, you'll be asked to connect to the Tor network. In most cases, clicking "Connect" will suffice, but if you are in a country with **internet restrictions** (such as China), you may need to use **bridges** or **pluggable transports** to bypass censorship.
4. **Browsing the Dark Web**:
   Once Tor is running, you can begin browsing websites that end in

.onion (the dark web's domain suffix). These websites can only be accessed through Tor, and they provide a **secure**, **encrypted connection**.

Step 2: Using a VPN for Enhanced Security

While Tor provides strong anonymity, combining it with a **VPN** (Virtual Private Network) offers **additional layers of protection** and helps safeguard your identity even further.

Why Use a VPN with Tor?

- **Hides Your Tor Usage**: Using a VPN before connecting to Tor makes it harder for anyone monitoring your internet traffic (like your Internet Service Provider or government authorities) to know you're using Tor in the first place.
- **Protects Your IP Address**: Even though Tor hides your IP address by routing your traffic through multiple relays, a VPN ensures that your **real IP address** is **hidden** even before the traffic reaches the Tor network.
- **Bypasses Censorship**: Some countries actively block Tor. A VPN can help you bypass these restrictions by masking your connection and making it appear as though you're accessing the internet from a different country.

How to Set Up a VPN with Tor:

1. **Choose a Reliable VPN Provider**:
   Select a **reputable VPN** that values **privacy** and **security**. Providers like **ExpressVPN**, **NordVPN**, and **ProtonVPN** are popular choices that offer strong encryption and no-logs policies.
2. **Install the VPN**:
   Download and install the VPN software on your device. Most VPN providers offer easy-to-follow installation guides for different operating systems.
3. **Connect to the VPN**:
   Once installed, launch the VPN app, choose a server location

(preferably outside of your country for extra privacy), and connect to the VPN.
4. **Launch Tor Browser**:
   After connecting to the VPN, open the **Tor browser**. Now, your internet traffic is first encrypted by the VPN and then routed through Tor, providing double encryption for enhanced anonymity.

Step 3: Ensuring Encryption for Sensitive Data

Encryption is the process of converting data into a secure format so that only authorized parties can access it. Encryption ensures that your sensitive information—such as emails, messages, or files—is **protected from prying eyes**.

How to Encrypt Communications

To maintain privacy while communicating online, you need to use **end-to-end encryption** for your messages and emails.

1. **Encrypted Email Services**:
   - **ProtonMail** and **Tutanota** offer **end-to-end encrypted email** services. This means that only the sender and the recipient can read the email's content—no one else, not even the email provider, can decrypt the message.
2. **Encrypted Messaging Apps**:
   - Use **Signal** or **WhatsApp** for encrypted text messages and calls. These apps provide **end-to-end encryption**, ensuring that no third party can intercept or read your messages.
3. **File Encryption**:
   For sensitive files, use tools like **VeraCrypt** or **BitLocker** (on Windows) to encrypt files before sending or storing them. These tools will ensure that only those with the correct decryption key can access your files.

Step 4: Additional Security Tools for Enhanced Privacy

While **Tor**, **VPNs**, and **encryption** are fundamental for securing your browsing, there are additional tools that can further enhance your security and privacy while using the dark web.

Privacy-Focused Search Engines:

Traditional search engines like **Google** track your searches and build profiles based on your activity. On the dark web, it's crucial to use privacy-focused search engines that don't track your searches or store personal data.

- **DuckDuckGo**: A search engine that does not track or profile users. You can use DuckDuckGo's **.onion** version for privacy while browsing the dark web.
- **StartPage**: Another search engine that ensures privacy by not tracking your search history. It also provides search results from Google without the tracking.

Secure File Sharing:

- **OnionShare**: This tool allows you to **share files** securely over the Tor network. It ensures that files are transferred without compromising your privacy and anonymity.
- **Whisper Systems**: You can use this for encrypted file transfers if you're exchanging sensitive documents.

Using NoScript with Tor:

While **Tor** offers strong security, some dark web websites might attempt to run **malicious scripts** or **JavaScript** that can compromise your security. **NoScript** is a browser extension that helps block these scripts from running, making your browsing more secure.

1. **Install NoScript**: Tor Browser comes with **NoScript** pre-installed, which helps block potentially harmful scripts on websites.
2. **Configuring NoScript**: You can configure NoScript to block JavaScript on specific websites or allow it only on trusted sites.

WebRTC is a protocol used by browsers to enable real-time communication (such as video and audio calls). However, it can also **leak your real IP address** despite using Tor or a VPN. Make sure WebRTC is disabled in your browser settings to prevent potential leaks.

Visual Aid: Secure Browsing with Tor and VPN

Here's a simple diagram illustrating how **Tor** and a **VPN** work together to ensure secure browsing:

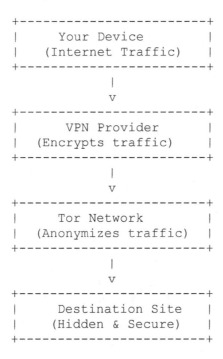

```
+-----------------------+
|     Your Device       |
|   (Internet Traffic)  |
+-----------------------+
            |
            v
+-----------------------+
|     VPN Provider      |
|   (Encrypts traffic)  |
+-----------------------+
            |
            v
+-----------------------+
|     Tor Network       |
|  (Anonymizes traffic) |
+-----------------------+
            |
            v
+-----------------------+
|    Destination Site   |
|   (Hidden & Secure)   |
+-----------------------+
```

In this setup, your **internet traffic** first goes through the **VPN** (which encrypts and anonymizes it), then it passes through **Tor**, which further anonymizes your connection by routing it through multiple nodes. Finally, your **destination website** cannot trace your real IP address or location.

The dark web can be a useful space for privacy, security, and anonymity, but it's also a place where threats and risks can lurk. Setting up **secure browsing** through tools like **Tor**, **VPNs**, and **encryption** ensures that your online activities remain protected.

4.3: Tools for Enhanced Security (e.g., Privacy-Focused Search Engines)

When it comes to browsing the **dark web** or navigating the **surface web** securely, it's crucial to use the right set of tools. While **Tor** and **VPNs** provide strong layers of protection, there are other tools you can use to enhance your **security** and **privacy** even further. These tools focus on protecting your **personal information**, minimizing **tracking**, and ensuring your browsing activity remains private.

In this section, we will focus on a few key tools that can help you maintain security while browsing online, with a particular focus on **privacy-focused search engines**, **encrypted communications**, and **file sharing tools**. By integrating these tools into your browsing habits, you can significantly reduce the risks associated with online activities.

Why Enhance Your Security?

The internet today is increasingly becoming a place where **personal data** is constantly being collected, tracked, and profiled. Websites and advertisers gather a lot of information about you, such as:

- **Browsing habits**
- **Search queries**
- **Location data**
- **Device information**

This data is often used to create detailed profiles, which are then sold or used to serve you targeted ads. Worse, it can be exploited by malicious actors. **Enhanced security tools** give you the power to prevent this kind of tracking, keep your information private, and ensure that you're not exposed to unnecessary risks.

---

1. Privacy-Focused Search Engines

One of the most common ways websites track you is through search engines. Google, for example, logs everything you search, and its algorithms build a profile on you. On the dark web, where anonymity is key, traditional search engines are not ideal because they track every click and query.

Why Use Privacy-Focused Search Engines?

Privacy-focused search engines ensure that your **search activity** is not recorded or profiled. They don't track you, store your personal information, or sell your data to advertisers. These search engines also protect your **identity** by offering anonymity during browsing.

Popular Privacy-Focused Search Engines:

1. **DuckDuckGo**:
    o DuckDuckGo is one of the most widely-used **privacy-first search engines**. It doesn't track your searches or store personal information. Unlike Google, DuckDuckGo does not create a **search history** or personalize your results based on past behavior.
    o **Dark Web Version**: DuckDuckGo offers a **.onion** version that is specifically designed for use with Tor, ensuring complete privacy on the dark web.
    o **How It Works**: DuckDuckGo scrapes results from a variety of sources, including Yahoo, Bing, and its own search index, without collecting or storing any personal information.
2. **StartPage**:
    o StartPage is another great privacy-focused search engine that pulls results from **Google** but without tracking your

personal information or storing search history. It's often considered the best way to access Google's results without compromising privacy.

- o **How It Works**: When you search on StartPage, your queries are sent to Google, but Google doesn't have access to your personal information because **StartPage acts as a middleman**. The results you get are completely unfiltered, offering privacy without sacrificing search quality.

3. **Qwant**:
   - o Qwant is a European-based search engine that emphasizes privacy and does not track user data. It provides a privacy-focused alternative to both Google and Bing.
   - o **How It Works**: Qwant indexes websites using its own crawler and doesn't store personal data or use tracking cookies.

How to Set Up Privacy-Focused Search Engines:

- To use **DuckDuckGo** or **StartPage** on Tor, simply type their **.onion URLs** in the Tor browser's address bar. The **.onion versions** of these search engines ensure maximum privacy and are encrypted through the Tor network.
  - o **DuckDuckGo**: https://3g2upl4pq6kufc4m.onion
  - o **StartPage**: https://startpage.com

Using these search engines not only protects your privacy but also ensures that your searches on the dark web or surface web are **not logged** or **profiled**.

---

2. Encrypted Communication Tools

Encryption is a crucial tool for ensuring your communications remain private. Whether you're sending emails, chatting with someone online, or transferring files, **encrypted communication** ensures that only you and your recipient can access the information.

Many online communication methods, such as **email** and **messaging apps**, are vulnerable to hacking, surveillance, and unauthorized access. Using encrypted communication ensures that even if someone intercepts your message, they cannot read it without the decryption key.

Popular Encrypted Communication Tools:

1. **ProtonMail**:
   - ProtonMail is a secure email provider that offers **end-to-end encryption**. This means that only the sender and the recipient can read the email contents. Even ProtonMail's administrators cannot access your emails.
   - **How It Works**: ProtonMail uses **OpenPGP** encryption to protect email content. Additionally, all emails are stored in an encrypted format in ProtonMail's servers.
   - **Tip**: Use ProtonMail's **.onion** version to securely send encrypted emails through the Tor network.
2. **Signal**:
   - Signal is a highly secure messaging app that provides **end-to-end encryption** for both text messages and voice calls. It's recommended by many privacy advocates and experts because it's open-source and has been independently audited.
   - **How It Works**: Signal uses the **Signal Protocol** to encrypt messages and calls, ensuring that only the sender and receiver can decrypt and read them.
3. **WhatsApp**:
   - WhatsApp also offers end-to-end encryption, which means that the company cannot access your messages. While WhatsApp does store metadata (who you are communicating with and when), it ensures that your messages are protected from eavesdropping.

Setting Up Encrypted Communication:

- For **ProtonMail**, create an account on their website, and if using Tor, access the **.onion version** for added security.
- **Signal**: Install the app on your phone, register with your phone number, and begin sending encrypted messages.

- **WhatsApp**: Ensure that your encryption settings are enabled by default (this is usually automatic for messages sent between WhatsApp users).

These tools give you **confidentiality** and ensure that **third parties** cannot access your conversations.

---

3. Secure File Sharing Tools

Sharing files securely is another crucial aspect of maintaining privacy online. Sometimes, you may need to send **sensitive files** that need to remain **protected** from interception.

Why Use Secure File Sharing?

Regular file-sharing services may expose your personal data, leaving your files vulnerable to hackers, government surveillance, or unauthorized access. **Encrypted file-sharing tools** help ensure that only the intended recipient can access your files.

Popular Secure File Sharing Tools:

1. **OnionShare**:
   - **OnionShare** allows you to securely share files over the **Tor network**. The service provides **anonymous peer-to-peer file sharing** with strong encryption.
   - **How It Works**: You upload your file to **OnionShare**, and it creates a **unique .onion URL** that only the intended recipient can access. The files are transferred without using a central server, making the process **more secure**.
2. **Tresorit**:
   - Tresorit is a cloud storage service that offers **end-to-end encryption**. It's designed for securely storing and sharing sensitive files.
   - **How It Works**: Tresorit uses **zero-knowledge encryption**, which means they cannot access your files, even if they wanted to. You hold the encryption keys.

How to Use OnionShare:

1. Download and install **OnionShare** from https://onionshare.org.
2. Select the file(s) you want to share and choose the **"Start Sharing"** option. OnionShare will generate a **.onion URL**.
3. Send the generated URL to your recipient via a secure channel (e.g., ProtonMail). The recipient can then access and download the file using Tor.

---

4. Avoiding Online Tracking with Privacy Tools

One of the best ways to enhance your security is by blocking trackers and advertisements that monitor your online behavior.

Why Block Trackers?

Trackers are used by websites and advertisers to collect data about your browsing habits. This data can be used to build profiles, target ads, or even exploit your personal information.

Privacy Tools to Block Trackers:

1. **uBlock Origin**:
   - **uBlock Origin** is an open-source browser extension that blocks **ads**, **trackers**, and other intrusive scripts. It's lightweight and customizable, making it one of the most popular privacy tools available.
   - **How It Works**: It uses **filter lists** to block known trackers and malicious scripts that can compromise your security.
2. **Privacy Badger**:
   - Developed by the **Electronic Frontier Foundation (EFF)**, **Privacy Badger** automatically detects and blocks third-party trackers on websites.
   - **How It Works**: Privacy Badger analyzes tracking patterns and blocks trackers that seem to be following you across different websites.

Visual Aid: Enhancing Security with Tools

Here's a flowchart to help you visualize the different tools used to enhance security:

```
+--------------------------------+        +------------------
          ----------+         +-----------------------------+
   |       Start with VPN         | ---> |       Tor Browser
          | ----> |  Privacy-Focused Search Engines |
   | (Hides IP and encrypts traffic)|        |       (Anonymity &
      Encryption) |          |        (DuckDuckGo, StartPage)     |
+--------------------------------+        +------------------
          ----------+         +-----------------------------+
                 |                            |
                            |
                 v                            v
                            v
+--------------------------------+        +------------------
          ----------+         +-----------------------------+
   |    Use Encrypted Communication|        |   Secure File
      Sharing       |        |   Block Trackers (uBlock)     |
   |     (ProtonMail, Signal)       |        |     (OnionShare,
      Tresorit)    |        |     (Privacy Badger)           |
+--------------------------------+        +------------------
          ----------+         +-----------------------------+
```

By combining **Tor**, **VPNs**, **privacy-focused search engines**, **encrypted communication**, and **file-sharing tools**, you can create a powerful, multi-layered defense to protect your privacy and security while browsing the dark web or engaging in everyday online activities.

The tools and practices we discussed in this section ensure that your **identity**, **data**, and **communications** remain safe from surveillance, interception, and unwanted exposure. In an era where privacy concerns are at an all-time high, securing your browsing habits is not only smart—it's essential.

By following these **secure browsing practices** and integrating these tools into your daily online activities, you can confidently explore the internet without worrying about threats and vulnerabilities.

Chapter 5: Navigating the Dark Web for Beginners

The **dark web** can be an exciting and sometimes daunting space, especially for beginners. While it offers many benefits, like access to **uncensored information**, **privacy**, and **secure communication**, it's also home to a variety of risks, including **malicious websites**, **fraud**, and **illegal activities**. In this chapter, we'll guide you step by step through the process of **navigating the dark web safely**, teaching you how to find valuable resources, identify trustworthy websites, and avoid common pitfalls.

Let's explore the **fundamentals** of navigating the dark web, starting with an introduction to **dark web websites**, followed by the **best practices for searching**, **recognizing secure websites**, and **avoiding potential dangers**.

5.1: Introduction to Dark Web Websites

The **dark web** is often shrouded in mystery, with many people associating it with **illicit activities** like drug trafficking, hacking, and illegal markets. However, the dark web is much more than just a platform for these activities. It is also a space for **privacy**, **freedom of speech**, and **anonymity** in environments where these rights are under threat.

At the heart of the dark web are the **websites** that operate using **.onion** domains, which are only accessible through specific software, such as **Tor** (The Onion Router). In this section, we will take a deep dive into what **dark web websites** are, how they differ from traditional websites, and the unique features that set them apart. We will also look at the potential benefits and challenges of accessing these sites.

What Are Dark Web Websites?

Dark web websites are websites that are part of the **deep web** and use a special **.onion** domain suffix. These websites are **not indexed** by traditional search engines like **Google** or **Bing**. Instead, they are part of a network that can only be accessed using specialized tools like **Tor**. Here are some defining characteristics of these websites:

- **.onion Domain**: Unlike conventional websites that end with .com, .org, or .net, dark web websites use **.onion** as their domain extension. This extension signifies that the website is only accessible through the **Tor network**.
- **Anonymity and Encryption**: Dark web websites are often used to protect the **identity** and **location** of both users and website owners. Tor encrypts users' connections and routes them through multiple relays across the globe, ensuring that no single entity can trace the user's activity back to them.
- **Specialized Browser**: To access **.onion websites**, you need a specialized browser, like **Tor Browser**, which routes your internet traffic through the **Tor network** and ensures anonymity.
- **Access to Hidden Services**: These sites may host content that is hidden from regular search engines for privacy or security reasons. This includes everything from **secure communication platforms**, to **censorship-resistant websites**, and **privacy-focused services**.

How Do Dark Web Websites Work?

Dark web websites rely on the **Tor network** to provide anonymity and security. The **Tor network** uses a method known as **onion routing**, which involves encrypting and routing internet traffic through several nodes (relays) around the world.

1. **Onion Routing**: When you visit a dark web website, your data is encrypted multiple times and sent through several Tor nodes. Each relay only decrypts one layer of the data, so no single node knows both the **origin** and **destination** of the traffic.
2. **Multi-Layer Encryption**: This layered encryption process ensures that your **identity**, **location**, and **browsing activity** remain hidden, making it nearly impossible for anyone to track or intercept your data.

3. **Hidden Services**: In the Tor network, websites are hosted as **hidden services**, which means their IP addresses and physical locations are obscured, unlike traditional websites that can be located through standard IP addresses.

Real-World Example:

- **ProtonMail**: ProtonMail is a secure, encrypted email service that offers both a regular web-based version and a **.onion** version for users who want to ensure even greater privacy and anonymity. By using the **.onion** version of ProtonMail, users can communicate without worrying about being surveilled by governments or hackers.

What Makes Dark Web Websites Different from Regular Websites?

Dark web websites differ from traditional websites in several key ways:

1. Privacy and Anonymity

The primary difference between dark web websites and regular websites is **privacy**. Dark web sites prioritize protecting users' **identities** and **activities**. Unlike conventional websites that may track your **IP address**, **location**, and **browsing history**, dark web sites use **Tor's encryption** to ensure that this information is not easily exposed.

- **Regular Websites**: When you visit a typical website, your **IP address** is exposed, making it possible for websites to track your browsing habits and even pinpoint your **physical location**.
- **Dark Web Websites**: Websites on the dark web, accessed via **Tor**, hide your **IP address**, making it virtually impossible to trace your activities. The website's **onion domain** is also hidden, so you cannot directly access the site without Tor.

Unlike traditional websites, which can be accessed through standard browsers like Chrome, Safari, or Firefox, **dark web sites** are only accessible through **Tor** or other specialized browsers that support the **.onion** domain.

- **Regular Websites**: Any modern browser (like Google Chrome or Safari) can access standard websites by simply typing the domain (e.g., google.com).
- **Dark Web Websites**: To access dark web sites, you need the **Tor browser**, which routes your traffic through the Tor network. This process of routing and encryption ensures that your activities are kept private and secure.

3. Hosting and Data Security

Dark web websites are typically **self-hosted** and are often run by individuals or groups who wish to remain **anonymous**. The **.onion** domain also ensures that the server's real **IP address** and location remain hidden.

- **Regular Websites**: Most websites are hosted by service providers like **GoDaddy** or **Amazon Web Services**. These hosting services log user activities and may be required to provide data to law enforcement agencies upon request.
- **Dark Web Websites**: Hosting a dark web website via **Tor** means the website owner's physical location and server information are **hidden**. Even if the website is taken down, it's hard for authorities to track the individual or group behind the site.

Why Are People Drawn to Dark Web Websites?

While many associate the dark web with **illegal activities**, it's important to recognize that not all dark web websites are criminal. Many users turn to the dark web for reasons like:

1. Privacy and Censorship Resistance

In countries with **strict censorship**, the dark web is used to access information that may be otherwise blocked. Users in **authoritarian regimes** or countries with internet restrictions use the dark web to communicate, share ideas, and access news without government interference.

- **Case Study: The Arab Spring (2010-2012)**: Activists in countries like **Egypt** and **Tunisia** used the dark web to bypass government censorship, organize protests, and share information. The Tor network provided a secure way to circumvent the regime's attempts to monitor and block communication.

2. Whistleblowing and Journalism

Dark web websites also serve as platforms for **whistleblowers** and **journalists** to communicate securely. Platforms like **SecureDrop** allow journalists to receive documents and information from anonymous sources without revealing the identities of those involved.

- **Example**: WikiLeaks uses dark web sites to accept **anonymous submissions** from whistleblowers, allowing them to expose corruption, human rights violations, and governmental misconduct while staying protected.

3. Secure Communication

Some users, especially those in high-risk professions, need a secure way to communicate without being monitored. Dark web websites provide a space for **encrypted messaging** and **file-sharing**, which is vital for both journalists and activists.

How to Find Reliable Dark Web Websites

While there are **valuable websites** on the dark web, it's important to be cautious and know where to look for **trusted** resources.

1. Trusted Directories

Websites like **The Hidden Wiki** offer directories of **.onion sites** that can be useful for beginners. However, always verify any website before engaging, as some directories may list both legitimate and malicious sites.

2. Reputable Platforms

Some reputable platforms, like **ProtonMail** and **SecureDrop**, have official **.onion sites** for enhanced privacy and security. These websites are widely recognized for their legitimacy.

3. Community Feedback

User reviews and feedback on forums or communities dedicated to the dark web can help you identify **safe and legitimate** sites. Many dark web forums discuss the latest tools, services, and websites, providing firsthand experiences with their **security** and **legitimacy**.

Visual Aid: How the Dark Web Works

Here's a simplified diagram to help visualize how dark web websites operate:

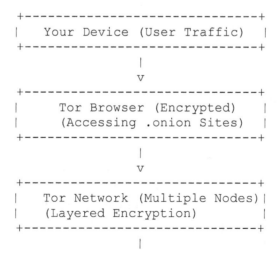

```
+------------------------------+
|   Your Device (User Traffic) |
+------------------------------+
               |
               v
+------------------------------+
|     Tor Browser (Encrypted)  |
|     (Accessing .onion Sites) |
+------------------------------+
               |
               v
+------------------------------+
|   Tor Network (Multiple Nodes)|
|     (Layered Encryption)     |
+------------------------------+
               |
```

```
                    v
    +-----------------------------+
    |      .onion Website         |
    |      (Hidden Services)      |
    +-----------------------------+
```

In this diagram, your internet traffic is first encrypted by the **Tor browser**, routed through multiple nodes in the **Tor network**, and finally reaches the **.onion** website, which ensures that both your **identity** and the website's **location** remain hidden.

The **dark web** is a fascinating, complex space that serves various purposes, from ensuring **privacy** and **freedom of speech** to providing secure platforms for **whistleblowing** and **anonymous communication**. While it's true that some dark web sites are used for illegal activities, many others are legitimate and offer essential services for those who need privacy, anonymity, and freedom from surveillance.

5.2: How to Search the Dark Web Safely

Searching the **dark web** can be an intriguing experience, but it requires careful steps to ensure your **security** and **privacy**. Unlike traditional web browsing, where you can simply use **Google** or **Bing** to search for anything, searching the dark web requires specialized tools and techniques. This guide will show you how to safely search the dark web while protecting your identity and avoiding potential risks.

Understanding the Dark Web Search Landscape

The **dark web** is home to a wealth of information and resources—some of it entirely legal and valuable, while some of it might be harmful or illicit. Here's a quick overview of the key elements you need to understand:

1. **Dark Web Search Engines**: Unlike the surface web, dark web websites are not indexed by standard search engines like **Google** or **Bing**. Instead, dark web search engines like **DuckDuckGo**, **Ahmia**, and **NotEvil** are designed to help you find **.onion** websites.
2. **.onion Domains**: Websites on the dark web use **.onion** domain names. These sites are hidden from traditional search engines and can only be accessed using **Tor** or other specialized browsers.
3. **Anonymity and Encryption**: Search engines on the dark web are built to maintain **user anonymity**. When using Tor, your **IP address** is hidden, and your browsing is encrypted, making it difficult for third parties to track your activities.
4. **Risks**: Searching the dark web exposes you to certain risks, such as stumbling across **malicious websites**, **fraudulent activities**, or **illegal content**. It's essential to follow the right protocols and use the correct tools to minimize these risks.

Step-by-Step Guide to Safe Searching on the Dark Web

Now that you have an overview, let's go through the key steps you need to take to search the dark web safely.

Step 1: Set Up Secure Browsing Using Tor

To access the dark web, you'll need the **Tor browser**, which routes your traffic through the **Tor network** to anonymize your browsing activity.

1. **Download Tor Browser**:
   Go to the official Tor Project website at *https://www.torproject.org* and download the browser for your operating system. It's available for **Windows, macOS**, and **Linux**. Avoid downloading it from third-party sites to prevent malicious software.
2. **Install Tor Browser**:
   Follow the installation instructions. The process is simple, and once it's installed, you'll be ready to browse securely.
3. **Connect to Tor**:
   Once the browser is installed, open it. The first time you open Tor,

you'll need to connect to the Tor network by clicking on the **"Connect"** button. If you're in a region with internet restrictions, you may need to configure the browser to use **bridges** or other methods to bypass censorship.

4. **Browse Using Tor**:
    After connecting, you can start searching the dark web using **.onion** domains. Tor automatically protects your identity, but keep in mind that you should still be cautious about personal information and avoid logging into accounts that could expose your identity.

Step 2: Use Privacy-Focused Search Engines

Since **Google** and **Bing** don't index dark web sites, you need specialized **dark web search engines** that are compatible with **.onion** domains. These search engines offer privacy and anonymity while helping you find reliable content.

1. **DuckDuckGo**:
    DuckDuckGo is a **privacy-focused search engine** that doesn't track your searches or collect personal data. It also has a **dark web version** accessible through Tor. To access it, type: `http://3g2upl4pq6kufc4m.onion` in the Tor browser's address bar.
    - o **Benefits**: No search tracking, respects privacy, and provides relatively clean search results for the dark web.
    - o **Usage Tip**: Use DuckDuckGo for **general queries** and information gathering on the dark web.
2. **Ahmia**:
    Ahmia is another search engine that specializes in **.onion** websites. It provides a **clean interface** and indexes a wide range of dark web sites.
    - o **Benefits**: Provides results from **Tor** websites and is one of the most popular dark web search engines.
    - o **Usage Tip**: Ahmia also features a **clean web version** for surface web results. To access it via Tor, visit: `http://msydqstlz2kzerdg.onion`.
3. **NotEvil**:
    NotEvil is a dark web search engine that provides **uncensored search results** from the **dark web**. It is **privacy-conscious** and focuses on maintaining user anonymity.

- Benefits: It's straightforward to use and provides access to many **onion sites** not available on other search engines.
- **Usage Tip**: Use NotEvil for deeper searches, especially if DuckDuckGo doesn't yield enough results.

Step 3: Conduct Your Search with Caution

Now that you're equipped with the Tor browser and a privacy-focused search engine, here are some best practices for conducting searches on the dark web:

1. **Use Keywords Carefully**:
   Search queries should be **general** to avoid stumbling upon illegal sites. If you're looking for something like a **privacy tool**, use specific keywords like "**secure email**" or "**encrypted communication**." Avoid searching for terms that are related to illegal content.
2. **Look for .onion Extensions**:
   Always ensure that the websites you visit end in **.onion**. These sites are unique to the dark web and can only be accessed through Tor. If a website does not use this extension, it's likely not a dark web site, and you should be cautious about visiting it.
3. **Check for HTTPS Encryption**:
   Just like regular websites, it's important to check for **HTTPS** encryption on dark web websites. Even on the dark web, some sites may not use proper security, making them vulnerable to hacking or data interception.
4. **Avoid Clicking on Suspicious Links**:
   While browsing, avoid clicking on links that seem suspicious or too good to be true. Many scam sites exist on the dark web, attempting to lure users into downloading malicious files or engaging in fraudulent activities.

Step 4: Use Security Measures for Extra Protection

When searching the dark web, it's essential to take additional steps to safeguard your **privacy** and **security**. Here are some key practices:

1. **Use a VPN (Virtual Private Network)**:
   While Tor does an excellent job at providing anonymity, combining it with a **VPN** provides an extra layer of security. A

VPN will **hide your real IP address** from anyone monitoring your internet traffic, even if they're watching the Tor network. This is particularly important if you're concerned about government surveillance or want to ensure your traffic is encrypted.

2. **Avoid Personal Information**:
   Never provide **real names**, **email addresses**, or any other personal information on the dark web unless you're absolutely sure that the site is trustworthy and legitimate. This includes signing up for accounts, subscribing to services, or engaging in any form of transaction.

3. **Use a Secure Email Provider**:
   If you need to sign up for any services or communicate with others on the dark web, use an **encrypted email provider** like **ProtonMail** or **Tutanota**. These services offer end-to-end encryption, ensuring that your emails remain private.

4. **Install Security Software**:
   Ensure your system is **secure** by installing reliable **antivirus** and **anti-malware** software. This protects you from potential threats when downloading files or interacting with unknown websites.

Visual Aid: How to Safely Search the Dark Web

Here's a simple flowchart to visualize the steps for **safe searching** on the dark web:

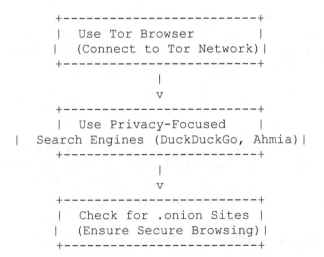

```
        +-------------------------+
        |   Use Tor Browser       |
        |  (Connect to Tor Network)|
        +-------------------------+
                    |
                    v
        +-------------------------+
        |  Use Privacy-Focused    |
      | Search Engines (DuckDuckGo, Ahmia)|
        +-------------------------+
                    |
                    v
        +-------------------------+
        |  Check for .onion Sites |
        |  (Ensure Secure Browsing)|
        +-------------------------+
```

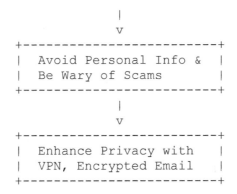

```
                    |
                    v
     +-------------------------+
     | Avoid Personal Info &   |
     | Be Wary of Scams        |
     +-------------------------+
                    |
                    v
     +-------------------------+
     | Enhance Privacy with    |
     | VPN, Encrypted Email    |
     +-------------------------+
```

Step 5: Dealing with Search Results Safely

While you're searching the dark web, you may encounter various types of results—some legitimate and others potentially dangerous. Here's how to handle them:

1. **Trusted Sources**: Always trust **well-known and reputable sources**. Sites like **SecureDrop** (for whistleblowers) or **ProtonMail** are good examples of reliable dark web services.
2. **Verify Website Authenticity**: Check if the site you're visiting has an **HTTPS connection** (for encrypted connections) and a **reliable reputation** in privacy or security forums before interacting with it.
3. **Stay Away from Suspicious Content**: If a site offers **illegal services**, contains **adult content**, or asks for **personal data**, it's best to avoid it. The dark web has its share of dangerous and illicit sites that can lead to trouble if you engage with them.

Searching the dark web safely requires the right tools, practices, and mindset. By using the **Tor browser**, privacy-focused search engines, and securing your connection with a **VPN**, you can explore the dark web with confidence. However, you must always remain cautious, avoid clicking on suspicious links, and refrain from providing personal information. By following these steps and practicing safe browsing habits, you can ensure that your dark web experience is **secure** and **anonymous**.

As with any powerful tool, the dark web requires responsibility. With the right precautions, it can be a valuable space for accessing **secure communication**, **uncensored information**, and **privacy-respecting services**.

5.3: Identifying Safe and Secure Websites on the Dark Web

Navigating the **dark web** safely involves more than just knowing how to access **.onion** sites—it's about knowing **which sites are safe** to interact with and which sites could pose significant **risks** to your **privacy** and **security**. The anonymity and encryption offered by the dark web are powerful tools for protecting your identity, but they also make it easy for malicious actors to hide their activities. This section will help you **identify trustworthy and secure websites** on the dark web, giving you the tools to explore this space with confidence.

Why Identifying Safe Websites Matters

The dark web is a **huge** and **unregulated** space. While there are many legitimate websites that offer valuable resources, there are also a large number of **malicious websites** that can put you at risk for things like **identity theft**, **malware**, or even **scams**. Many websites on the dark web operate without any oversight, making it essential to exercise caution when interacting with unknown sites.

By knowing how to identify **safe websites**, you can avoid scams, stay protected from potential **cyberattacks**, and use the dark web for its many **legitimate purposes**, such as **secure communication**, **censorship resistance**, and **privacy tools**.

Key Factors to Identify Safe and Secure Websites on the Dark Web

When you're exploring the dark web, there are several key factors that can help you identify whether a site is safe and secure. These factors can help you avoid **malicious actors**, **fraudulent sites**, and **illegal content**.

---

1. Use Reputable Directories

One of the easiest ways to find safe websites on the dark web is to start with **trusted directories**. These directories curate lists of verified **.onion** sites, often organized by category (e.g., **secure communication**, **whistleblowing platforms**, **research resources**).

Trusted Directories:

- **The Hidden Wiki**: This is one of the most well-known directories on the dark web, providing links to a variety of **.onion** sites. However, it's important to verify any site listed here, as not all sites on The Hidden Wiki are trustworthy. Some links might point to **dangerous** or **illegal** sites.
- **DarkWebLinks**: Another directory that lists **.onion** sites, though it's always good practice to verify these sites before interacting with them.

Note: Be cautious with any dark web directory you use. Some of these directories may link to sites that are **unverified** or **unsafe**. Always cross-reference multiple sources and verify before interacting with any site.

How to Use Directories Safely

- **Step 1**: Use a trusted directory like **The Hidden Wiki** or **DarkWebLinks**.
- **Step 2**: Copy the **.onion** URL of a site from the directory.

- **Step 3**: Open the link in **Tor** and ensure that the website is accessible and functions properly. Look for signs of legitimacy, like **encrypted connections** (indicated by **HTTPS**).

---

2. Check for HTTPS Encryption

Even though dark web websites use the **Tor network** for encryption, you should still check for **HTTPS** in the address bar when you visit a site. Websites with **HTTPS** (HyperText Transfer Protocol Secure) use additional encryption to protect data during transmission between your browser and the website. This adds an extra layer of security.

Why HTTPS Matters:

- **Data Integrity**: Ensures that the data you send to and receive from the website isn't altered or tampered with.
- **Authentication**: Verifies that the website you're interacting with is legitimate and not a **man-in-the-middle** impersonating a trusted site.
- **Privacy**: Helps protect sensitive information like passwords, usernames, and personal data from being intercepted.

Example: When visiting **ProtonMail's .onion** version, the address should show:

```
https://protonmail[.]onion
```

If the website doesn't use HTTPS, this could be a red flag.

---

3. Verify Website Authenticity

A website may appear legitimate, but that doesn't guarantee it's safe. Here's how you can verify if a website is trustworthy:

1. **Check for Reviews**: Dark web forums, **Reddit**, and other dark web-related discussion platforms often have threads where users discuss **trusted** and **dangerous websites**. Reading these reviews can give you insight into the reliability of the site.

- o **Example**: Sites like **Reddit's DarkNetMarkets** subreddit provide reviews on **marketplaces** and **services** on the dark web, which can give you an idea of the site's reputation.
2. **Research the Website's Purpose**: A website's purpose and what it offers are often good indicators of whether it's legitimate. Trusted **.onion** sites are typically focused on privacy, secure communication, or information-sharing, and they generally provide details about how to use their services securely.
   - o **Legitimate Example**: **SecureDrop** is a trusted **whistleblower** submission platform that allows anonymous communication between journalists and sources. The website clearly describes its services and usage, ensuring transparency.
3. **Look for Contact Information**: Legitimate websites will often provide a **secure contact method** for inquiries, like a **secure chat** or **email address**. Be cautious if a site lacks clear contact methods or if they ask for sensitive personal information right away.

---

4. Avoid Unnecessary Personal Information Requests

A major sign of a **malicious** or **fraudulent website** on the dark web is when the site asks for **personal information** that should never be needed. For example:

- **Asking for credit card information**
- **Requesting your full name or address**
- **Asking for your phone number** or other identifiable details

Legitimate dark web sites, particularly those focused on privacy or security, will never ask for this type of information. They often use **pseudonyms** or **temporary usernames** instead of requiring real names.

Example: Avoid signing up for **dark web marketplaces** that require payment details or personal identification unless they're **well-known** and **reliable** (e.g., **ProtonMail**).

While dark web websites can sometimes have a rough or basic design due to their focus on **functionality** over aesthetics, **malicious websites** often have suspicious characteristics. Pay attention to these factors:

1. **Website Design**: Scam sites might have **poor design**, broken links, or pages with **suspicious downloads**.
2. **Functional Links**: If a website's links don't work or lead to **error pages**, this could indicate that the site is not legitimate or it's intentionally hiding something.
3. **Excessive Pop-ups or Ads**: If you're bombarded with pop-ups, ads, or download prompts, it's a good indication that the site may not be safe.

---

6. Use Reputable Services and Platforms

Stick to well-known and **trusted platforms** in the dark web ecosystem. Services like **ProtonMail** (for secure email), **Whonix** (for privacy-focused operating systems), and **SecureDrop** (for anonymous document submission) are examples of trusted platforms that are often used by individuals and organizations in need of secure communication.

- **SecureDrop**: An **.onion** platform used by major news outlets like **The Washington Post** and **The Guardian** for whistleblowing and document submissions.
- **ProtonMail**: A secure, **end-to-end encrypted email service** that provides a **.onion** version for even higher security and anonymity.

These services are **widely trusted** and offer robust **privacy protection** for their users.

Visual Aid: Identifying Safe Websites on the Dark Web

Here's a flowchart summarizing the steps to identify safe websites on the dark web:

```
+---------------------------------------+
|   Use Trusted Directories (The Hidden Wiki)  |
+---------------------------------------+
                    |
                    v
+---------------------------------------+
|      Look for HTTPS (Encryption)      |
|      (Check for secure connections)   |
+---------------------------------------+
                    |
                    v
+---------------------------------------+
|      Verify Website's Authenticity    |
|      (Check for reviews and feedback) |
+---------------------------------------+
                    |
                    v
+---------------------------------------+
|  Avoid Sites Asking for Personal Information |
|      (Don't provide sensitive data)   |
+---------------------------------------+
                    |
                    v
+---------------------------------------+
|   Check Website Design & Functionality |
|   (Look for functional links, clear layout) |
+---------------------------------------+
                    |
                    v
+---------------------------------------+
|      Stick to Reputable Services      |
|      (ProtonMail, SecureDrop, etc.)   |
+---------------------------------------+
```

While the dark web can offer **valuable resources**, it also presents a unique set of risks that can jeopardize your **privacy**, **security**, and even **legal standing**. By following the steps outlined in this guide—using **trusted directories**, ensuring **HTTPS encryption**, verifying the **authenticity** of websites, avoiding **personal information requests**, and sticking to **reputable services**—you can reduce these risks and confidently navigate the dark web.

5.4: How to Avoid Common Pitfalls on the Dark Web

The **dark web** is a space where privacy and anonymity are prioritized, but it's also filled with potential risks. While there are many legitimate, privacy-respecting services on the dark web, there are also a significant number of **malicious actors**, **fraudulent sites**, and **illegal content**. The key to navigating the dark web safely is to understand these risks and take proactive steps to **avoid common pitfalls**.

Why Avoiding Pitfalls Matters

When you venture onto the dark web, the stakes are high. Since **traditional protections** (like website tracking and data protection laws) don't apply, it's easy to fall victim to **scams**, **malware**, **identity theft**, or **encounter illegal content**. Understanding the **dangers** and **precautionary measures** will help ensure that your dark web experience remains both **safe** and **productive**.

---

1. Malicious Links and Scams

One of the most prevalent risks on the dark web is encountering **malicious websites** or **scam links**. Unlike the surface web, which is largely regulated, the dark web is **unpoliced**, which means that malicious sites can easily set up shop and trick users into providing personal information or engaging in illegal activity.

How to Avoid Malicious Links:

- **Don't Click on Unverified Links**: One of the most important rules for safe browsing on the dark web is to **never click** on

unverified links. If you found a link via a search engine or a forum, make sure that it's from a trusted source.

Example: If you're using a dark web directory (like **The Hidden Wiki**), **double-check the site's reputation** before clicking any links. **Avoid clicking links** in pop-ups, ads, or unsolicited messages.

- **Use Trusted Search Engines**: Always rely on reputable, **privacy-focused search engines** (like **DuckDuckGo's .onion version**, **Ahmia**, or **NotEvil**) to search for dark web resources. These engines index **legitimate** sites and filter out harmful or malicious links.
- **Check for HTTPS**: Just like with any internet browsing, you should always ensure that the website is using **HTTPS**. If a site asks for sensitive information and doesn't have encryption, it's likely a scam.

Example:

When browsing a dark web **marketplace**, if the site asks for **credit card information** or other **personal details** and it doesn't show HTTPS in the URL, exit immediately. These sites are likely **phishing** or attempting to steal your information.

---

2. Encountering Illegal Content

The dark web is infamous for hosting **illegal content**. Whether it's **drugs**, **weapons**, or **stolen data**, there are parts of the dark web where illegal activities flourish. While accessing these areas is dangerous and unlawful, the real danger lies in **accidentally stumbling upon** illegal sites, which could get you in trouble with law enforcement.

How to Avoid Encountering Illegal Content:

- **Stick to Trusted Websites**: Use reputable sites that you know are legitimate. For example, websites like **ProtonMail's .onion** or

SecureDrop (used by journalists for whistleblower submissions) are great examples of legal, safe websites.

- **Be Careful with Search Terms**: Avoid searching for sensitive or illegal terms like **"black market"** or **"drugs for sale"**. Use more neutral search queries like **"secure email"** or **"whistleblowing platforms"**.
- **Follow Community Recommendations**: Always check dark web **forums** and **communities** for reviews and recommendations. Users often post warnings about potentially illegal sites or scams.

Case Study: Silk Road Takedown

The infamous **Silk Road** marketplace, which operated on the dark web, allowed users to buy and sell illegal goods. Its downfall in 2013 by the FBI serves as a reminder that law enforcement is actively monitoring the dark web for illegal activities. Even if you unintentionally land on an illegal website, you could be at risk of investigation.

To avoid this, always avoid interacting with marketplaces that deal in **illicit goods** or engage in activities that feel suspicious.

---

3. Malware and Cybersecurity Threats

The dark web is a breeding ground for **malware** and **viruses**, which are often used to **steal personal information** or **compromise your device**. Malicious websites can infect your system just by visiting, or by prompting you to **download harmful files** or **click on pop-up ads**.

How to Protect Yourself from Malware:

- **Keep Your Software Updated**: Make sure that your operating system, **Tor browser**, and any security tools (like antivirus programs) are always up to date. This will help prevent attackers from exploiting known vulnerabilities.
- **Use Antivirus and Anti-Malware Software**: Always use a reputable antivirus software. This will provide an extra layer of

protection by detecting and blocking malware or malicious scripts before they can harm your system.

- **Avoid Downloading Files from Unknown Sources**: Never download **files** or **attachments** from unverified dark web sites. Even files that seem harmless can be laced with malware or viruses designed to steal your data or compromise your device.
- **Use Virtual Machines (VMs)**: If you're particularly concerned about security, consider browsing the dark web using a **virtual machine**. A VM allows you to browse in a contained environment where potential malware cannot affect your primary operating system.

Example:

If you're accessing a **dark web market**, and you're prompted to download a file for **"secure access"** or a **"software update"**, don't download it unless it's from a trusted site like **ProtonMail's .onion** version. **Refrain from downloading any files** from an unverified source.

---

4. Identity Exposure and Data Leaks

One of the most common risks when browsing the dark web is the potential exposure of your **personal identity** or **data leaks**. Inadvertently revealing your identity can happen if you log into **personal accounts** (like Gmail or Facebook), use **real names** or **photos**, or inadvertently give away information via **form fields** or **chats**.

How to Prevent Identity Exposure:

- **Use Pseudonyms**: When signing up for services or forums on the dark web, always use **pseudonyms** or **temporary usernames**. Never use your **real name** or anything that could be used to identify you.
- **Avoid Logging into Personal Accounts**: **Never log into email accounts**, **social media**, or other **personal platforms** while browsing the dark web. This can directly link your dark web activities to your real-world identity.

- **Use Secure, Anonymous Services**: Always use **secure, encrypted email providers** (like **ProtonMail** or **Tutanota**) and **secure chat applications** (like **Signal**) for communication. These services are designed to protect your identity and maintain your privacy.
- **Use a VPN**: A **VPN** (Virtual Private Network) adds an extra layer of protection by **masking your IP address** and **encrypting your internet traffic**. This will make it much harder for anyone to trace your dark web activities back to you.

5. Fraudulent Websites and Financial Scams

The dark web is notorious for being a haven for **financial scams** and **fraudulent websites** that seek to steal your **cryptocurrency, bank details**, or other financial assets. These scams often present themselves as **marketplaces, investment opportunities**, or **get-rich-quick schemes**.

How to Avoid Financial Scams:

- **Never Send Money without Verifying the Site**: If a website asks for cryptocurrency or financial information, ensure that it's a **reputable** and **legitimate** service. Always double-check that the site is authentic by verifying its **.onion address**, reading user reviews, and ensuring that **HTTPS** encryption is present.
- **Avoid Unsolicited Offers**: Never respond to unsolicited **advertisements, emails**, or **messages** offering **investment opportunities** or **quick cash**. These are often fraudulent attempts to steal your money.
- **Use Secure Payment Methods**: When engaging in any financial transactions on the dark web, always use **secure methods** such as **cryptocurrency** (e.g., Bitcoin) and avoid using your **personal credit card** or other identifiable financial details.

Visual Aid: Pitfalls to Avoid on the Dark Web

Here's a visual aid summarizing the key pitfalls to avoid on the dark web and how to handle them:

```
+-------------------------------------------+
|          Malicious Links & Scams          |
|    - Use verified links                   |
|    - Avoid clicking on pop-ups or ads     |
|    - Check for HTTPS and reviews          |
+-------------------------------------------+
                     |
                     v
+-------------------------------------------+
|          Encountering Illegal Content     |
|    - Stick to trusted websites            |
|    - Avoid searching for illicit content  |
|    - Verify websites with community reviews|
+-------------------------------------------+
                     |
                     v
+-------------------------------------------+
|          Malware & Cybersecurity Threats  |
|    - Use up-to-date antivirus software    |
|    - Avoid downloading untrusted files    |
|    - Consider using a Virtual Machine (VM)|
+-------------------------------------------+
                     |
                     v
+-------------------------------------------+
|          Identity Exposure & Data Leaks   |
|    - Use pseudonyms and temporary usernames|
|    - Don't log into personal accounts     |
|    - Use encrypted communication tools    |
+-------------------------------------------+
                     |
                     v
+-------------------------------------------+
|          Financial Scams & Fraudulent Sites |
|    - Avoid sending money to unverified sources|
|    - Always use secure payment methods      |
|    - Be cautious of "get-rich-quick" schemes|
+-------------------------------------------+
```

Navigating the dark web can be a rewarding experience, but it requires **vigilance**, **precaution**, and an understanding of the **potential risks**. By following the steps outlined in this guide—avoiding **malicious links**, staying clear of **illegal content**, and taking measures to **protect your**

identity and **data**—you can significantly reduce the risks associated with dark web browsing.

The key to a successful dark web experience is to be **informed**, **cautious**, and **prepared**. With the right tools, practices, and mindset, you can safely explore the dark web for **privacy-focused services**, **secure communication**, and other **valuable resources**, while steering clear of common pitfalls.

Part 3: Intermediate Level – Navigating Online Safely and Recognizing Threats

Chapter 6: Identifying Cyber Threats on the Dark Web

The **dark web** is an anonymous, often unregulated space that attracts both privacy-conscious users and malicious actors. While many individuals use the dark web to protect their **freedom of speech** or **secure communication**, others use it for **illegal activities**, including **cybercrime**. As you navigate the dark web, it's essential to be aware of common **cyber threats** and understand how **cybercriminals** operate. In this chapter, we'll explore the **most common cyber threats** you'll encounter on the dark web, how **cybercriminals** operate in this space, and the steps you can take to **recognize** and **avoid** scams and attacks.

6.1: Common Cyber Threats (Malware, Ransomware, Phishing)

The dark web is infamous for hosting illicit activities, but it's not just the legal concerns you need to worry about. Cyber threats such as **malware**, **ransomware**, and **phishing** are all too common in the hidden corners of the internet. These threats can compromise your data, your device, and even your financial well-being.

In this guide, we'll break down these **common cyber threats** that are prevalent on the dark web, and provide you with practical steps to protect yourself from them.

What Are Cyber Threats on the Dark Web?

Cyber threats are essentially malicious activities intended to harm users, steal information, or disrupt systems. On the dark web, these threats are amplified due to the **anonymity** of users and the **lack of regulation**. The threats can manifest in many ways, but the most common ones you'll encounter include:

- **Malware**: Malicious software designed to damage or gain unauthorized access to a system.
- **Ransomware**: A form of malware that locks or encrypts your files and demands a ransom for access.
- **Phishing**: Fraudulent attempts to obtain sensitive information by pretending to be a trustworthy entity.

Understanding these threats and how to protect yourself is essential for navigating the dark web safely.

---

1. Malware: A Sneaky Intruder

Malware is short for **malicious software**, and it's one of the most prevalent threats on the dark web. Malware can come in many forms—viruses, worms, Trojans, rootkits, spyware, and more. These programs can be used to **steal personal information**, **spy on your activities**, or **damage your system**.

Types of Malware Common on the Dark Web:

1. **Trojan Horses**: These appear as legitimate software but carry harmful payloads that allow attackers to gain access to your system.
2. **Keyloggers**: These record everything you type on your device, which is especially dangerous for capturing **login credentials** and **personal data**.
3. **Spyware**: Spyware secretly monitors your actions and collects sensitive information, often without your consent.

How Malware Spreads on the Dark Web:

- **Malicious Websites**: Malware is often distributed via links to **infected websites**. For example, you might come across **fake**

.onion sites that offer software or tools for download, but in reality, these downloads contain malware.

- **Marketplaces**: Dark web marketplaces often sell **malware kits** and other tools that cybercriminals can use to launch attacks. These are sometimes sold for a premium in Bitcoin.
- **Email Phishing**: Cybercriminals often send links to malware via **phishing emails** or messages, luring victims into clicking on them and unwittingly downloading malicious software.

How to Protect Yourself from Malware:

1. **Use Antivirus Software**: Always have a reputable **antivirus program** running on your device. Set it to automatically update and scan for malware.
2. **Don't Download Unknown Files**: Avoid downloading software or files from untrusted websites on the dark web. If you must download something, ensure it's from a **trusted source** and double-check the file's integrity.
3. **Enable Browser Security**: Use **Tor's NoScript** feature to block potentially harmful scripts that may be executed on infected sites.

---

2. Ransomware: A Digital Hostage

Ransomware is a particularly dangerous type of malware because it encrypts your files and demands a **ransom** (often in cryptocurrency) for the decryption key. It can cause significant damage to individuals and organizations by locking them out of their own data.

How Ransomware Works on the Dark Web:

- **Ransomware-as-a-Service (RaaS)**: On the dark web, some **cybercriminals offer ransomware as a service**. This means anyone with malicious intent can purchase a **ransomware toolkit** to launch attacks against individuals or businesses.
- **Phishing Emails**: Attackers often deliver ransomware through **phishing emails**. Once the victim clicks on an infected link or

opens a malicious attachment, ransomware is downloaded and installed on their system.

The Ransomware Process:

1. **Infection**: The user clicks on a malicious email attachment, or downloads a file from an infected website on the dark web.
2. **Encryption**: The ransomware locks files on the user's computer or network.
3. **Ransom Demand**: A ransom note is displayed, demanding a cryptocurrency payment (e.g., **Bitcoin**) to decrypt the files.
4. **Decryption (or not)**: After payment, the attacker may send the decryption key to the victim to restore their files—or they may not, leaving the victim with **irreversibly encrypted data**.

How to Protect Yourself from Ransomware:

1. **Back Up Your Files**: Regularly back up important files to a **secure external drive** or cloud storage. This ensures that if your files are encrypted, you can restore them without paying the ransom.
2. **Keep Your Software Updated**: Regularly update your **operating system** and **software** to patch security vulnerabilities that ransomware may exploit.
3. **Don't Pay the Ransom**: If you do become infected with ransomware, avoid paying the ransom. There's no guarantee that the attacker will provide the decryption key.
4. **Use Anti-Ransomware Software**: Many antivirus programs now offer specific tools to detect and prevent ransomware attacks.

---

3. Phishing: The Bait-and-Switch Attack

Phishing is a method used by cybercriminals to **steal sensitive information**, such as **login credentials**, **credit card numbers**, and **personal details**. In phishing attacks, the attacker masquerades as a legitimate entity, such as a trusted service, and tricks the victim into entering confidential data on a fake website.

- **Fake Login Pages**: One common phishing technique on the dark web is setting up fake **login pages** for well-known services (e.g., **ProtonMail, Bitcoin exchanges**). These sites look identical to the original but are designed to capture your login credentials.
- **Malicious Emails**: Phishing emails are often sent with a link to a malicious **.onion** site that appears legitimate but is actually designed to steal your information.

Phishing Attack Example:

Imagine receiving an email claiming to be from **ProtonMail** offering a free service upgrade. The email contains a link to a login page where you're asked to input your **username** and **password**. However, this page is a **fake** designed to capture your credentials.

How to Recognize Phishing:

1. **Check the URL**: Always verify the **.onion URL** of any website. If the address doesn't match the official site or includes **extra characters**, be cautious.
2. **Look for HTTPS**: Genuine websites use HTTPS to encrypt traffic. Ensure that the site you visit has **HTTPS** (not HTTP) and is properly encrypted.
3. **Don't Trust Suspicious Links**: Avoid clicking on **links** in unsolicited emails or messages. These may lead to phishing websites.
4. **Enable Two-Factor Authentication (2FA)**: Use **2FA** on your accounts to add an extra layer of protection in case your credentials are stolen.

Visual Aid: Common Cyber Threats on the Dark Web

Here's a visual aid summarizing the common cyber threats you may encounter on the dark web:

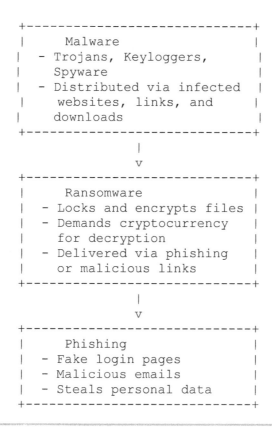

```
+------------------------------+
|          Malware             |
|  - Trojans, Keyloggers,      |
|    Spyware                   |
|  - Distributed via infected  |
|    websites, links, and      |
|    downloads                 |
+------------------------------+
               |
               v
+------------------------------+
|         Ransomware           |
|  - Locks and encrypts files  |
|  - Demands cryptocurrency    |
|    for decryption            |
|  - Delivered via phishing    |
|    or malicious links        |
+------------------------------+
               |
               v
+------------------------------+
|          Phishing            |
|  - Fake login pages          |
|  - Malicious emails          |
|  - Steals personal data      |
+------------------------------+
```

How to Protect Yourself from These Cyber Threats

1. **Use a Secure Browser**: Always browse the dark web using the **Tor browser**. This ensures that your traffic is encrypted, and your identity remains anonymous.
2. **Regular Software Updates**: Keep your operating system, **Tor browser**, and any security software updated to protect against known vulnerabilities.
3. **Backup Your Data**: Regularly back up important files to a secure location so that ransomware can't hold your data hostage.
4. **Be Cautious with Downloads**: Avoid downloading software, files, or any other content from untrusted or suspicious dark web websites.
5. **Stay Informed**: Keep yourself updated on the latest **cybersecurity threats** and **dark web scams**. Join cybersecurity forums or read reports from trusted security sources.

The **dark web** can be a dangerous space, but with the right tools and knowledge, you can protect yourself from common cyber threats like **malware, ransomware**, and **phishing**. Always approach the dark web with caution, use security best practices, and stay vigilant about the websites you visit and the files you download. By following these strategies, you'll be better equipped to **navigate the dark web safely** and avoid the risks associated with cybercrime.

6.2: How Cybercriminals Operate on the Dark Web

The **dark web** is a hidden part of the internet that offers **anonymity**, making it an ideal environment for **cybercriminals** to operate with relative impunity. In this chapter, we'll delve into how cybercriminals use the dark web to conduct illicit activities, the tools they use, and the tactics they employ to avoid detection. Understanding how cybercriminals operate in this space is essential for both individuals and organizations to protect themselves from falling victim to their schemes.

How Cybercriminals Exploit the Dark Web for Illicit

Activities

The **dark web** enables a range of illicit activities due to its **anonymity** and **lack of regulation**. While legitimate users turn to the dark web for privacy and freedom of speech, cybercriminals leverage the platform for illegal activities like **fraud, data theft, drug trafficking**, and **hacking**. Here's how they do it:

1. Cybercriminal Marketplaces and Forums

One of the most common ways cybercriminals operate on the dark web is through **marketplaces** and **forums**. These are the equivalent of online stores and discussion spaces, but they cater specifically to **illegal goods and services**. Here, cybercriminals can buy, sell, or trade anything from **stolen data** to **malware**.

How Marketplaces Work:

- **Anonymity**: Transactions on dark web marketplaces are often conducted using **cryptocurrencies** (such as **Bitcoin** or **Monero**) to ensure the identity of buyers and sellers remains hidden.
- **Variety of Goods**: These marketplaces sell a variety of illegal items, including **stolen credit card information**, **malware kits**, **drugs**, and even **weaponry**.
- **Escrow Services**: To build trust between buyers and sellers, many marketplaces use **escrow services**. The buyer's funds are held in escrow until the transaction is completed, at which point the seller is paid.

Example: The infamous **Silk Road** marketplace was one of the first large dark web markets that allowed users to buy illegal goods with Bitcoin. Although it was shut down by the FBI in 2013, many similar marketplaces continue to thrive.

How Cybercriminals Use Marketplaces:

- **Selling Malicious Tools**: Cybercriminals can sell or purchase **malware**, **ransomware**, and **botnets** that can be used for **cyberattacks**. These tools often come with detailed instructions on how to deploy them.
- **Data Theft**: Stolen data, including **login credentials, credit card information**, and **personal identification details**, is regularly traded on these platforms. Buyers often use this data for **identity theft** or **fraud**.
- **Money Laundering**: Criminals use the dark web to launder money, converting stolen funds into cryptocurrencies to hide their tracks.

2. Ransomware and Cyber Extortion

Ransomware is a particularly lucrative tool for cybercriminals operating on the dark web. By encrypting a victim's files or locking them out of their system, cybercriminals demand **ransom payments** (often in cryptocurrency) in exchange for the decryption key.

How Ransomware is Sold on the Dark Web:

- **Ransomware-as-a-Service**: Cybercriminals can purchase or rent **ransomware kits** on the dark web. These services are known as **Ransomware-as-a-Service (RaaS)**, allowing anyone—even those with minimal technical expertise—to launch **ransomware attacks**.
- **Targeting Businesses**: Many dark web actors target **businesses**, often demanding **larger ransoms** based on the victim's perceived ability to pay.
- **Phishing and Malware**: Ransomware is often delivered via **phishing emails** or **malicious websites** where users are tricked into downloading it.

Case Study: The WannaCry ransomware attack in 2017 affected over 200,000 computers across 150 countries, causing significant damage to organizations worldwide. WannaCry was linked to vulnerabilities in Windows systems that were exploited using tools believed to have been stolen from the NSA and distributed on the dark web.

---

3. Hacking and Data Breaches

Cybercriminals on the dark web regularly trade **hacking tools** and **exploit kits** designed to take advantage of vulnerabilities in software or systems. These tools are used to **break into systems**, steal data, or cause damage to the target network.

How Cybercriminals Exploit Systems:

- **Zero-Day Exploits**: Cybercriminals can purchase **zero-day vulnerabilities** (flaws in software that are unknown to the vendor) on the dark web. These exploits allow them to **compromise systems** without detection, giving them full access to sensitive data.

- **Botnets and Distributed Denial-of-Service (DDoS)**: Some cybercriminals sell access to **botnets**—networks of compromised computers that can be used to launch large-scale **DDoS attacks**.
- **Password Cracking**: Stolen login credentials, often obtained through data breaches, are sold on dark web marketplaces. Cybercriminals can use these credentials for **identity theft** or **account takeover**.

Case Study: The Equifax data breach in 2017, one of the largest data breaches in history, exposed the personal data of over 140 million people. Hackers exploited a known vulnerability in Apache Struts software, which was widely discussed on dark web forums before the breach. The stolen data, including names, birthdates, addresses, and Social Security numbers, was later sold on dark web marketplaces.

---

4. Fraud and Identity Theft

Fraud is rampant on the dark web, with cybercriminals regularly buying and selling stolen personal data to commit various types of fraud, including **identity theft**, **credit card fraud**, and **social engineering** attacks.

How Fraud is Facilitated on the Dark Web:

- **Stolen Credit Cards**: Cybercriminals buy stolen credit card information on the dark web and use it to make **fraudulent purchases**.
- **Fake IDs**: Cybercriminals on the dark web sell **fake identification documents** that can be used for **identity theft**, committing fraud, or carrying out other illegal activities.
- **Social Engineering Attacks**: With access to stolen personal data, cybercriminals can launch **social engineering** attacks, such as **phishing** or **vishing**, to further exploit their victims.

Example: Fraudulent websites on the dark web offer stolen credit card details for as little as a few dollars. Once acquired, cybercriminals can use these details to make illegal transactions, often purchasing luxury goods or even cryptocurrency.

How Cybercriminals Avoid Detection

Cybercriminals on the dark web rely heavily on the anonymity and encryption provided by **Tor** to operate without fear of detection. However, they also use several techniques to further cover their tracks and avoid law enforcement agencies. Here's how:

1. Cryptocurrency:

- **Cryptocurrency transactions** are widely used on the dark web to conduct **anonymous** payments. **Bitcoin** and **Monero** are the most popular cryptocurrencies, as they offer **greater anonymity** than traditional bank transfers.
- **Cryptocurrency mixers**: To obscure the origin and destination of funds, cybercriminals often use **cryptocurrency mixing services**, which break up transactions into smaller parts and send them through multiple addresses to mask the transaction trail.

2. Escrow Services:

- On dark web marketplaces, **escrow services** are commonly used to ensure that **buyers** and **sellers** fulfill their obligations. These services act as intermediaries that hold payments in escrow until the transaction is complete, helping to build trust between parties and reducing the risk of scams.

3. Anonymity Networks (Tor, I2P):

- **Tor**: The **Tor network** routes internet traffic through multiple layers of encryption, providing users with **anonymity** and masking their **IP addresses**. This makes it difficult for law enforcement to trace activities back to cybercriminals.
- **I2P**: Another privacy-focused network, **I2P**, is sometimes used by cybercriminals as an alternative to Tor. I2P offers decentralized, **censorship-resistant services**, making it harder for authorities to monitor activities.

4. Hidden Services:

- Cybercriminals often host their websites as **hidden services** on the dark web. These sites are **not indexed by traditional search**

engines, and their **IP addresses** are **obfuscated**, making it nearly impossible to trace the physical location of the server.

Visual Aid: How Cybercriminals Operate on the Dark Web

To help visualize how cybercriminals operate on the dark web, here's a simplified flowchart:

```
+-------------------------------+
|      Dark Web Marketplaces    |
| - Selling illegal goods (e.g. |
|   malware, stolen data)       |
| - Anonymous transactions (via |
|   cryptocurrency)             |
+-------------------------------+
                |
                v
+-------------------------------+
|      Hacking & Exploits       |
| - Buying zero-day exploits    |
| - Malware for system breaches |
| - Phishing kits               |
+-------------------------------+
                |
                v
+-------------------------------+
|     Ransomware-as-a-Service   |
| - Renting ransomware tools    |
| - Attacking individuals/businesses|
+-------------------------------+
                |
                v
+-------------------------------+
|     Money Laundering & Fraud  |
| - Using cryptocurrency mixers |
| - Buying stolen credit cards  |
| - Fake IDs and social engineering|
+-------------------------------+
```

The **dark web** provides a haven for cybercriminals to operate with anonymity and without significant fear of law enforcement detection. By understanding the various methods used by these criminals—such as **dark web marketplaces**, **ransomware**, **hacking tools**, and **fraudulent schemes**—you can better equip yourself to **stay safe** while exploring the dark web.

6.3: How to Recognize and Avoid Scams on the Dark Web

The **dark web** is home to both **legitimate** and **illegitimate** services, and unfortunately, scams are rampant in this space. From fake marketplaces to fraudulent services, the dark web is filled with risks that can cost you money, data, or even your identity. But with the right knowledge and a healthy dose of skepticism, you can learn how to recognize and avoid these scams effectively. In this guide, we'll walk through the **most common scams** on the dark web, how to spot them, and practical steps you can take to protect yourself.

Why Scams Are Common on the Dark Web

The **anonymity** and **lack of regulation** provided by the dark web make it an ideal environment for scammers. Many users of the dark web are looking for **privacy-focused services**, **secure communication platforms**, or **uncensored content**, making them vulnerable to scams. Additionally, the **lack of oversight** means that **fraudulent actors** can easily set up fake websites, market malicious products, or sell non-existent services.

Scams can come in many forms:

- **Fake marketplaces** selling counterfeit goods.
- **Phishing sites** designed to steal personal information.
- **Malicious software** or ransomware sold under the guise of legitimate products.

- **Financial scams** that promise high returns but only result in stolen cryptocurrency.

Recognizing Common Scams on the Dark Web

Before you click a link or make a purchase on the dark web, it's essential to know how to spot potential scams. The most common types of scams include **fake marketplaces**, **phishing schemes**, and **malware**.

---

1. Fake Marketplaces and Fraudulent Products

One of the most common scams on the dark web is the **fake marketplace**, where you may find offers for **drugs**, **malware**, or **stolen data** that either don't exist or are of poor quality. Cybercriminals use fake marketplaces to steal cryptocurrency or personal data.

Signs of a Fake Marketplace:

- **No Reviews or User Feedback**: If a marketplace doesn't have any reviews or user feedback, it's likely a scam. Legitimate dark web marketplaces often have a **reputation system** or at least some indication of trustworthiness.
- **Too-Good-to-Be-True Prices**: If something is priced **much lower** than market value, it might be a scam. Fraudulent sellers often advertise "too good to be true" deals to lure victims.
- **Unprofessional Website Design**: Scammers often create poorly designed websites with broken links, lots of pop-ups, or a lack of basic security features (e.g., no **HTTPS**).
- **Unclear Terms of Service**: Legitimate marketplaces often have clear terms of service, privacy policies, and support contact options. If these are missing or vague, the site might not be trustworthy.

1. **Check Reviews and Reputation**: Always check **trusted forums** and **discussion boards** for feedback on a marketplace. Websites like **Reddit** (DarkNetMarkets) and **dark web communities** can provide insights from experienced users.
2. **Use Escrow Services**: Trusted marketplaces use **escrow services** to hold payment until both the buyer and seller fulfill their obligations. Avoid sites that don't offer escrow services for transactions.
3. **Start with Small Transactions**: If you must use a new marketplace, begin with a **small purchase** to test its legitimacy. If the transaction goes smoothly, you can make larger purchases.

---

2. Phishing Scams

Phishing on the dark web works much like phishing on the surface web. Cybercriminals create fake **login pages** that look identical to legitimate sites in order to steal your login credentials or other sensitive information.

How Phishing Works on the Dark Web:

- **Fake Login Pages**: Cybercriminals often create fake login pages for **email services**, **marketplaces**, or **social media** sites on the dark web. These fake sites appear identical to real sites, but when you log in, your credentials are captured and used for **identity theft** or **account takeover**.
- **Malicious Links**: Phishing scams often come in the form of **unsolicited messages** or emails that contain links to **fake sites** designed to steal your information.

How to Avoid Phishing Scams:

1. **Verify the URL**: Always verify that the website you are visiting is the **correct** .onion address. Even a minor variation in the URL could indicate a phishing site.
2. **Enable Two-Factor Authentication (2FA)**: For any accounts you create on the dark web, always enable **2FA** to provide an

additional layer of security, even if your login credentials are compromised.

3. **Use Password Managers**: Password managers can help you ensure that you're logging into the correct site, as they will only fill in login details for sites with the correct domain.

---

3. Malware and Ransomware

Malware (malicious software) is commonly sold or distributed on the dark web. Cybercriminals use it for a range of activities, including **data theft**, **hacking**, and **ransomware attacks**. Malware is often hidden within **malicious downloads**, **infected links**, or **fake software updates**.

Signs of Malware Distribution:

- **Suspicious Download Links**: Be wary of any download links that seem suspicious or out of place. Malware is often distributed through **free software** or **cracked programs** advertised on dark web marketplaces.
- **Pop-up Ads or Forced Downloads**: Malware is often pushed via pop-up ads or forced downloads when you visit certain websites on the dark web. These can install harmful software onto your device.
- **Fake Software or Updates**: Some scams involve offering **free software** or **security updates**, but these downloads can actually install malware onto your system.

How to Avoid Malware:

1. **Avoid Downloading Suspicious Files**: Do not download any files or software from untrusted sources. Stick to well-known, reputable services for anything you need.
2. **Use Antivirus and Anti-Malware Software**: Always have **antivirus** and **anti-malware software** installed on your device, and make sure they are updated regularly. This can detect and block malicious downloads before they can infect your system.
3. **Use Virtual Machines (VMs)**: If you're particularly concerned about security, consider using a **virtual machine** to browse the dark web. A VM isolates your main system from any potential threats and limits the impact of malware.

Steps to Recognize and Avoid Scams on the Dark Web

Now that you know the most common scams on the dark web, let's explore a **step-by-step guide** to help you avoid falling victim to them.

Step 1: Verify the Legitimacy of the Website

Before interacting with any dark web site:

- **Check the URL**: Ensure the site is using a **legitimate .onion** address. Double-check that the URL matches the official site and isn't a slight variation used by scammers.
- **Look for HTTPS**: Ensure the site uses **HTTPS** encryption, even though **.onion sites** already have encryption via Tor. The extra encryption layer helps protect your data.
- **Check Reviews**: Look up the site on dark web forums, Reddit, and other platforms where users report their experiences. Feedback from other users can help you determine if a website is trustworthy.

Step 2: Be Cautious of Offers that Are Too Good to Be True

If something sounds **too good to be true**, it probably is. Be skeptical of:

- **Unrealistically low prices** on products like drugs, electronics, or software. Scammers often offer **unbelievably cheap deals** to lure victims.
- **Too-good-to-be-true services**: Be wary of services offering huge **financial gains** or **instant rewards**, especially when they ask for **upfront payments** in cryptocurrency.

When making a transaction on the dark web:

- **Use Cryptocurrency**: Always use a secure, anonymous cryptocurrency like **Bitcoin** or **Monero** for transactions. Never use **credit cards** or **bank transfers** on the dark web, as these methods can expose your identity.
- **Check for Escrow Services**: Reputable dark web marketplaces use **escrow services** to protect buyers and sellers. If a website does not provide this, it could be a scam.

Step 4: Protect Your Identity and Data

Your identity is your most valuable asset on the dark web:

- **Use a VPN**: Always use a **VPN** (Virtual Private Network) alongside **Tor** to hide your real IP address and further protect your anonymity.
- **Avoid Personal Information**: Never share personal details like your **full name**, **address**, **phone number**, or **email** on the dark web unless absolutely necessary.

Visual Aid: How to Recognize and Avoid Dark Web Scams

Here's a simple flowchart to help you spot and avoid scams on the dark web:

```
+-----------------------------------+
|      Step 1: Verify Website Legitimacy|
|   - Check the URL                 |
|   - Look for HTTPS encryption      |
|   - Check reviews and reputation   |
+-----------------------------------+
```

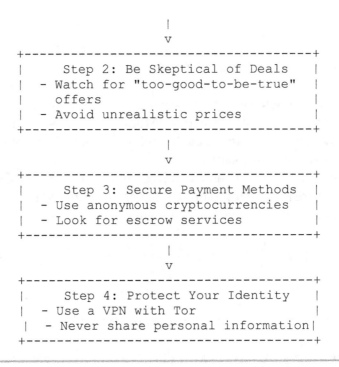

```
                          |
                          v
      +------------------------------------+
      |       Step 2: Be Skeptical of Deals |
      |  - Watch for "too-good-to-be-true"  |
      |    offers                           |
      |  - Avoid unrealistic prices         |
      +------------------------------------+
                          |
                          v
      +------------------------------------+
      |      Step 3: Secure Payment Methods |
      |  - Use anonymous cryptocurrencies   |
      |  - Look for escrow services         |
      +------------------------------------+
                          |
                          v
      +------------------------------------+
      |      Step 4: Protect Your Identity  |
      |  - Use a VPN with Tor               |
      |  - Never share personal information |
      +------------------------------------+
```

Navigating the dark web requires **vigilance** and **caution**. While it can be a valuable resource for privacy, communication, and secure transactions, it's also rife with scams. By following the steps outlined in this guide— **verifying websites**, **avoiding unrealistic deals**, **using secure payment methods**, and **protecting your identity**—you can significantly reduce the risks and have a safer experience on the dark web.

Stay skeptical, always prioritize **security** and **anonymity**, and remember that **too good to be true** often is. The dark web may have its dangers, but with the right precautions, it can be navigated securely and responsibly.

Chapter 7: Safe Practices for Online Security

In today's digital world, **online security** is more important than ever. Whether you are accessing the **dark web** or browsing the surface web, it's essential to protect your **identity, personal information**, and **digital accounts**. Cyber threats like **identity theft, hacking**, and **phishing** are rampant, but there are many steps you can take to safeguard yourself. In this chapter, we'll cover **best practices for online security**, focusing on protecting your identity, using **encrypted communication**, and ensuring **strong password security**.

7.1: How to Protect Your Identity and Personal Information

In today's digital age, protecting your **identity** and **personal information** is more critical than ever. With **cybercriminals, identity thieves**, and **phishers** constantly on the lookout for vulnerable targets, it's essential to adopt proactive measures to safeguard your personal data. This chapter will break down the key steps and strategies you can take to protect yourself online—whether you're navigating the **dark web** or simply browsing the **surface web**.

Why Protecting Your Identity Is Essential

Your **personal information** is valuable. It includes things like your **name, email address, phone number, address**, and even your **biometric data**. Once this information is compromised, it can be used for **identity theft, financial fraud**, or **unauthorized access to your accounts**.

Example: A few years ago, a **major data breach** exposed millions of people's personal information from a popular social media platform.

Cybercriminals used this data to carry out **identity theft**, stealing money from users' bank accounts and using their information to open **credit cards** in their names.

By following best practices for protecting your identity, you can reduce your risk of falling victim to such attacks.

1. Use Anonymity Tools to Mask Your Identity

When browsing online, especially on the **dark web**, maintaining your **anonymity** is crucial. This means hiding your real-world identity, such as your **IP address** and **location**, from malicious actors or surveillance systems.

1.1 Tor Browser

Tor (The Onion Router) is the most widely used tool for maintaining anonymity online. It works by **routing your internet traffic** through several layers of encryption, ensuring that your activity is **masked** and **untraceable**.

- **How it works**: When you use Tor, your internet traffic is passed through a network of **volunteer-operated relays** before reaching its destination. This makes it difficult to trace back to you or your physical location.
- **Advantages**:
  - **Anonymizes IP address**: Tor hides your real IP address, making it harder to track your browsing activity.
  - **Bypasses censorship**: Tor helps you access content that may be blocked or censored in certain countries or regions.

Steps to Use Tor for Anonymity:

1. **Download the Tor Browser**: Go to the official Tor Project website and download the **Tor Browser** for your operating system.

2. **Install and Set Up**: Follow the installation instructions and choose the **"Connect"** option to connect to the Tor network.
3. **Start Browsing Anonymously**: Once connected, you can start browsing the web with **improved privacy**. The Tor browser will ensure that your internet traffic is encrypted and routed through multiple layers to hide your identity.

Key Consideration:

While Tor enhances **privacy**, it's still essential to follow **good security practices**, such as avoiding logging into personal accounts with real names.

1.2 Use a VPN (Virtual Private Network)

While **Tor** provides anonymity, pairing it with a **VPN** adds an additional layer of protection. A **VPN** encrypts your internet connection and routes it through a remote server, making it more difficult for anyone to track your online activity.

- **How it works**: A VPN **masks your IP address** by making it appear as though you are browsing from a different location (sometimes in a completely different country). This means that even if someone is monitoring your network traffic, they won't be able to trace it back to you.
- **Advantages**:
    - **Extra privacy**: A VPN provides an additional layer of encryption on top of Tor, making it harder for third parties to monitor your activity.
    - **Prevents tracking**: A VPN prevents websites from tracking your real IP address, which can be used for profiling or location-based tracking.

How to Use a VPN Alongside Tor:

1. **Choose a Reputable VPN**: Select a **reliable** and **privacy-focused VPN provider** (e.g., **ExpressVPN, NordVPN**).
2. **Install the VPN Software**: Download and install the VPN app on your device.

3. **Connect to the VPN**: Before opening Tor, connect to the VPN server of your choice. This ensures that your connection is encrypted right from the start.
4. **Use Tor**: After establishing a VPN connection, launch Tor and begin browsing anonymously with added security.

Key Consideration:

Make sure your **VPN service doesn't log** any of your activity. Some VPNs log user data, which can be problematic if privacy is a priority.

---

2. Avoid Using Real Names and Personal Information

When engaging with services or websites on the internet—especially on the dark web—avoid using your real identity whenever possible.

2.1 Use Pseudonyms for Online Accounts

A **pseudonym** is a fictitious name that doesn't tie back to your **real-world identity**. By using pseudonyms for your online accounts, you prevent cybercriminals from associating your online activity with your actual name.

How to Use Pseudonyms:

1. **Create a Unique Identity**: When signing up for online services, create an account using a **name that's not connected to your real identity**.
2. **Use a Separate Email**: Use a **disposable email** for accounts that don't require personal communication or tie-ins to your personal life. Services like **ProtonMail** or **Guerrilla Mail** offer temporary, anonymous email addresses.

Whether you're on the **dark web** or browsing social media, **personal data** like your **phone number, home address**, or **birthdate** can be used to **target you** in scams, **phishing** attacks, or **identity theft**.

Steps to Protect Personal Data:

- **Limit Data Sharing**: Share as little **personal information** as possible. Use **anonymous accounts** and **temporary addresses** for anything that doesn't need your real information.
- **Check Privacy Settings**: On social media or any service you use, always review your **privacy settings** to ensure that your personal information isn't visible to the public.

---

3. Use Secure Communication Channels

When sharing information online—especially sensitive information like **passwords** or **financial data**—make sure to use secure and **encrypted communication channels**. These services ensure that your messages are safe from eavesdropping or interception.

3.1 Use Encrypted Messaging Apps (e.g., Signal)

Signal is one of the most trusted encrypted messaging apps that uses **end-to-end encryption** to protect your messages and calls.

- **Why Signal is Secure**:
  - **End-to-End Encryption**: Only you and the recipient can read the message; not even Signal can decrypt it.
  - **Minimal Data Collection**: Signal collects very little data on users, ensuring privacy.

1. **Download Signal**: Install the **Signal app** from the **App Store** (iOS) or **Google Play Store** (Android).
2. **Set Up**: Register using your phone number (Signal doesn't store messages on its servers).
3. **Start Communicating**: Send encrypted messages, make secure calls, and enjoy private communication.

Key Consideration:

While **Signal** offers **top-notch security**, it's essential that you also maintain a **secure device** (i.e., using **strong passwords** or **biometrics** for your phone) to further protect your messages.

3.2 Encrypt Your Email with PGP

PGP (Pretty Good Privacy) is a widely used encryption standard for securing email messages. By encrypting your emails, you can ensure that only the intended recipient can read the contents.

How PGP Works:

- **Public Key**: The recipient provides you with their **public key** to encrypt the message.
- **Private Key**: The recipient uses their **private key** to decrypt the message.

How to Use PGP:

1. **Install GPG Software**: Use software like **Gpg4win** or **OpenPGP** to generate your own **public/private key pair**.
2. **Set Up Your Email Client**: Many secure email providers, like **ProtonMail**, have built-in PGP support. Alternatively, use PGP with your **standard email client** by installing plugins like **Enigmail**.
3. **Encrypt Emails**: Use the recipient's **public key** to encrypt emails before sending them.

Key Consideration:

PGP is highly effective but requires a bit of setup. Always keep your **private key** secure—if someone gains access to it, they could read your encrypted messages.

---

4. Use Secure Wi-Fi and Avoid Public Networks

When browsing online, especially when accessing sensitive sites or services, always use a **secure Wi-Fi network**. Avoid **public Wi-Fi** whenever possible, as it is more vulnerable to attacks.

4.1 Use VPN on Public Networks

Public networks are notoriously insecure and can be targeted by cybercriminals. When connecting to **public Wi-Fi**, always use a **VPN** to encrypt your connection.

Why Use VPN on Public Wi-Fi:

- **Encryption**: A VPN encrypts your internet traffic, ensuring that hackers cannot intercept your data, even on untrusted networks.
- **Privacy**: It hides your IP address, making it difficult for attackers to trace your activity.

Visual Aid: Key Steps to Protect Your Identity

Here's a simple flowchart summarizing how to protect your identity and personal information:

```
+----------------------------------------+
| Step 1: Use Anonymity Tools            |
| - Tor Browser                          |
```

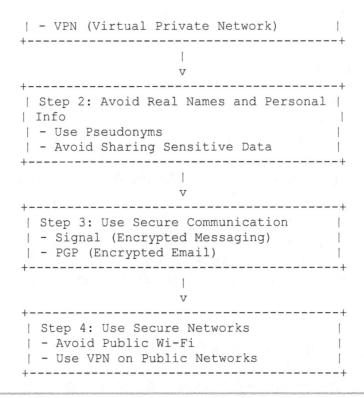

```
| - VPN (Virtual Private Network)        |
+----------------------------------------+
                    |
                    v
+----------------------------------------+
| Step 2: Avoid Real Names and Personal  |
| Info                                   |
| - Use Pseudonyms                       |
| - Avoid Sharing Sensitive Data         |
+----------------------------------------+
                    |
                    v
+----------------------------------------+
| Step 3: Use Secure Communication       |
| - Signal (Encrypted Messaging)         |
| - PGP (Encrypted Email)                |
+----------------------------------------+
                    |
                    v
+----------------------------------------+
| Step 4: Use Secure Networks            |
| - Avoid Public Wi-Fi                   |
| - Use VPN on Public Networks           |
+----------------------------------------+
```

Protecting your **identity** and **personal information** is vital in today's interconnected world. By using **anonymity tools** like **Tor** and **VPNs**, **avoiding real names** in non-secure environments, **encrypting communications** with tools like **Signal** and **PGP**, and **securing your Wi-Fi connections**, you can significantly reduce the risks of identity theft, fraud, and hacking.

7.2: Using Encrypted Communications (e.g., PGP, Signal)

In today's increasingly interconnected world, **secure communication** is essential to protecting your **privacy** and safeguarding sensitive data. Whether you are sharing personal information, discussing confidential business matters, or simply wanting to ensure your conversations are private, encryption plays a vital role in keeping your data secure.

In this guide, we will explore **encrypted communication** methods, specifically **PGP (Pretty Good Privacy)** and **Signal**, both of which are highly trusted and widely used for ensuring privacy in digital communications. This chapter will walk you through the concepts, use cases, and **step-by-step instructions** on setting up and using these tools effectively.

What is Encryption and Why It Matters?

Encryption is the process of converting **plain text** into **ciphertext** (an unreadable format) using an encryption algorithm. Only the intended recipient, who has the correct decryption key, can convert the ciphertext back into readable information.

In simple terms, encryption ensures that even if your communication is intercepted, it cannot be read or tampered with by unauthorized parties. Whether you're sending a **text message**, **email**, or **making a voice call**, using encryption ensures that your information remains **private**.

1. Using PGP (Pretty Good Privacy) for Encrypted

Emails

PGP is one of the most widely used standards for encrypting **email messages**. It provides a secure way to exchange messages by using **asymmetric encryption**, which involves a pair of keys: one for **encryption** (the public key) and one for **decryption** (the private key).

How PGP Works

PGP relies on **two keys**:

- **Public Key**: This key is shared with others and used to **encrypt** a message before sending it. The public key can be distributed freely.
- **Private Key**: This key is kept **secret** and used to **decrypt** messages that were encrypted with the matching public key.

PGP Key Pair:

- You generate a pair of keys—**a private key** (which remains on your device) and **a public key** (which you share with others).
- When someone sends you an encrypted message, they use your **public key** to encrypt it.
- You use your **private key** to decrypt the message when it reaches you.

Setting Up PGP for Encrypted Email Communication

Step 1: Install PGP Software

You can use various software solutions to set up PGP, such as **Gpg4win**, **GpgTools**, or **OpenPGP**. Here's how you can set up PGP on your system:

1. **Download and Install Gpg4win** (Windows) or **GpgTools** (Mac) from their respective websites.
2. **Set up your keypair**:
   - Follow the installation prompts to generate a **PGP keypair**.
   - Choose a **strong passphrase** for your private key to ensure its security.

Step 2: Integrating PGP with Your Email Client

Many popular email services and clients allow PGP integration, either natively or with plugins. Let's use **Thunderbird** (an open-source email client) with the **Enigmail plugin** as an example:

1. **Install Thunderbird** and the **Enigmail plugin**.
2. Open **Thunderbird**, then go to the **Enigmail setup wizard** to configure your **PGP keys**.

3. Once configured, you can now encrypt your emails using your **public key** and decrypt messages you receive using your **private key**.

- **To encrypt an email**: When composing an email in Thunderbird, you can simply click the **"Encrypt"** button before sending the email. This will use the recipient's **public key** to encrypt the message.
- **To decrypt an email**: If you receive an encrypted email, Thunderbird will automatically use your **private key** to decrypt it. You will be prompted to enter your passphrase.

Benefits of Using PGP for Email Encryption

- **Confidentiality**: Even if someone intercepts your email, they cannot read its contents unless they have the private key.
- **Authentication**: PGP also provides **digital signatures**, ensuring that the email was indeed sent by the expected person.
- **Integrity**: PGP ensures that the content of the email has not been altered during transmission.

---

2. Using Signal for Secure Messaging and Calls

Signal is a **free, open-source messaging app** that provides **end-to-end encryption** for texts, voice calls, and video calls. Signal has gained popularity due to its **simplicity**, **high security**, and the fact that it **doesn't collect** unnecessary metadata.

How Signal Encryption Works

Signal uses **end-to-end encryption**, meaning the messages are encrypted on the sender's device and only decrypted on the recipient's device. Even **Signal's servers** don't have access to the contents of your messages.

- **Asymmetric Encryption**: Signal uses **asymmetric encryption** for exchanging keys. It securely generates a **unique encryption key** for each message, ensuring that each one is securely transmitted.
- **Forward Secrecy**: Every message has a **new encryption key**, which means that if an attacker obtains one key, they cannot decrypt previous or future messages.

Signal uses the **Signal Protocol**, which is widely recognized as one of the most secure messaging protocols available.

Setting Up Signal for Secure Messaging

Step 1: Install Signal

- Download and install the **Signal app** from the **Google Play Store** (for Android) or **App Store** (for iOS).
- Open the app and register using your **phone number**. Signal doesn't store your messages on its servers, so it only requires your phone number for identification.

Step 2: Sending Encrypted Messages

1. **Create a Contact**: Add a contact to Signal by using their phone number.
2. **Send Encrypted Messages**: Type a message and send it as usual. Signal automatically encrypts it using **end-to-end encryption**.
3. **Voice and Video Calls**: You can also make encrypted **voice and video calls** to your contacts by tapping the phone or video camera icon.

Step 3: Encrypted Group Chats

Signal also allows for **group chats** that are fully encrypted. You can create a group and add members, and all messages exchanged within the group are securely encrypted, ensuring that only group members can access them.

- **Strong Encryption**: Signal's **end-to-end encryption** guarantees that only the recipient can read the message.
- **Metadata Minimization**: Signal stores minimal metadata, so it doesn't track your contacts or message content.
- **Free and Open-Source**: As an open-source project, Signal's code is publicly available, allowing for transparency and constant scrutiny by security experts.
- **No Ads**: Signal doesn't display ads, ensuring a **privacy-respecting** user experience.

Case Study: Why Signal is Trusted by Experts

Signal is widely recommended by **security experts**, including Edward Snowden, who use it to communicate securely. Unlike other messaging platforms that may collect data or store logs, Signal is trusted because of its **open-source code** and the **strong encryption standards** it employs.

For example, in **2016**, Signal was used to communicate securely during the **United States presidential election**. Journalists, political activists, and public figures trusted Signal to ensure their **private conversations** remained confidential and protected from surveillance.

3. Best Practices for Encrypted Communications

To make the most of encrypted communication, follow these best practices:

- Whether you're using **PGP** for email or **Signal** for messaging, **password protection** is essential for securing your encryption keys. Use a **long, complex password** for your **private key** in PGP and set a **strong passcode** for Signal.

2. Regularly Update Your Encryption Tools

- Keep your **PGP software** (e.g., Gpg4win, OpenPGP) and **Signal** app up to date. This ensures that you benefit from the latest security enhancements and protection against new vulnerabilities.

3. Verify Key Fingerprints

- When exchanging PGP keys, always **verify key fingerprints** with the person you're communicating with. This ensures that you're using the **correct public key** and helps protect against **man-in-the-middle attacks**.

4. Enable Two-Factor Authentication (2FA)

- Many encrypted communication platforms, including Signal, offer **two-factor authentication (2FA)**. Enabling 2FA adds an extra layer of security, ensuring that even if someone obtains your password, they won't be able to access your account without the second factor (usually a **code** sent to your phone).

Visual Aid: How Encrypted Communication Works

Here's a simple flowchart to visualize how **PGP encryption** and **Signal messaging** work:

```
+----------------------------------+
|        PGP Encryption Flow        |
+----------------------------------+
                 |
                 v
```

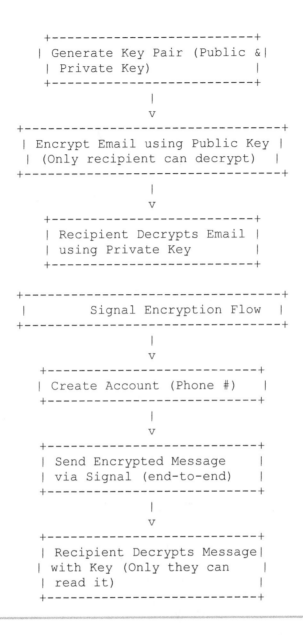

```
+--------------------------+
| Generate Key Pair (Public &|
| Private Key)             |
+--------------------------+
             |
             v
+----------------------------------+
| Encrypt Email using Public Key |
| (Only recipient can decrypt)   |
+----------------------------------+
             |
             v
   +--------------------------+
   | Recipient Decrypts Email |
   | using Private Key        |
   +--------------------------+

+----------------------------------+
|       Signal Encryption Flow     |
+----------------------------------+
             |
             v
   +--------------------------+
   | Create Account (Phone #) |
   +--------------------------+
             |
             v
   +--------------------------+
   | Send Encrypted Message   |
   | via Signal (end-to-end)  |
   +--------------------------+
             |
             v
   +--------------------------+
   | Recipient Decrypts Message|
   | with Key (Only they can  |
   | read it)                 |
   +--------------------------+
```

In today's digital age, **encrypted communication** is not just an option; it's a necessity. Tools like **PGP** for emails and **Signal** for messaging provide robust solutions for **protecting your privacy** and keeping your communications secure.

7.3: Best Practices for Password Security and Two-Factor Authentication

In the digital age, **password security** and **two-factor authentication (2FA)** are the cornerstones of protecting your personal information, online accounts, and sensitive data. With the increasing number of data breaches, cyberattacks, and identity theft, it's more important than ever to follow best practices for securing your passwords and enabling **2FA** to strengthen your online security.

In this guide, we'll walk through the best practices for creating and maintaining strong passwords, as well as implementing **two-factor authentication**. Whether you're securing an email account, social media, or financial platform, the steps outlined here will significantly reduce your vulnerability to attacks.

Why Password Security and 2FA Are Crucial

Your **password** is the primary defense against unauthorized access to your accounts. A weak or reused password is like leaving your front door wide open to burglars. Even worse, **password breaches** are rampant, with **millions of passwords** leaked every year from **data breaches**.

To further protect your accounts, **two-factor authentication (2FA)** adds a second layer of security. Even if a hacker obtains your password, they won't be able to access your account without the second form of authentication, often something you physically have—like your phone or an authentication app.

1. Best Practices for Password Security

A strong, unique password is the first line of defense for any online account. Let's go over the best practices for creating and managing passwords effectively.

1.1 Create Strong, Unique Passwords

The first step to securing your accounts is to **create strong passwords**. A strong password is one that is difficult for hackers or automated systems to guess.

What Makes a Strong Password?

- **Length**: The longer the password, the harder it is to crack. A password should be at least **12 characters** long.
- **Complexity**: Use a mix of **uppercase** and **lowercase letters**, **numbers**, and **special characters** (e.g., !, #, $, %).
- **Avoid Dictionary Words**: Passwords based on common words (e.g., "password123") are easy to guess using dictionary attacks.
- **Unpredictability**: A combination of random characters is best. For example, "Xz8$eRm@92!Qb" is much stronger than "password123".

Example of a Strong Password:

- **Strong**: `S#b2kz!8LmX7@3`
- **Weak**: `password123`

Why is Length Important?

Longer passwords take exponentially longer to crack. For example, a 12-character password made up of random letters, numbers, and symbols could take centuries to crack using brute-force methods.

How to Create a Strong Password:

1. **Avoid Personal Information**: Don't use easily guessable information like your **name**, **birthdate**, or **favorite sports team**.

2. **Use a Password Generator**: If you're unsure about creating a strong password, use a **password generator** to create random, complex passwords.

- **Password Manager**: Tools like **1Password**, **LastPass**, and **Bitwarden** can generate, store, and automatically fill in strong, unique passwords for each of your accounts.

1.2 Use Unique Passwords for Every Account

Reusing the same password across multiple accounts increases the risk of a **cascade failure**. If a hacker gains access to one account, they could try the same password on other accounts (a technique known as **credential stuffing**).

Why You Should Use Unique Passwords:

- **One Breach, One Account**: If your password is reused across multiple sites and one of those sites is compromised, hackers could gain access to **all your accounts**.
- **Minimize Risk**: Using unique passwords ensures that if one account is compromised, your other accounts remain secure.

How to Manage Unique Passwords:

- **Password Manager**: A **password manager** can store and automatically generate unique passwords for every account you create. This way, you don't need to remember every single password, only the one for the password manager.

1.3 Avoid Storing Passwords in Insecure Locations

Writing passwords down on paper or storing them in **text files** on your computer is a huge security risk. If someone gains access to that physical note or file, they can easily retrieve all your passwords.

- **Password Managers**: As mentioned, password managers encrypt your passwords and store them in one place, making it easy to access securely.
- **Encrypted Files**: If you must store passwords on your computer, ensure that the file is **encrypted** using software like **VeraCrypt**.

---

2. Best Practices for Two-Factor Authentication (2FA)

Two-factor authentication (2FA) adds an essential layer of protection to your online accounts. It requires something you know (your password) and something you have (usually a mobile device or authentication app) to log in.

2.1 Types of Two-Factor Authentication

There are several methods of **2FA**, each offering varying levels of security.

1. SMS-based Authentication

- **How it Works**: After entering your password, you receive a **one-time code** via text message (SMS) to enter.
- **Pros**: Easy to set up and use.
- **Cons**: Vulnerable to **SIM swapping** and **man-in-the-middle attacks**. It's better than nothing, but not the most secure option.

2. Authenticator Apps (Recommended)

- **How it Works**: You use an app like **Google Authenticator**, **Authy**, or **Microsoft Authenticator** to generate a time-based **one-time passcode** (TOTP). This code changes every 30 seconds and is required for login, along with your password.
- **Pros**: More secure than SMS since it isn't vulnerable to SIM swapping. The codes are only available on your phone.

- **Cons**: If you lose your phone, you may need to go through a recovery process to regain access.

- **How it Works**: A **hardware token** (like **Yubikey**) is a physical device that you plug into your computer or phone to authenticate your login.
- **Pros**: The most secure form of 2FA. It's nearly impossible for hackers to steal since it requires physical access to the device.
- **Cons**: Requires buying a physical device and carrying it with you.

2.2 How to Set Up Two-Factor Authentication

Step 1: Choose a 2FA Method

Decide which form of 2FA works best for you. For the highest security, consider using an **authenticator app** or a **hardware token**.

Step 2: Enable 2FA on Your Accounts

Most services support 2FA, including **Google**, **Facebook**, **Twitter**, and **ProtonMail**. Here's how to enable 2FA for your Google account:

1. Go to your **Google Account** settings.
2. Under the **Security** tab, find **2-Step Verification** and click **Get Started**.
3. Choose the method (Google Authenticator, text message, or a hardware key).
4. Follow the prompts to finish setup.

Step 3: Backup Codes

Many services provide **backup codes** in case you lose access to your 2FA method (like losing your phone). Print or store these codes in a secure location.

Repeat the process for any other online accounts you have. If they support 2FA, it's essential to enable it to ensure your data is as secure as possible.

2.3 How to Keep 2FA Secure

- **Backup Your Recovery Codes**: Always store your **backup codes** somewhere secure (but not online) in case you lose access to your 2FA device.
- **Use a Password Manager**: Many password managers, such as **1Password** and **Bitwarden**, also integrate with 2FA, allowing you to store both passwords and 2FA codes in one encrypted location.
- **Avoid Shared Devices**: Never use 2FA on a public or shared device. Always ensure your phone or computer is secured and private.

Visual Aid: Best Practices for Password Security and

2FA

Here's a visual representation summarizing the best practices for **password security** and **2FA**:

```
+-------------------------------------+
|        Step 1: Create Strong        |
|        and Unique Passwords         |
| - Use 12-16 characters              |
| - Mix uppercase, lowercase,         |
|   numbers, and symbols              |
| - Avoid personal information        |
+-------------------------------------+
                  |
                  v
+-------------------------------------+
|        Step 2: Use a Password       |
|        Manager for Storage          |
| - Store unique passwords            |
```

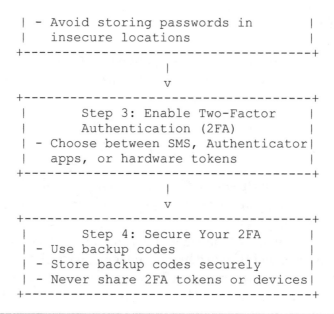

```
| - Avoid storing passwords in       |
|   insecure locations               |
+-------------------------------------+
                  |
                  v
+-------------------------------------+
|       Step 3: Enable Two-Factor     |
|       Authentication (2FA)          |
| - Choose between SMS, Authenticator |
|   apps, or hardware tokens          |
+-------------------------------------+
                  |
                  v
+-------------------------------------+
|       Step 4: Secure Your 2FA       |
| - Use backup codes                  |
| - Store backup codes securely       |
| - Never share 2FA tokens or devices |
+-------------------------------------+
```

Case Study: The Importance of 2FA in High-Profile Hacks

In **2019**, **Twitter** experienced a high-profile **hacking incident** where several **verified accounts** were compromised. The hackers gained access by using **SIM swapping**, which allowed them to intercept SMS-based 2FA codes and access accounts. This event led many high-profile figures to adopt stronger 2FA methods, such as **authenticator apps** or **hardware tokens**, in the aftermath.

This case emphasizes the need for **stronger forms of 2FA** and serves as a warning that even if you use **SMS-based 2FA**, it might not be enough to keep your accounts safe.

In conclusion, **password security** and **two-factor authentication** are foundational practices in protecting your **digital identity** and **online accounts**. By using strong, unique passwords, adopting a password manager, and enabling 2FA, you're taking critical steps toward keeping your information secure.

Chapter 8: Staying Anonymous While Browsing the Dark Web

When it comes to the **dark web**, **anonymity** is crucial. Whether you're there for privacy reasons, to access secure communications, or to explore information that's censored or restricted, protecting your identity and activity is key. Cybercriminals, surveillance systems, and even government agencies may be trying to track your online presence. In this chapter, we'll explore the essential tools and techniques for staying **anonymous** while browsing the dark web and other parts of the internet. We'll also discuss how to **protect your privacy**, mitigate tracking technologies, and ensure that your activities remain untraceable.

8.1: Tools for Anonymity: VPNs, Proxy Servers, and Tor

When browsing the internet, especially the **dark web**, anonymity is essential to ensure that your identity, location, and online activity remain private. Whether you're concerned about online surveillance, preventing tracking, or avoiding targeted advertising, using **VPNs**, **proxy servers**, and **Tor** are the best ways to maintain your privacy. In this guide, we'll delve into these tools, explain how they work, and how you can use them effectively to stay anonymous online.

1. VPNs (Virtual Private Networks)

A **VPN** is one of the most effective tools for securing your internet connection and masking your online identity. It creates a **secure, encrypted tunnel** between your device and a **remote server**, ensuring that no one—whether it's hackers, advertisers, or even your ISP—can see what you're doing online.

- **Encryption**: VPNs encrypt your data, ensuring that your internet traffic is secure and unreadable by third parties.
- **IP Masking**: By routing your traffic through a remote server, VPNs mask your **real IP address** and replace it with one from the VPN server, making it difficult to trace your activities.
- **Geo-Spatial Anonymity**: VPNs allow you to **change your virtual location** by connecting to servers in different countries, allowing you to **bypass geo-restrictions** (e.g., accessing content restricted in your region).

Setting Up and Using a VPN

1. **Choose a VPN Provider**: There are many VPN services available, with **paid services** generally offering better privacy and performance. Some popular options include **ExpressVPN**, **NordVPN**, and **CyberGhost**. Make sure to choose a VPN with a **no-logs policy** to ensure that your activity isn't tracked or recorded.
2. **Install the VPN Software**: Download and install the VPN application on your device. Most VPNs support multiple platforms (Windows, macOS, Android, and iOS).
3. **Connect to a VPN Server**: Open the VPN app and choose a server location. It could be a **nearby server** for better performance, or a **farther server** for **anonymity**.
4. **Browse Securely**: Once connected to the VPN, you can start browsing the internet with **encryption** in place and your IP address hidden.

Pros of Using a VPN:

- **Encryption** keeps your data private.
- **IP masking** hides your real location and activity.
- Can **bypass geo-blocked content**.
- **Secure public Wi-Fi**: Protects you from eavesdropping on unsecured networks like coffee shops or airports.

- **Potential slowdowns**: The encryption and routing process can slow down your connection, though high-quality VPNs mitigate this.
- **Not completely anonymous**: Some VPNs may still log data, so always choose a VPN with a **no-logs policy**.

---

2. Proxy Servers

A **proxy server** acts as an intermediary between your device and the internet. When you use a proxy, your requests to websites go through the proxy server, which makes the request on your behalf. The website then responds to the proxy, which sends the response back to you.

How Proxy Servers Work

- **IP Masking**: The primary function of a proxy server is to **mask your IP address**. Websites see the proxy's IP address instead of yours, offering a basic level of **anonymity**.
- **No Encryption**: Unlike VPNs, most proxies don't **encrypt** your internet traffic. While they hide your IP address, your traffic is still **vulnerable to interception** if someone is monitoring the network.

Types of Proxy Servers

1. **HTTP Proxy**: Used primarily for web browsing. It only works with **HTTP traffic**.
2. **SOCKS Proxy**: More versatile than HTTP proxies, SOCKS proxies can handle any type of traffic, including **email** and **file transfers**.

Setting Up and Using a Proxy Server

1. **Choose a Proxy Provider**: Select a **reliable proxy provider** like **ProxyMesh** or **HideMyAss**.

2. **Configure Your Device**: Enter the proxy details (usually the server IP and port number) into your device's network settings.
3. **Start Browsing**: Once connected, your requests will go through the proxy, masking your real IP address.

Pros of Using a Proxy:

- **Basic anonymity** by hiding your real IP address.
- **Faster than VPNs** for browsing since there's no encryption involved.

Cons of Using a Proxy:

- **No encryption**: Your traffic is not encrypted, so it's vulnerable to monitoring or hacking.
- **Not ideal for security-sensitive activities** like banking or email.
- **Less reliable**: Proxies may leak data or provide inconsistent performance.

---

3. Tor (The Onion Router)

Tor is a **free, open-source software** that ensures **total anonymity** by routing your internet traffic through a **network of volunteer-operated relays**. The unique feature of Tor is that it **encrypts your data multiple times**, making it **extremely difficult** for anyone to trace your activity back to you.

How Tor Works

- **Onion Routing**: Tor's architecture is based on **onion routing**, where your data is encrypted in multiple layers (like an onion). Each relay along the path removes one layer of encryption, but no single relay knows the complete path.
- **Exit Nodes**: The final node in the Tor network is called the **exit node**, where your encrypted data is decrypted and sent to the destination website. While the exit node can see your traffic, it doesn't know who you are (because your IP is hidden).

1. **Download and Install the Tor Browser**: Go to the official **Tor Project website** and download the **Tor Browser**. It's available for all major operating systems (Windows, macOS, Linux).
2. **Connect to the Tor Network**: Once installed, open the Tor browser and click **"Connect"** to establish a connection to the Tor network.
3. **Start Browsing**: Once connected, you can start browsing websites anonymously. Tor also allows you to access **.onion** sites, which are only accessible through the Tor network.

Pros of Using Tor:

- **Complete anonymity**: Tor is designed to hide your identity and activity.
- **Bypasses censorship**: Tor helps you access blocked or censored content, including dark web sites.
- **Free**: Tor is completely free and open-source.

Cons of Using Tor:

- **Slower speeds**: Because Tor routes your traffic through multiple relays, it's generally slower than regular browsing.
- **Exit node risk**: Although your data is encrypted, **exit nodes** can still see unencrypted traffic, which could expose sensitive data if you visit an unsecured website.

How to Use VPN, Proxy, and Tor Together

While each of these tools is powerful on its own, you can combine them for added privacy. Here's how:

1. **VPN + Tor**:
   - **Why use both**: By using a **VPN** before connecting to **Tor**, you add an additional layer of security and ensure your ISP can't see that you're using Tor.

- **How to set it up**: First, connect to a VPN server. Once connected, open the **Tor Browser** to access the Tor network. Your traffic will be encrypted twice—once by the VPN and once by Tor.

2. **VPN + Proxy**:
    - **Why use both**: Using a **VPN** with a **proxy** can provide extra anonymity when surfing the web. The **VPN** encrypts your traffic, while the **proxy** masks your IP address.
    - **How to set it up**: First, connect to the VPN, then configure your device or browser to route traffic through the proxy.

Visual Aid: How VPN, Proxy, and Tor Work

Here's a simple diagram to show how **VPN**, **proxy servers**, and **Tor** work:

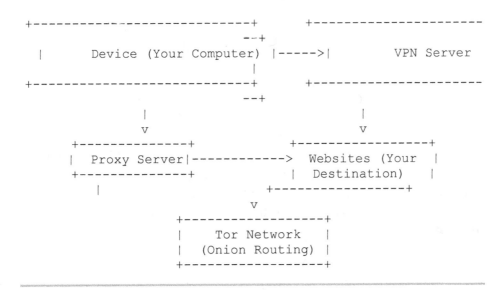

Case Study: Using Tor for Privacy

Consider the case of **whistleblowers** or **journalists** operating in countries with oppressive regimes. **Tor** is widely used by these individuals to protect their identity and communicate securely. In one instance, **Edward Snowden**, the famous whistleblower, used **Tor** to communicate securely with journalists while avoiding detection by the U.S. government.

By using Tor, Snowden ensured that his communications remained **anonymous** and **encrypted**, despite being under intense scrutiny. This example highlights the power of Tor in maintaining privacy and freedom of speech, especially in high-risk situations.

Conclusion: Choosing the Right Tool for Anonymity

Each tool—**VPN**, **proxy servers**, and **Tor**—offers distinct advantages and can be used depending on your needs.

- **VPNs** provide **robust security** with encryption and are ideal for general privacy, especially when bypassing geo-restrictions or using public Wi-Fi.
- **Proxy servers** offer basic **IP masking** but lack encryption, making them less secure for sensitive activities.
- **Tor** offers **maximum anonymity** but at the cost of slower browsing speeds, making it ideal for those who prioritize privacy over speed.

In many cases, using a **combination** of these tools (such as **VPN + Tor**) can offer the highest level of security and anonymity. Whether you're navigating the dark web or just trying to protect your online privacy, the tools discussed in this chapter will help you achieve a higher level of **anonymity** and **security** in your online activities.

8.2: Using Secure Email Services and Anonymous Payment Methods

When navigating the **dark web** or engaging in any privacy-focused activities, the need for **secure communication** and **anonymous**

transactions is crucial. Email and payment methods are two essential components of this, and ensuring that they are both **secure** and **anonymous** is critical to maintaining privacy. In this chapter, we'll explore how to use **secure email services** and **anonymous payment methods** to protect your personal information and maintain anonymity.

---

1. Secure Email Services: Protecting Your Communication

Traditional email providers such as **Gmail**, **Yahoo**, or **Outlook** are not designed with privacy in mind. These services track your activity, store your data, and may even be subject to government surveillance. For **secure communication**, using a **privacy-focused email service** is essential. These services offer **end-to-end encryption**, ensuring that only you and the recipient can read your messages.

Why Secure Email Services Are Important

- **End-to-End Encryption**: Ensures that only the sender and recipient can read the contents of the email. Even the service provider cannot access your messages.
- **No Data Logging**: Secure email providers typically don't log user activity, meaning they don't store your IP address or email metadata.
- **Protection from Surveillance**: These services offer better protection against surveillance and data mining, particularly when communicating about sensitive topics.

1.1 Secure Email Providers

Several **secure email services** are available, each offering varying levels of protection, anonymity, and features. Let's explore the most commonly used services:

1. **ProtonMail**

- o **End-to-End Encryption**: ProtonMail encrypts emails by default, and it doesn't store your data or IP address.
- o **Swiss Privacy Laws**: ProtonMail is based in Switzerland, a country with strong privacy laws.
- o **Free & Paid Versions**: ProtonMail offers a free plan with limited storage and a paid plan with more features.

Setting Up ProtonMail:

4. Go to the **ProtonMail website** and create an account.
5. Choose a **username** and **password**. No personal information is required to sign up.
6. Once your account is created, you can start sending and receiving **encrypted emails**.
7. ProtonMail automatically encrypts your emails when sending them to other ProtonMail users.

Example:

- o **Scenario**: If you're working as a journalist, **ProtonMail** is ideal for keeping your communication secure and private from potential surveillance.
2. **Tutanota**
   - o **Open-Source**: Tutanota is open-source, meaning its source code is available for inspection, which increases transparency and security.
   - o **No Ads or Tracking**: Tutanota does not show ads or track your usage, further protecting your privacy.
   - o **End-to-End Encryption**: Like ProtonMail, Tutanota provides end-to-end encryption for all messages, even for non-Tutanota users.

Setting Up Tutanota:

3. Visit **Tutanota's website** and sign up for a free account.
4. Choose your email address and password.
5. Tutanota offers a **mobile app** that you can install for easy access on the go.
6. Start sending encrypted emails directly from your Tutanota inbox.
3. **Mailfence**

- o **PGP Encryption**: Mailfence offers integrated support for **PGP encryption**, ensuring that only the intended recipient can read the email.
- o **Strong Privacy Policies**: Based in Belgium, Mailfence adheres to the strict privacy regulations of the European Union.
- o **Free & Paid Options**: The free version provides basic email functionality, while the paid plans offer **more storage** and additional features like **calendar** and **document signing**.

Setting Up Mailfence:

3. Go to **Mailfence.com** and register for an account.
4. Configure your **PGP key** settings to enable encrypted communication.
5. Use the provided tools to encrypt and decrypt your emails.

1.2 Best Practices for Secure Email Usage

- **Enable Two-Factor Authentication (2FA)**: Adding an extra layer of protection by requiring a second form of identification (like a code sent to your phone) makes it harder for hackers to access your account.
- **Be Cautious with Attachments**: While ProtonMail and other services encrypt emails, **attachments** are not automatically encrypted unless specifically done so. Use a service like **Encrypted File Store** to encrypt any attachments before sending them.
- **Verify Keys for Encryption**: If you're using PGP encryption (like in **Mailfence**), always verify the recipient's public key to avoid man-in-the-middle attacks.

---

2. Anonymous Payment Methods: Protecting Your

Financial Privacy

In the digital age, traditional payment methods like **credit cards** and **bank transfers** leave a trail that can link back to your identity. If you wish to maintain **financial privacy** or remain **anonymous** while purchasing goods or services online—whether on the dark web or elsewhere—using **anonymous payment methods** is essential.

Why Anonymous Payments Are Important

- **Privacy**: Anonymous payment methods prevent anyone from linking your real identity to a transaction.
- **Security**: Some payment methods offer **extra protection** against fraud and theft.
- **Accessing Restricted Services**: Certain websites may only accept anonymous payments to ensure the privacy of their users.

2.1 Anonymous Payment Methods

Here are the most common anonymous payment methods that provide **privacy** and **security**:

1. **Cryptocurrencies (Bitcoin, Monero, etc.)**
   - **Bitcoin**: While Bitcoin is not **completely anonymous**, it offers a higher level of privacy than traditional payment methods. However, the Bitcoin blockchain is transparent, meaning transactions can be traced back to specific wallets if proper precautions are not taken.
   - **Monero**: A privacy-centric cryptocurrency that **completely anonymizes** transaction details, including the sender and recipient. Monero is often the preferred choice for **high anonymity** transactions.
   - **How to Use**: You can use **Bitcoin** or **Monero** to make anonymous payments. Simply transfer the cryptocurrency to the merchant's wallet address and ensure that your wallet is **untraceable**.

   Setting Up Bitcoin:

4. Download a **Bitcoin wallet** (e.g., **Electrum**, **Exodus**) and create a wallet.
5. **Buy Bitcoin** through a secure exchange or peer-to-peer network.

6.   Use **Tor** and a **VPN** to **protect your identity** while making transactions.

7.   Transfer the Bitcoin to the merchant's wallet address for your purchase.

8.   Download the **Monero Wallet** from the official website.

9.   Use a **decentralized exchange** or **peer-to-peer trading** to buy Monero.

10.   Send Monero to the merchant or recipient's Monero address for completely anonymous transactions.

2. **Gift Cards**
    o **Anonymous Prepaid Gift Cards**: Some online merchants accept gift cards as a form of payment. These gift cards can be purchased **in-store** with cash and used online without revealing your identity.
    o **How to Use**: Buy a gift card from a local retailer (such as **Amazon**, **Visa**, or **Mastercard** gift cards). You can then use the gift card details to make online purchases **anonymously**.

Best Practices for Using Gift Cards:

    o **Use cash** to buy the gift cards at a store, ensuring there's no direct link to your identity.
    o Avoid using gift cards for high-value transactions unless you're sure the merchant accepts them anonymously.

3. **Prepaid Debit Cards**
    o **Prepaid Debit Cards** are similar to gift cards but are often reloadable. These cards can be purchased with **cash** at a retail store and used for **online transactions** without revealing your personal information.
    o **How to Use**: Purchase a prepaid card like **NetSpend** or **Green Dot**, which can be loaded with a specified amount of money. Use it like a regular debit card to make online purchases.

Best Practices for Using Prepaid Cards:

    o Buy the cards in **cash** to maintain privacy.

o   Ensure that the prepaid card does not require personal identification or a **social security number** to register.

---

3. How to Maintain Privacy When Using Secure Email and Anonymous Payments

To maximize your **privacy**, you should implement a **multi-layered approach** to secure email and payment methods. Here's how you can combine both:

1. **Use Tor with Secure Email**: When sending encrypted emails, use the **Tor Browser** to anonymize your connection. This ensures that your IP address is masked and cannot be traced.
2. **Use Cryptocurrencies for Payments**: Pay for services with **Bitcoin** or **Monero** through the **Tor network** for **complete anonymity**.
3. **Avoid Linking Personal Information**: Never use your **real name, address**, or **phone number** when signing up for secure email services or making anonymous payments. Always create **pseudonymous accounts**.

Visual Aid: Using Secure Email and Anonymous Payment Methods

Here's a visual guide to ensure you maintain **privacy** and **security**:

```
+-------------------------------+
|  Step 1: Use Secure Email     |
|  - ProtonMail, Tutanota       |
|  - End-to-end encryption      |
+-------------------------------+
                |
```

```
                      v
+-------------------------------+
|  Step 2: Use Anonymous Payment|
|  - Bitcoin, Monero, Gift Cards |
|  - Avoid using personal info   |
+-------------------------------+
                |
                v
+-------------------------------+
|  Step 3: Combine Tor + VPN    |
|  - Hide your IP address        |
|  - Encrypt your connection     |
+-------------------------------+
```

Case Study: Journalists and Activists Using Secure

Email and Anonymous Payments

Consider the case of **journalists** and **activists** operating under oppressive regimes, where privacy and security are paramount. These individuals use services like **ProtonMail** and **Tutanota** to ensure their communication is private, encrypted, and free from government surveillance.

Additionally, they use **Monero** to make anonymous donations and payments to support their work, ensuring that their financial transactions cannot be traced back to them. The combination of **secure email** and **anonymous payment methods** allows them to operate without fear of being identified or censored.

In the digital age, privacy is more important than ever, especially when interacting with the dark web or engaging in sensitive communications. By using **secure email services** like **ProtonMail** and **Tutanota**, and making payments with **cryptocurrencies** or **prepaid cards**, you can protect your identity and ensure that your actions remain private.

8.3: Understanding and Mitigating Tracking Technologies

In an era where **data is king**, your online activities are constantly being tracked, analyzed, and monetized by corporations, governments, and other entities. Whether you're browsing the surface web or the dark web, **tracking technologies** are always at work, collecting data about your online behavior. While this can lead to **personalized experiences** (like ads tailored to your interests), it also compromises **privacy** and **anonymity**.

---

1. Understanding Tracking Technologies

Tracking technologies are methods used to **identify**, **monitor**, and **collect data** on your online behavior. These technologies can be broadly divided into several categories, each with its own unique mechanism for gathering data.

1.1 Types of Tracking Technologies

Here are some of the most common types of tracking technologies you'll encounter online:

1. Cookies

- **What They Are**: Cookies are small text files stored in your browser that hold information about your visit to a website, such as login credentials, preferences, and browsing history.
- **Why They're Used**: Cookies are used to **remember users**, keep you logged in, personalize your experience, and track your behavior across websites for **advertising** and **analytics**.

2. Web Bugs / Pixels

- **What They Are**: A **web bug** (or **pixel tag**) is a small, invisible image or piece of code embedded in a webpage or email. It tracks whether a user has visited a particular page or opened an email.

- **Why They're Used**: Web bugs are used by advertisers to track the **effectiveness** of their campaigns, and by websites to monitor user activity.

3. Browser Fingerprinting

- **What It Is**: Browser fingerprinting involves collecting **information about your device and browser** configuration (such as screen resolution, installed plugins, fonts, and more). This information is used to create a unique "fingerprint" of your device, which can be used to track you even if you delete cookies or use an incognito window.
- **Why It's Used**: Fingerprinting is used by advertisers and websites to track users without the use of cookies. It's also used for **security purposes** to detect fraud or suspicious activity.

4. IP Tracking

- **What It Is**: Your **IP address** is a unique identifier assigned to your device when you connect to the internet. It reveals your **geographical location** and can be used to track your online behavior across websites.
- **Why It's Used**: IP tracking is used to **monitor your location** for advertising, geolocation services, and security purposes.

5. Device Tracking

- **What It Is**: Device tracking is the use of unique identifiers, such as **device IDs** (on mobile phones) or **MAC addresses** (for Wi-Fi), to track your behavior across different websites and apps.
- **Why It's Used**: Companies track devices to build more accurate **user profiles** and deliver targeted advertisements.

---

2. Mitigating Tracking Technologies

Now that we understand how tracking technologies work, let's explore how to mitigate or block them to protect your **privacy** while browsing online. The strategies below will help you avoid being **tracked**, whether you're on the **surface web** or the **dark web**.

2.1 Using Privacy-Focused Browsers and Extensions

Your browser is your primary gateway to the internet, and it's also the primary **tool** for trackers to monitor your activity. Luckily, there are **privacy-focused browsers** and browser extensions that can significantly reduce your online footprint.

1. Privacy-Focused Browsers

- **Brave Browser**: Brave is a **privacy-oriented browser** that blocks trackers and ads by default. It also offers an integrated **Tor** option for anonymous browsing and rewards users with **BAT tokens** (Basic Attention Tokens) for viewing privacy-respecting ads.
- **Tor Browser**: The **Tor browser** is a must-have tool for anyone seeking **maximum privacy**. It routes your traffic through the **Tor network**, which anonymizes your browsing activity by **encrypting** your data and bouncing it through a series of **volunteer-operated nodes**. Tor also disables **JavaScript** by default to help mitigate browser fingerprinting.
- **Firefox with Privacy Add-ons**: Firefox, when used with privacy-focused extensions like **uBlock Origin**, **Privacy Badger**, and **NoScript**, can become a powerful tool for **tracking protection**.

2. Browser Extensions

- **uBlock Origin**: uBlock Origin is a **lightweight** ad blocker that can also block **third-party trackers**. It is highly customizable and effective in blocking most trackers from collecting your data.
- **Privacy Badger**: Developed by the **Electronic Frontier Foundation** (EFF), Privacy Badger blocks trackers that **violate privacy** policies. It learns to block trackers based on your browsing activity, making it a **smart choice** for automatic protection.
- **NoScript**: NoScript is a browser extension that blocks **JavaScript, Java, Flash**, and other potentially dangerous content from running on websites. It helps mitigate risks from malicious **web bugs** and **fingerprinting** techniques.

2.2 Managing Cookies and Local Storage

Cookies and local storage are widely used to track your browsing activity. To prevent tracking, you can take several steps to manage cookies and other storage technologies.

1. Delete or Block Cookies

- **Use Browser Settings**: Most modern browsers allow you to **block** or **delete cookies** through the settings. You can opt to block **third-party cookies**, which are often used for tracking, while allowing first-party cookies necessary for website functionality.
- **Use Private Browsing / Incognito Mode**: Incognito mode disables cookie storage, meaning your browsing session will not leave traces on your local device. However, it's worth noting that this doesn't stop trackers from monitoring your activity online.

2. Use Cookie Management Extensions

- **Cookie AutoDelete**: This extension automatically deletes cookies after each session, preventing persistent cookies from tracking you.
- **ClearURLs**: This extension automatically removes tracking parameters from URLs, which can often be used to track your browsing activity.

2.3 Using VPNs for IP Address Masking

A **VPN** (Virtual Private Network) is one of the most effective tools for masking your real **IP address** and hiding your online activity. By routing your traffic through a remote server, a VPN **conceals your IP address** and prevents websites from tracking you based on location.

Setting Up and Using a VPN

1. **Choose a Reputable VPN Provider**: Popular providers like **ExpressVPN**, **NordVPN**, or **ProtonVPN** offer **strong encryption** and **no-logs policies**, ensuring your online activity remains private.
2. **Install the VPN**: After subscribing to a VPN service, download the app for your operating system and log in.

3. **Connect to a Server**: Choose a **server location** and connect. Your **IP address** will now appear as the server's, effectively hiding your real IP.

Why VPNs Are Effective Against Tracking:

- **Masks Your IP Address**: By replacing your real IP address with the VPN server's, websites cannot link your activities to your physical location.
- **Encryption**: A VPN encrypts your internet traffic, making it difficult for trackers or hackers to see what you're doing online.

2.4 Mitigating Browser Fingerprinting

Browser fingerprinting is a method of tracking users based on their unique browser configurations. Even if you use **Tor** or a **VPN**, fingerprinting can still identify you.

How to Mitigate Fingerprinting:

- **Use Tor**: The Tor network is specifically designed to make every user appear the same, mitigating fingerprinting. The **Tor Browser** does this by standardizing your browser's **user-agent**, **screen resolution**, and other characteristics, making your activities **indistinguishable** from others.
- **Use Privacy-Focused Browsers**: Browsers like **Brave** and **Firefox**, when used with privacy extensions like **Privacy Badger** or **NoScript**, reduce the effectiveness of fingerprinting by limiting the amount of data that can be collected about your browser.
- **Disable JavaScript**: Many fingerprinting techniques rely on JavaScript to gather information about your device and browser. Disabling JavaScript (using **NoScript** or **Tor**) can help prevent these techniques.

Visual Aid: Mitigating Tracking Technologies

Here's a flowchart summarizing how to mitigate tracking technologies effectively:

```
+------------------------------+
|    Step 1: Use Privacy Browser|
|    - Tor, Brave, Firefox     |
|    - Use Privacy Extensions  |
+------------------------------+
              |
              v
+------------------------------+
|    Step 2: Manage Cookies    |
|    - Block Third-Party Cookies|
|    - Use Cookie Management    |
|      Extensions (e.g., uBlock)|
+------------------------------+
              |
              v
+------------------------------+
|    Step 3: Mask IP Address    |
|    - Use a VPN               |
|    - Choose VPN with No-Logs  |
+------------------------------+
              |
              v
+------------------------------+
|    Step 4: Mitigate Fingerprint|
|    - Use Tor or Privacy Browsers|
|    - Disable JavaScript       |
+------------------------------+
```

Case Study: How Activists and Journalists Protect Their Privacy

Consider the case of **activists** in repressive countries, where the internet is heavily censored and monitored. They rely on **secure email** services, **Tor**, and **VPNs** to protect their communication and online activities from government surveillance. By using these tools in combination, they can **bypass censorship** and maintain **privacy**, even while engaging in high-risk activities such as **protesting** or **exposing government corruption**.

One famous example is **Edward Snowden**, the former NSA contractor who used **Tor** to communicate securely with journalists during his whistleblowing activities. Snowden also used **encrypted email** services like **ProtonMail** to ensure that his communication was private and secure.

As technology evolves, so too do the methods used by companies, governments, and cybercriminals to track and collect data about you. By understanding the types of **tracking technologies** used today, and implementing strategies like using **secure email services**, employing a **VPN**, managing **cookies**, and mitigating **browser fingerprinting**, you can protect your **privacy** and maintain **anonymity** online.

Part 4: Advanced Level – Analyzing Cybercriminal Operations

Chapter 9: Understanding Cybercrime on the Dark Web

The **dark web**—an encrypted and often anonymous part of the internet—has earned a reputation as a haven for **illegal activities**. While it is true that the dark web offers valuable resources for those seeking **privacy** and **freedom of expression**, it is also a hub for **cybercrime**. From **drug markets** to **weapon trades**, and **hacking services**, the dark web has enabled a range of illegal enterprises to thrive under the radar of authorities.

9.1: Types of Cybercrime: Drug Markets, Weapon Trade, Hacking Services

The **dark web** has gained notoriety for being a breeding ground for illegal activities. Among the most prominent cybercrimes that thrive in this hidden, encrypted part of the internet are the **drug trade**, **weapon markets**, and **hacking services**. These illegal activities are facilitated by the anonymity and privacy that the dark web provides, allowing individuals to engage in illicit transactions without easily being traced by law enforcement.

In this guide, we'll dive into each of these types of cybercrime, explaining how they operate, the risks involved, and offering a clearer understanding of their impact on society. We will also discuss specific examples and case studies to highlight how these criminal activities unfold in real-world scenarios.

1. Drug Markets on the Dark Web

The **dark web drug trade** is one of the most well-known illegal activities that flourishes within anonymous marketplaces. These drug markets mirror legitimate e-commerce platforms, with buyers and sellers using encrypted websites to interact.

How Drug Markets Operate

Drug marketplaces on the dark web function much like online shopping platforms. These platforms connect buyers and sellers, allowing users to browse **drug listings**, make **purchases**, and arrange for **delivery**, all while maintaining anonymity. Typically, these transactions are conducted using **cryptocurrencies** like **Bitcoin** or **Monero**, which provide users with added privacy and security.

Key Features of Dark Web Drug Markets:

- **Anonymity**: Users communicate through encrypted messaging systems, and transactions are conducted using cryptocurrencies, making it harder for authorities to track activities.
- **Escrow Systems**: Many markets use **escrow services** to protect buyers and sellers. The buyer's funds are held in escrow until they confirm the receipt of the product, minimizing fraud.
- **Drug Categories**: Drugs sold range from **marijuana** to **synthetic drugs**, including highly dangerous substances like **fentanyl**, **MDMA**, and **ecstasy**.

Risks and Challenges:

- **Law Enforcement Targeting**: Law enforcement agencies are increasingly targeting these dark web markets, employing **undercover agents** to infiltrate and dismantle such operations.
- **Fraud**: While escrow systems provide some protection, buyers are still at risk of receiving counterfeit or low-quality products.
- **Health Hazards**: Some of the drugs sold on these markets can be **laced** with dangerous substances, leading to potentially life-threatening consequences.

Example: Silk Road

One of the most famous dark web marketplaces was **Silk Road**, launched in 2011. It was the first major platform dedicated to the sale of illegal goods, primarily drugs. Its founder, **Ross Ulbricht**, operated under the pseudonym **Dread Pirate Roberts**, and the marketplace facilitated millions of transactions until it was shut down in 2013. The Silk Road was a prime example of how dark web drug markets function, offering a wide range of illicit substances while using cryptocurrency for payment to keep transactions untraceable.

---

2. Weapon Trade on the Dark Web

The **illegal weapon trade** is another major type of cybercrime that thrives on the dark web. Dark web marketplaces also provide a platform for individuals to **buy** and **sell firearms**, **ammunition**, and **explosives**, all while maintaining their anonymity.

How Weapon Markets Operate

The process of buying and selling weapons on the dark web is largely similar to drug transactions. Sellers list firearms, accessories, and other weapons for sale, and buyers make purchases using cryptocurrencies.

Key Features of Dark Web Weapon Trade:

- **Anonymous Transactions**: Like the drug trade, the weapon trade operates in much the same way, with encrypted communications and cryptocurrency transactions ensuring privacy for both parties.
- **Variety of Weapons**: The market for firearms and weapons includes everything from **handguns**, **assault rifles**, and **ammunition** to **explosives** and **military-grade equipment**.
- **Secrecy and Delivery**: Sellers often disguise the true nature of their goods in **regular packages** to avoid detection by law enforcement.

Risks and Challenges:

- **Legal Consequences**: The purchase of illegal firearms is heavily monitored by law enforcement. If caught, buyers face **severe legal consequences**, including imprisonment.
- **Fraudulent Transactions**: Like drug markets, weapon trade platforms are prone to **fraud**. Sellers may never deliver the

promised goods, and buyers may lose their cryptocurrency in a scam.

- **Dangerous Products**: Many of the weapons sold on the dark web are not **regulated** and may be dangerous or malfunctioning. There's also the risk of **stolen weapons** being sold to criminals.

Example: AlphaBay

AlphaBay was another massive dark web marketplace that catered to illegal activities, including the **sale of firearms** and **explosives**. Launched in 2014, AlphaBay allowed sellers to list weapons, explosives, and counterfeit goods, while buyers were able to complete transactions through **Bitcoin**. The platform was taken down by law enforcement in 2017, but not before it became a notorious hub for weapon sales.

3. Hacking Services on the Dark Web

The dark web also hosts a booming market for **hacking services**. Criminals, organizations, and even **nation-states** seeking to conduct **cyberattacks** often turn to the dark web to hire hackers or purchase hacking tools.

How Hacking Services Operate

Hacking services on the dark web are typically offered by **cybercriminals** who have the skills to carry out cyberattacks. These services can range from **distributed denial-of-service (DDoS)** attacks to **data breaches** and **identity theft**.

Key Features of Dark Web Hacking Services:

- **Hack-for-Hire**: Cybercriminals offer their services to anyone willing to pay, including **corporate espionage**, **stalking**, and **financial fraud**.
- **Malware and Ransomware**: Many hackers sell **malware**, including **ransomware** that can be used to **encrypt data** and demand payment from victims.

- **DDoS Attacks**: Hackers sell access to **botnets**, which can be used to overwhelm and crash websites through **distributed denial-of-service attacks**.

Risks and Challenges:

- **Legal Repercussions**: Using hacking services is illegal and can lead to **serious criminal charges**. Individuals who engage in cybercrime face both legal and financial consequences if caught.
- **Security**: Many hackers are untrustworthy, and hiring them may result in further compromise of your systems. There's also the risk of being scammed if the hacker doesn't complete the job.

Example: Ransomware as a Service (RaaS)

A notable example of dark web cybercrime is the **Ransomware-as-a-Service (RaaS)** model. Criminals can purchase **ransomware kits** from dark web markets, which come with all the tools needed to launch a ransomware attack. These kits have made ransomware attacks increasingly accessible to individuals with little technical expertise. Many **businesses** have been affected by these types of attacks, paying hefty ransoms to regain access to their encrypted data.

Visual Aid: Flow of Cybercrime on the Dark Web

To better understand how the types of cybercrime on the dark web operate, here's a simple flowchart to visualize how these illicit markets work:

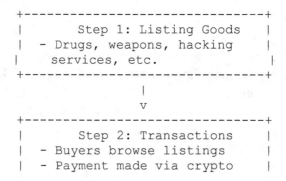

```
+-------------------------------+
|       Step 1: Listing Goods   |
|    - Drugs, weapons, hacking  |
|      services, etc.           |
+-------------------------------+
                |
                v
+-------------------------------+
|       Step 2: Transactions    |
|    - Buyers browse listings   |
|    - Payment made via crypto  |
|                               |
```

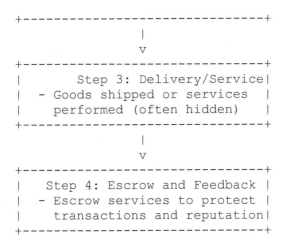

```
         +------------------------------+
                        |
                        v
         +------------------------------+
         |       Step 3: Delivery/Service|
         |   - Goods shipped or services |
         |     performed (often hidden)  |
         +------------------------------+
                        |
                        v
         +------------------------------+
         |   Step 4: Escrow and Feedback |
         |   - Escrow services to protect|
         |     transactions and reputation|
         +------------------------------+
```

Cybercrime on the dark web is a multifaceted and dangerous activity that has widespread implications for society. Whether it's the **drug trade**, the **illegal weapon market**, or **hacking services**, each type of cybercrime undermines security, trust, and the rule of law.

For law enforcement, tracking and dismantling these operations is a monumental task due to the **anonymity** and **decentralization** of the dark web. However, as demonstrated by high-profile takedowns of platforms like **Silk Road** and **AlphaBay**, authorities are increasingly getting better at infiltrating these illicit markets.

For individuals, the risks of engaging in these illegal activities are severe—ranging from **legal consequences** to being defrauded by malicious actors. The dark web, while offering anonymity, also harbors criminal activities that can have profound effects on people's lives and on the broader world.

9.2: How Dark Web Criminals Organize and Operate

The **dark web** offers anonymity, which is why it has become a hub for a range of **illicit activities**. Whether it's the **sale of illegal goods** or the **provision of cybercriminal services**, dark web criminals have created highly organized systems that allow them to operate with relative impunity. In this guide, we'll explore how dark web criminals organize their operations, focusing on the **structure of their networks**, the **tools they use**, and how they manage to evade detection.

Understanding these operations provides crucial insights into both the **motives** of dark web criminals and the **challenges** law enforcement faces in trying to infiltrate and dismantle such networks.

---

1. Organizational Structure of Dark Web Criminals

While it may seem like dark web criminals are isolated, many work within highly **structured** and **organized networks**. These networks enable them to **minimize risk**, ensure **continuity of operations**, and scale up their activities. Here's how these groups often operate:

1.1 Decentralization and Anonymity

Dark web criminals rely heavily on **decentralized** systems to hide their identities and avoid detection. The anonymity provided by **Tor** and other privacy tools like **I2P** makes it difficult to track individuals back to their physical locations. This decentralization ensures that, even if one node is taken down, the network can continue to function.

- **No Central Server**: Unlike traditional criminal enterprises that rely on central hubs (e.g., a leader or a headquarters), dark web criminals often operate through **distributed networks**. This means that there's no single point of failure.
- **Pseudonyms and Fake Identities**: Criminals in the dark web typically use **pseudonyms** and fake identities to further obscure their real-world identity. This prevents law enforcement from identifying key players in the network.
- **Encrypted Communication**: Most dark web criminals use encrypted messaging services to communicate securely. These messages are often routed through networks like **Signal** or **ProtonMail**, providing an extra layer of protection.

1.2 Hierarchy and Specialization

While dark web operations are decentralized, many of them still have a **hierarchical structure**. This hierarchy is usually organized in a way that makes it harder for law enforcement to infiltrate the network and shut it down.

- **Leaders/Organizers**: These individuals act as the **key decision-makers**. They often control the flow of money, resources, and goods in the dark web marketplace. They may have **multiple marketplaces** running simultaneously, each serving a different purpose (e.g., drugs, weapons, counterfeit IDs).
- **Middlemen and Moderators**: These individuals handle the **day-to-day operations** of the dark web marketplaces. They are responsible for overseeing transactions, resolving disputes, and ensuring that both buyers and sellers follow the marketplace's rules.
- **Vendors and Buyers**: These are the individuals who buy and sell goods and services on the dark web. Vendors range from large-scale suppliers of illegal products to smaller, independent operators. Buyers, on the other hand, may be purchasing anything from illicit substances to hacking tools.

1.3 Distributed Operations

Criminals often specialize in a particular aspect of the dark web ecosystem to minimize risk and maximize efficiency. The ecosystem includes:

- **Drug Trade**: Some groups focus solely on the **illegal drug market**, sourcing products from suppliers and selling them on the dark web.
- **Hacking Services**: Other groups specialize in providing **hacking tools** or offering **cybercrime-for-hire** services. These can range from **DDoS attacks** to **ransomware** deployment.
- **Counterfeit Goods**: A different subset of dark web criminals focuses on selling **counterfeit goods** such as fake IDs, passports, or credit cards.

This **division of labor** allows dark web criminals to operate more efficiently and minimize exposure to law enforcement.

2. Tools and Technologies Used by Dark Web Criminals

The **tools** and **technologies** used by dark web criminals are a vital part of their operations. These tools not only help them maintain **anonymity** but also allow them to scale and optimize their criminal activities.

2.1 Cryptocurrencies: The Backbone of Dark Web Transactions

Cryptocurrencies, such as **Bitcoin**, **Monero**, and **Ethereum**, have become the preferred form of **payment** on the dark web. They provide several advantages, such as **anonymity**, **security**, and **ease of use**.

- **Bitcoin**: While Bitcoin is widely used on the dark web, it's not as anonymous as many people believe. Bitcoin transactions are **publicly recorded** on the blockchain, meaning they can potentially be traced back to an individual if their identity is linked to their wallet.
- **Monero**: This privacy-focused cryptocurrency offers a higher degree of **anonymity** than Bitcoin. Monero uses **ring signatures** and **stealth addresses** to conceal the sender, receiver, and amount involved in a transaction, making it a popular choice for dark web criminals.

How Cryptocurrencies Facilitate Criminal Activities:

- **Anonymity**: Cryptocurrencies are pseudonymous, allowing users to conduct transactions without revealing their identities.
- **Global Transactions**: Cryptocurrencies are not bound by borders or regulations, making it easy for criminals to **conduct international transactions**.

2.2 Encryption Tools and Services

In addition to cryptocurrencies, dark web criminals rely on various **encryption tools** to ensure their communications remain private.

- **Tor**: Tor, the most popular tool for anonymous browsing, routes internet traffic through a series of **randomly chosen relays** to obscure the user's **IP address**. Tor also allows users to access **.onion** sites, which are only accessible through the Tor network.
- **I2P**: The Invisible Internet Project (I2P) is another anonymity network that provides **end-to-end encryption** for communications. While less widely used than Tor, it's still popular for criminal operations, particularly when users want to avoid Tor's detection.

How Tor and I2P Protect Criminal Operations:

- **Hiding Identities**: These networks mask the user's location and IP address, making it nearly impossible to trace internet activity back to a real-world identity.
- **Access to Hidden Services**: Criminals use **.onion** and **.i2p** domains to host their illegal services. These domains are not indexed by traditional search engines, which makes it harder for authorities to detect illegal activity.

2.3 Dark Web Marketplaces

Most dark web criminal operations take place within **marketplaces** designed for buying and selling illicit goods. These marketplaces are often run with the same features as legitimate e-commerce platforms, including user ratings, product listings, and search functions.

- **Escrow Systems**: These systems hold the buyer's payment in **escrow** until the transaction is completed, reducing the risk of fraud.
- **Reputation Systems**: Sellers and buyers leave feedback about their transactions, building a **reputation** that helps protect against fraud.

3. How Criminals Evade Law Enforcement

Evading law enforcement is a primary concern for dark web criminals, and they employ a range of strategies to stay one step ahead of authorities. Let's explore some of the most common techniques used:

3.1 Use of Secure Communication Channels

Dark web criminals rely on encrypted communication tools to maintain confidentiality. These tools protect them from being intercepted by law enforcement agencies or other malicious actors.

- **Encrypted Messaging**: Services like **ProtonMail**, **Tutanota**, and **Signal** allow for **end-to-end encryption**, ensuring that only the intended recipient can read the messages.
- **Encrypted Calls**: Platforms like **WhatsApp** and **Signal** also offer **encrypted voice and video calls**, which criminals use to discuss deals and avoid detection.

3.2 Operating in Multiple Jurisdictions

Many dark web criminals operate in countries where **cybercrime laws** are weak or not enforced. By setting up operations in multiple jurisdictions, they create more **complex layers of defense** that law enforcement must navigate.

- **Offshore Hosting**: Criminals may host their dark web marketplaces or services on servers in countries with **relaxed data privacy laws** or **low extradition agreements**. This makes it harder for international law enforcement agencies to shut down the operation.

3.3 Use of Anonymized Networks for Censorship Resistance

The dark web's use of **anonymized networks** like Tor and I2P helps criminals avoid detection by **traditional law enforcement** methods. Since these networks prevent anyone from knowing the **source** or **destination** of the traffic, they offer an effective method for conducting illegal activities with a lower risk of being traced.

4. Case Study: How the FBI Took Down Silk Road

One of the most famous case studies in understanding how dark web criminals operate is the **Silk Road** investigation. This marketplace, created by **Ross Ulbricht**, was one of the first dark web platforms where criminals could buy and sell illegal goods, including drugs, weapons, and hacking tools.

How Silk Road Operated:

- Silk Road was a **marketplace** that used **Bitcoin** as its payment method and **Tor** for anonymous browsing.
- **Escrow systems** and **reputation systems** helped facilitate transactions and protect both buyers and sellers.
- **Ross Ulbricht** ran the operation under the pseudonym **Dread Pirate Roberts**, and his organization was highly structured, with **moderators** handling disputes and organizing the flow of goods.

Law Enforcement Takedown:

The FBI took down the Silk Road in 2013 after **investigating Ulbricht** for over two years. They used a combination of traditional investigative techniques, including **undercover agents**, **seizing Bitcoin** associated with illegal transactions, and **tracking IP addresses** to find Ulbricht's real identity.

Ulbricht was arrested in 2013 and convicted in 2015 for **money laundering**, **computer hacking**, and **conspiracy to traffic narcotics**. His arrest sent a strong message that dark web criminals, no matter how decentralized or anonymous, could eventually be caught.

Dark web criminals operate in highly organized, decentralized networks that take full advantage of the **anonymity** and **privacy** that dark web technologies like **Tor** and **cryptocurrencies** provide. These networks are built on trust and reputation, with criminals using sophisticated encryption tools and **secure communication channels** to protect themselves from law enforcement.

9.3: Case Studies of Major Dark Web Crimes (e.g., Silk Road, AlphaBay)

The dark web has become infamous for hosting a range of illegal activities, from **drug markets** and **weapon trades** to **cybercrime services**. Over the years, several major dark web marketplaces have emerged, each playing a significant role in the **illicit trade** of goods and services. While these platforms thrive under the radar, they also attract the attention of law enforcement, who work tirelessly to infiltrate, dismantle, and prosecute those responsible.

In this guide, we'll explore **two of the most notorious dark web crime hubs**: **Silk Road** and **AlphaBay**. We'll dive into how these marketplaces operated, the **criminal activities** they enabled, and how law enforcement ultimately took them down. These case studies will also provide insight into the **structure** and **organization** of dark web criminal enterprises.

---

1. Silk Road: The Dark Web's First Major Marketplace

Silk Road is perhaps the most famous dark web marketplace and a prime example of how criminals use the dark web to conduct illicit activities. Launched in 2011 by **Ross Ulbricht**, Silk Road allowed individuals to buy and sell illegal goods, primarily drugs, using **Bitcoin** for transactions. Silk Road became the blueprint for future dark web marketplaces and made headlines around the world due to its scale and eventual takedown.

How Silk Road Operated

Silk Road wasn't just a marketplace; it was a **complete ecosystem** for criminals to engage in anonymous transactions. Here's a breakdown of how it worked:

- **Anonymity and Encryption**: Silk Road was hosted on the **Tor network**, ensuring that users' **IP addresses** were masked and their browsing activity was hidden. Tor's **onion routing** made it extremely difficult for authorities to trace the site back to its operators.

- **Bitcoin as Payment**: One of the key aspects of Silk Road was its use of **Bitcoin** as a payment method. Bitcoin transactions are pseudonymous, which means that while they are recorded on the blockchain, they don't reveal personal details about the buyer or seller unless tied to a real-world identity.
- **Escrow Service**: To protect both buyers and sellers, Silk Road used an **escrow service**. When a buyer made a purchase, the cryptocurrency was held in escrow until the seller confirmed delivery of the goods. If there was a dispute, the **moderators** would intervene to resolve the issue.

Types of Products Sold on Silk Road:

- **Drugs**: The primary commodity traded on Silk Road was **illicit drugs**. Everything from marijuana to **fentanyl** (a potent opioid) was sold on the platform.
- **Fake IDs**: Silk Road also facilitated the sale of **counterfeit documents**, such as fake **passports**, **driver's licenses**, and other forms of identification.
- **Hacking Services**: Some sellers offered **hacking services**, such as **DDoS attacks**, malware, and stolen credit card data.

Silk Road's Reputation System

Silk Road employed a **reputation system** where users could rate each other after completing a transaction. This helped build **trust** between buyers and sellers, even in the absence of face-to-face interaction.

- **Feedback**: Buyers and sellers could leave reviews, providing valuable feedback on the quality of goods, reliability of sellers, and trustworthiness of buyers.
- **Escrow and Dispute Resolution**: The marketplace also had **moderators** who handled disputes between users, making sure that transactions went smoothly and reducing the risk of fraud.

In 2013, after a lengthy investigation by the **FBI**, **Silk Road** was seized, and its founder, **Ross Ulbricht**, was arrested. The investigation involved **undercover agents** who bought drugs, monitored the flow of cryptocurrency, and eventually linked Ulbricht to the operation.

Ulbricht was charged with **money laundering**, **computer hacking**, and **conspiracy to traffic narcotics**. Despite his claim that Silk Road was created as a tool for **freedom of speech** and **libertarian ideals**, the FBI took down the site, and Ulbricht was sentenced to **life in prison** without the possibility of parole.

Impact of Silk Road's Takedown

- **Shift to Other Platforms**: While Silk Road's seizure was a major blow, it did not end the **dark web drug trade**. Other marketplaces, such as **AlphaBay** and **Dream Market**, quickly took its place.
- **Legal Precedent**: The takedown of Silk Road set a **legal precedent** for how authorities could infiltrate and dismantle dark web criminal enterprises, leading to increased efforts against similar platforms.

---

2. AlphaBay: The Largest Dark Web Marketplace

(2014 - 2017)

AlphaBay was one of the largest dark web marketplaces for illegal goods and services. Launched in 2014, AlphaBay became a significant player in the dark web underworld, offering a range of illegal products, including drugs, weapons, counterfeit money, and hacking services.

How AlphaBay Operated

AlphaBay operated in a manner very similar to Silk Road but was **larger** and more **organized**. Its marketplace functioned as an **e-commerce**

platform, with **vendors** selling illegal items and **buyers** making purchases using cryptocurrencies. Here's how AlphaBay worked:

- **Wide Range of Illicit Products**: AlphaBay provided everything from **drugs, stolen data, fraudulent documents**, to **hacking services**. The platform had over **250,000 users** and hosted tens of thousands of vendors.
- **Cryptocurrency Transactions**: Just like Silk Road, AlphaBay used **Bitcoin** and **Monero** as payment methods, ensuring transactions were **anonymous**.
- **Escrow System**: AlphaBay utilized an **escrow service** similar to Silk Road's, which held the payment in escrow until the buyer confirmed the receipt of their purchase.
- **Reputation System**: AlphaBay also featured a **rating system** for buyers and sellers, giving users the opportunity to leave feedback and build **reputation** within the marketplace.

How AlphaBay Was Shut Down

In **July 2017**, the **FBI**, in collaboration with **international law enforcement**, took down AlphaBay. The website was seized, and its creator, **Alexandre Cazes**, was arrested. Tragically, Cazes was found dead in his jail cell shortly after his arrest in what was ruled a **suicide**.

Reasons for AlphaBay's Shutdown:

- **Massive Scale**: AlphaBay was one of the largest and most profitable dark web marketplaces, facilitating the sale of a wide variety of illegal goods and services.
- **International Cooperation**: The takedown of AlphaBay was a result of **coordinated efforts** by law enforcement agencies around the world. By working together, they were able to infiltrate the marketplace, track transactions, and ultimately arrest Cazes.
- **User Data**: After the takedown, law enforcement gained access to a significant amount of **user data**, including **chat logs, transaction details**, and **personal information**, which allowed them to trace and arrest many other dark web criminals.

- **Shift to Other Marketplaces**: Much like Silk Road's closure, AlphaBay's takedown didn't end the dark web criminal activity. Users quickly migrated to other platforms like **Hansa Market** and **Dream Market**.
- **Increased Law Enforcement Attention**: AlphaBay's seizure sent a clear message to dark web criminals that law enforcement agencies were actively targeting these marketplaces, leading to an increase in **investigative efforts**.

---

3. Other Notable Dark Web Marketplaces and Crimes

While **Silk Road** and **AlphaBay** were among the most famous dark web platforms, they weren't the only ones to have an impact. Here are a few other notable dark web crime hubs:

Dream Market

- **Description**: Dream Market was one of the largest successors to Silk Road and AlphaBay, hosting a wide range of illegal goods. It was seized by law enforcement in **2019**.

Hansa Market

- **Description**: Hansa Market was another major dark web marketplace that operated from **2015** until **2017**, when it was taken down by law enforcement. What made Hansa unique was its seizure by law enforcement **before** AlphaBay's shutdown. Authorities used Hansa as a **honeypot**, allowing them to track users as they migrated from AlphaBay.

The Hidden Wiki

- **Description**: The Hidden Wiki is an infamous dark web site that serves as a **directory** to many dark web sites, including **illicit marketplaces**, **hacking forums**, and **drug vendors**.

Conclusion: The Evolution of Dark Web Crime

The case studies of **Silk Road** and **AlphaBay** showcase how dark web criminals organize, operate, and evolve over time. While the takedown of these major platforms was a significant victory for law enforcement, it also highlighted the **complexity** of dark web criminal enterprises.

Dark web markets continue to pop up, offering a **wide range of illicit products and services**. However, authorities are becoming increasingly adept at infiltrating these platforms, collecting intelligence, and shutting them down.

As **cryptocurrencies**, **anonymity networks**, and **encryption** tools continue to evolve, it's likely that dark web crime will continue to adapt. The fight between dark web criminals and law enforcement is ongoing, and understanding how these marketplaces operate is essential for both users and authorities.

Chapter 10: Law Enforcement and Cybercrime Investigations

The dark web has been a game-changer for cybercriminals, providing them with a platform to operate outside the scrutiny of traditional surveillance. However, law enforcement agencies around the world have become increasingly adept at infiltrating and dismantling these dark web criminal operations. In this chapter, we'll explore how law enforcement tracks dark web criminals, examine high-profile takedowns, and discuss the **challenges** investigators face when tackling dark web crimes.

10.1: How Law Enforcement Tracks Dark Web Criminals

Tracking dark web criminals is one of the most complex challenges law enforcement agencies face today. The **dark web** offers a haven for criminal activity by providing **anonymity** and **cryptocurrency-based transactions**, which makes it difficult for authorities to trace illegal actions. However, over the years, law enforcement agencies have developed sophisticated methods to infiltrate and dismantle these operations.

In this guide, we'll take a detailed look at how **law enforcement** tracks dark web criminals, discussing key techniques, tools, and strategies used in **cybercrime investigations**. This chapter will also highlight how authorities manage to trace criminals despite the **anonymity** provided by the dark web.

---

1. Understanding the Dark Web and Its Challenges

The **dark web** is a part of the internet that is not indexed by traditional search engines. It's a **hidden network** that can only be accessed through special tools like **Tor** (The Onion Router) or **I2P** (Invisible Internet Project). While these tools ensure **privacy** for legitimate users, they also make it difficult for law enforcement to trace criminal activities.

Key challenges of tracking dark web criminals:

- **Anonymity**: Tools like **Tor** mask the user's **IP address**, making it difficult to trace online activity back to individuals.
- **Encryption**: Communications on the dark web are often **encrypted**, preventing authorities from reading messages without advanced decryption techniques.
- **Cryptocurrency Transactions**: Cryptocurrencies such as **Bitcoin** and **Monero** provide **financial anonymity**, making it harder for authorities to track and seize illicit funds.

Despite these challenges, law enforcement agencies have developed several methods to uncover and track dark web criminals. Let's explore the most effective strategies.

---

2. Key Methods Used by Law Enforcement to Track Dark Web Criminals

2.1 Traffic Correlation and Network Monitoring

One of the primary tools used by law enforcement to track dark web users is **traffic correlation**. Although Tor provides strong **anonymity** by bouncing traffic through multiple relays, **exit nodes** (the final stage of traffic leaving the Tor network) can sometimes reveal clues about the origin of the traffic.

How Traffic Correlation Works:

- **Exit Node Surveillance**: Law enforcement agencies may monitor traffic that exits through specific **Tor exit nodes**. While the traffic itself is encrypted, it can sometimes be **correlated** with patterns observed in other parts of the network.

- **Timing Analysis**: Investigators look for patterns in the **timing** of encrypted traffic. By comparing the time a message enters the network with when it exits, they can sometimes correlate activity between the two ends.

In the case of **Silk Road**, the FBI conducted **traffic correlation attacks** to trace **Ross Ulbricht**, the founder of the marketplace. By monitoring the **Tor network** and analyzing patterns between the data entering and exiting the network, they were able to identify the location of Ulbricht's activities, which eventually led to his arrest.

2.2 Blockchain Analysis Tools for Tracking Cryptocurrency

While **cryptocurrencies** provide a level of anonymity, they are not entirely untraceable. **Bitcoin**, for example, operates on a **public ledger** (the blockchain), which means every transaction is recorded and can be analyzed.

How Blockchain Analysis Works:

- **Public Ledger**: Bitcoin transactions are stored publicly on the blockchain. Law enforcement agencies use **blockchain analysis tools** such as **Chainalysis**, **Elliptic**, and **CipherTrace** to monitor these transactions and trace the flow of **illicit funds**.
- **Tainted Wallets**: By analyzing the transactions between different **Bitcoin wallets**, law enforcement can identify suspicious patterns, such as **wallets** linked to illegal activities (e.g., dark web marketplaces).
- **Tracing the Path**: Blockchain tools allow investigators to trace Bitcoin transactions back to exchanges or identifiable wallets. If those wallets are linked to known individuals, it becomes easier to identify dark web criminals.

Example: AlphaBay and Bitcoin Transactions

When **AlphaBay** was taken down in **2017**, law enforcement used **blockchain analysis** to track the flow of **Bitcoin** through the marketplace.

They were able to identify wallets associated with criminal activities and trace funds back to users, leading to several arrests.

2.3 Undercover Operations

Undercover operations are another critical technique for tracking and infiltrating dark web criminal networks. In these operations, law enforcement officers pose as **buyers**, **sellers**, or **service providers** within illicit dark web markets. These investigations require patience and strategic planning, as undercover agents often need to establish **trust** before they can gather critical information.

How Undercover Investigations Work:

- **Establishing Trust**: Law enforcement agents often begin by posing as legitimate users within dark web markets. They may establish a **positive reputation** by completing transactions and gaining the trust of other users.
- **Collecting Evidence**: As undercover agents participate in illicit transactions, they gather crucial evidence such as **messages**, **transaction records**, and **IP addresses**.
- **Infiltrating Seller Networks**: Agents often work to infiltrate **supply chains** and obtain valuable information about **drug suppliers**, **weapons sellers**, or **hackers** offering illegal services.

Example: AlphaBay Infiltration

During the takedown of **AlphaBay**, law enforcement agencies infiltrated the marketplace by posing as both buyers and sellers. This allowed them to gather enough evidence to take down the platform and arrest the administrators.

2.4 Human Intelligence (HUMINT) and Informants

Human intelligence, or **HUMINT**, plays a significant role in dark web investigations. By leveraging informants—people within dark web communities or even former criminals who turn on their peers—law enforcement can gain access to closed communities and critical information.

- **Informants**: Law enforcement may gain valuable information from informants who have been involved in dark web criminal activities. These informants can provide information on the **structure** of criminal organizations and help authorities understand the inner workings of dark web markets.
- **Infiltrating Communities**: In addition to undercover operations, **cyber detectives** may use **social engineering** to build relationships with dark web criminals. By engaging in conversation, they can gather valuable leads.

Example: Operation Disruptor

In **2020**, Operation Disruptor led to the arrest of over **170 people** globally, with the help of HUMINT. Investigators gathered intelligence from both undercover operations and informants, leading to coordinated takedowns of **drug trafficking operations** on dark web marketplaces.

2.5 Seizing the Dark Web Infrastructure

In some cases, law enforcement doesn't just rely on tracking criminals; they also go after the **dark web infrastructure** itself. By seizing the **servers** that host dark web marketplaces, authorities can shut down entire criminal networks and **gather evidence** at the same time.

How Seizing Infrastructure Works:

- **Coordinated Raids**: International cooperation is essential in seizing dark web servers. Law enforcement agencies around the world work together to track the physical locations of servers, sometimes coordinating raids to seize them.
- **Forensic Analysis**: After seizing servers, authorities conduct thorough forensic analysis to recover **user data**, transaction records, and other critical information.

In **2017**, the **Dutch National Police** seized **Hansa Market**, a major dark web marketplace. What made this case unique was that before seizing the market, law enforcement secretly operated the site for a month, collecting detailed **user data** before taking it offline.

---

3. Visual Aid: How Law Enforcement Tracks Dark Web Criminals

Here's a flowchart that summarizes the key strategies law enforcement uses to track dark web criminals:

```
        +--------------------------------+
        |    Step 1: Traffic Correlation |
        |    - Monitoring Tor Exit Nodes |
        |    - Identifying Timing Patterns|
        +--------------------------------+
                        |
                        v
        +--------------------------------+
        |    Step 2: Blockchain Analysis|
        |    - Tracking Bitcoin Wallets  |
        |    - Tracing Illicit Funds     |
        +--------------------------------+
                        |
                        v
        +--------------------------------+
        |    Step 3: Undercover Ops      |
        |    - Posing as Buyers/Sellers  |
        |    - Collecting Evidence       |
        +--------------------------------+
                        |
                        v
        +--------------------------------+
        |    Step 4: HUMINT (Informants)|
        |    - Gathering Intel from Inside|
        |    - Engaging with Communities |
        +--------------------------------+
                        |
                        v
```

```
+-------------------------------+
|   Step 5: Seizing Infrastructure|
|   - Coordinating Server Raids |
|   - Forensic Analysis         |
+-------------------------------+
```

Tracking dark web criminals is a multi-faceted challenge that requires a combination of advanced **technology**, **strategy**, and **international cooperation**. Law enforcement agencies around the world are increasingly capable of infiltrating dark web marketplaces, tracking cryptocurrency transactions, and using **undercover operations** to collect evidence and build cases against dark web criminals.

While the dark web remains a refuge for illegal activity, the **efforts** of law enforcement have resulted in significant successes in shutting down criminal operations, such as **Silk Road** and **AlphaBay**. However, with the continuous development of new privacy tools and the growing sophistication of dark web criminals, this remains an ongoing battle.

10.2: High-Profile Takedowns and Their Impact on Cybercrime

High-profile takedowns of dark web marketplaces have been pivotal in disrupting **cybercrime** and **illicit trade** on the dark web. These takedowns highlight the effectiveness of international cooperation, investigative techniques, and technological advancements in addressing the growing threat of cybercriminal activity online. This chapter explores some of the most significant takedowns of dark web marketplaces and their broader **impact on cybercrime**. By understanding the scale and execution of these takedowns, we can appreciate the challenges and successes of law enforcement in combating dark web crimes.

1. The Silk Road Takedown: The Beginning of the Dark Web Crackdown

1.1 The Rise of Silk Road

Launched in **2011** by **Ross Ulbricht** under the pseudonym **Dread Pirate Roberts**, **Silk Road** became the first major dark web marketplace catering exclusively to the sale of **illegal goods**, primarily **drugs**. Silk Road's design incorporated multiple features that enabled it to flourish for over two years, including **anonymous browsing via Tor** and **cryptocurrency payments** (Bitcoin), which ensured **transactional anonymity**.

1.2 How Silk Road Operated

Silk Road operated as a **peer-to-peer marketplace** where users could buy and sell items without ever meeting face-to-face. Sellers listed their illegal products (drugs, fake IDs, hacking tools), and buyers could browse these products, read **vendor reviews**, and make purchases using Bitcoin. The site included a **reputation system**, which ensured that trustworthy vendors gained credibility.

- **Cryptocurrency**: Silk Road's use of **Bitcoin** enabled users to complete transactions in a way that was **difficult to trace**. At the time, Bitcoin was seen as a **pseudonymous** digital currency, which made it a perfect tool for illicit transactions.
- **Escrow System**: To protect both buyers and sellers, Silk Road used an **escrow service**. Once a buyer made a purchase, the funds were held in escrow until the buyer confirmed receipt of the goods, after which the funds were released to the seller.

1.3 The Takedown of Silk Road

The takedown of Silk Road in **2013** marked the first major law enforcement victory in the fight against dark web criminal activities. The FBI and other international law enforcement agencies launched an extensive investigation into Silk Road and its creator, Ross Ulbricht. After gathering significant evidence, including the **tracking of Bitcoin transactions** and the **correlation of traffic patterns** on the Tor network, Ulbricht was arrested in **San Francisco** in **October 2013**.

- **Traffic Correlation**: Law enforcement employed a technique called **traffic correlation** to identify Ulbricht's **real-world location** and connect his online activity to his physical identity.
- **Bitcoin Transaction Tracking**: By tracing the flow of Bitcoin, investigators were able to connect the funds from Silk Road to Ulbricht's wallet and further gather evidence.

1.4 Impact of Silk Road's Takedown on Cybercrime

- **Disruption of the Drug Market**: The Silk Road takedown temporarily disrupted the dark web drug trade, but new marketplaces quickly rose to fill the gap.
- **Legal Precedent**: The takedown set a legal precedent for **tracking cryptocurrencies** and **infiltrating dark web marketplaces**. It also demonstrated that law enforcement agencies could infiltrate **anonymity networks** like Tor.
- **Public Awareness**: Silk Road's takedown brought attention to the **dangers of the dark web**, sparking global conversations about digital privacy, the regulation of cryptocurrencies, and cybercrime.

---

2. AlphaBay: The Largest Dark Web Marketplace (2014 - 2017)

2.1 AlphaBay's Rise to Prominence

Launched in **2014**, **AlphaBay** quickly became one of the most significant dark web marketplaces, offering a broad range of **illicit goods** including **drugs, weapons, hacking tools, stolen data**, and **counterfeit currency**. AlphaBay grew to host more than **250,000 users** and more than **40,000 vendors**, making it a highly attractive platform for cybercriminals.

- **Wide Range of Illicit Products**: AlphaBay's inventory included everything from **drugs** to **cyberattack services** (e.g., ransomware). It also offered **stolen credit card details** and **fake documents**.

- **Cryptocurrency Transactions**: Like Silk Road, AlphaBay used **Bitcoin** and **Monero** as payment methods, ensuring that transactions remained **private** and **difficult to trace**.

2.2 The Takedown of AlphaBay

In **July 2017**, after nearly three years of operation, **AlphaBay** was seized by a **coordinated international law enforcement operation** involving **Europol**, **FBI**, and other agencies. The platform was shut down, and its administrators were arrested.

One of the platform's administrators, **Alexandre Cazes**, was arrested in **Thailand**, but he was found dead in his prison cell shortly before the takedown.

Tactics Used for AlphaBay's Takedown:

- **Coordinated International Efforts**: The takedown was a **collaborative effort** between law enforcement agencies from **the United States**, **Canada**, **Thailand**, and **Europol**.
- **Hacking the Marketplace**: Unlike Silk Road, where investigators infiltrated the marketplace, law enforcement agencies seized **AlphaBay's infrastructure** and gained control of the platform before taking it offline.
- **Data Collection**: Authorities collected a **massive amount of data** from AlphaBay's servers, including **user logs, vendor information**, and **transaction histories**.

2.3 Impact of AlphaBay's Takedown on Cybercrime

- **Loss of Major Marketplace**: AlphaBay's takedown had a profound impact on the dark web, resulting in a **temporary shift** of users to other marketplaces like **Dream Market** and **Hansa Market**.
- **Global Crackdown**: The takedown demonstrated the ability of law enforcement agencies to dismantle large dark web operations and significantly **disrupt criminal economies**.
- **User Data Seized**: One of the most significant outcomes was the **collection of user data** from AlphaBay's servers, which led to the

identification of **hundreds of criminals** worldwide. This information has been used in ongoing investigations.

---

3. Operation Disruptor: A Coordinated Global Effort

3.1 What is Operation Disruptor?

Operation Disruptor was a **global law enforcement operation** launched in **2020** by **the FBI**, **Europol**, **the UK National Crime Agency**, and other international partners. The operation targeted criminals involved in **drug trafficking** and other illegal activities on the dark web. It resulted in the arrest of over **170 individuals** worldwide.

3.2 How Operation Disruptor Worked

- **Dark Web Infiltration**: Law enforcement agencies infiltrated **dark web marketplaces** and monitored transactions involving **illicit drugs** and **hacking tools**.
- **Seizing Assets**: As part of the operation, authorities seized **drugs** worth **$6.5 million** and **stolen goods** including **personal data** and **digital currency**.
- **Undercover Operations**: Investigators used **undercover agents** to buy illicit goods, collect evidence, and gain access to **criminal networks** operating on the dark web.

3.3 Impact of Operation Disruptor on Cybercrime

- **Major Arrests**: The operation resulted in **several high-profile arrests** and helped disrupt organized crime groups involved in **drug distribution** and **cybercrime**.
- **A Disruption to the Dark Web Economy**: Operation Disruptor had a significant impact on the dark web's **drug trade**, and authorities were able to shut down key platforms used for illicit transactions.
- **Ongoing Investigations**: The operation was not just a one-off success but part of an ongoing effort to monitor, infiltrate, and dismantle dark web criminal organizations.

4. Visual Aid: Key Steps in a High-Profile Dark Web Takedown

The following flowchart illustrates the typical steps involved in law enforcement's takedown of a dark web criminal network:

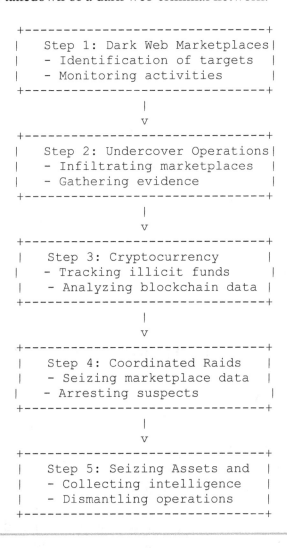

```
+-------------------------------+
|   Step 1: Dark Web Marketplaces|
|   - Identification of targets |
|   - Monitoring activities     |
+-------------------------------+
                |
                v
+-------------------------------+
|   Step 2: Undercover Operations|
|   - Infiltrating marketplaces |
|   - Gathering evidence        |
+-------------------------------+
                |
                v
+-------------------------------+
|   Step 3: Cryptocurrency      |
|   - Tracking illicit funds    |
|   - Analyzing blockchain data |
+-------------------------------+
                |
                v
+-------------------------------+
|   Step 4: Coordinated Raids   |
|   - Seizing marketplace data  |
|   - Arresting suspects        |
+-------------------------------+
                |
                v
+-------------------------------+
|   Step 5: Seizing Assets and  |
|   - Collecting intelligence   |
|   - Dismantling operations    |
+-------------------------------+
```

High-profile dark web takedowns like those of **Silk Road**, **AlphaBay**, and **Operation Disruptor** have shown that law enforcement agencies are becoming increasingly adept at infiltrating and dismantling dark web criminal operations. These operations not only disrupt illegal markets but also send a strong message to criminals operating in the shadows of the internet.

10.3: Challenges in Investigating Dark Web Crimes

The dark web is a complex and ever-evolving part of the internet, providing a haven for illegal activities. While law enforcement agencies have made significant strides in combating dark web crimes, the challenges of investigating these crimes remain formidable. From **anonymity networks** like **Tor** to **cryptocurrency payments**, the dark web presents unique hurdles that require specialized tools and techniques to overcome.

In this guide, we'll explore the main challenges law enforcement faces when investigating dark web crimes, discuss the limitations of current investigative methods, and highlight the continuous struggle to keep up with new technologies and tactics used by criminals.

1. Anonymity and Encryption: The Core Challenge

1.1 The Role of Anonymity in the Dark Web

The very foundation of the dark web is **anonymity**, which is achieved through tools like **Tor** and **I2P**. These networks are designed to **obfuscate** user identities and **protect** privacy, making it extremely difficult for law enforcement to trace online activities back to real-world individuals. This anonymity is essential for the dark web's appeal to criminals, as it allows them to carry out illegal activities such as **drug trafficking**, **weapons sales**, and **cybercrime** without fear of being identified or tracked.

- **Onion Routing**: Tor works by routing internet traffic through a series of **volunteer-operated nodes** (also known as relays). Each node decrypts a single layer of encryption, making it nearly impossible to track the origin or destination of the traffic.
- **Exit Nodes**: The final relay, called the **exit node**, is where the encrypted traffic exits the Tor network. Although Tor anonymizes the traffic through the relays, it doesn't necessarily encrypt traffic after it exits the network, making **exit nodes** a potential vulnerability.

Why Anonymity is a Challenge:

- **Obfuscated Identities**: Dark web criminals use **Tor** and **I2P** to mask their **IP addresses** and **geographical locations**, which makes it difficult for law enforcement to track them.
- **Layered Encryption**: The multiple layers of encryption in **Tor** make it hard for investigators to intercept and decrypt communications in real-time.
- **Countermeasures**: Criminals are aware of the risks of being identified and often take additional steps to anonymize their activity, such as using **VPNs** or **proxy servers** in conjunction with Tor.

---

2. Cryptocurrencies and Financial Anonymity

Cryptocurrencies, particularly **Bitcoin** and **Monero**, are the most common form of payment used on the dark web. While **Bitcoin** offers some degree of pseudonymity, **Monero** and other privacy coins go further, ensuring **complete anonymity** in transactions. Law enforcement faces a major challenge in tracking and tracing these transactions, especially when privacy coins are used.

2.1 Tracking Bitcoin Transactions

While Bitcoin's **public ledger** (the **blockchain**) makes it possible to trace transactions, it doesn't directly link those transactions to an individual's identity. This creates a challenge for investigators, as they need to correlate multiple data points to identify the individuals behind the wallets.

How Bitcoin Tracking Works:

- **Blockchain Analysis**: Tools like **Chainalysis** and **Elliptic** are used by law enforcement to trace the flow of Bitcoin through the blockchain. These tools can identify when Bitcoin transactions move between **wallets** and potentially link these wallets to real-world identities.
- **Tainted Wallets**: Some Bitcoin wallets are associated with known **criminal activities**. Investigators can track the movement of funds into and out of these wallets to build a case.

Limitations of Bitcoin Tracking:

- **Pseudonymity**: Bitcoin addresses are not inherently linked to real-world identities. Tracking the movement of funds doesn't necessarily lead to identifying the person behind the wallet.
- **Coin Mixing Services**: Criminals can use **coin mixing** or **coin tumbling** services to obscure the transaction trail. These services mix a user's coins with those of other users to break the link between wallets.

2.2 The Challenge of Privacy Coins (Monero, Zcash)

Monero, **Zcash**, and other privacy coins are designed to **conceal** transaction details such as the sender, receiver, and amount, making them **nearly impossible to trace** using traditional blockchain analysis techniques.

How Monero Works:

- **Ring Signatures**: Monero uses **ring signatures**, which mix the sender's transaction with others, creating a group of potential senders. This makes it **impossible** to identify the actual sender.

- **Stealth Addresses**: Monero's **stealth addresses** ensure that only the sender and recipient can see the actual address involved in the transaction, further obfuscating transaction details.
- **RingCT (Ring Confidential Transactions)**: This feature ensures that the transaction amounts remain hidden, providing complete **financial privacy**.

Why Monero is Difficult to Track:

- **Hidden Transaction Details**: Unlike Bitcoin, which records all transaction data on a public blockchain, Monero's **ring signatures** and **stealth addresses** make it impossible for law enforcement to analyze the transaction history or trace it to an individual.
- **Adoption by Criminals**: Many dark web criminals prefer Monero for its high level of anonymity, making it more challenging for authorities to track illicit payments.

---

3. Evolving Techniques and Countermeasures by Criminals

As law enforcement agencies develop new techniques to track criminals on the dark web, criminals continually adapt by employing new technologies and methods to evade detection.

3.1 Use of Encrypted Messaging Platforms

Many dark web criminals use encrypted messaging platforms such as **ProtonMail**, **Signal**, or **WhatsApp** to communicate securely. These platforms provide **end-to-end encryption**, ensuring that only the sender and recipient can read the messages.

Challenges of Tracking Encrypted Communications:

- **End-to-End Encryption**: Law enforcement cannot intercept and read encrypted communications on platforms like Signal and

WhatsApp without first gaining access to the device or compromising the encryption.

- **Secure Email Providers**: ProtonMail and other secure email services do not store user data or logs, making it challenging for authorities to monitor and track communications.

3.2 Use of VPNs and Proxy Servers

Criminals often use **VPNs (Virtual Private Networks)** and **proxy servers** to further obfuscate their **IP addresses** and **geographical locations**. By routing traffic through multiple servers across different countries, VPNs make it difficult for law enforcement to pinpoint the true location of dark web users.

Why VPNs and Proxies are a Challenge:

- **Obscured IP Address**: By masking the IP address, VPNs and proxy servers prevent authorities from using traditional IP tracking methods to identify and locate criminals.
- **International Jurisdictions**: VPNs often use servers located in countries with **relaxed privacy laws** or **weak cybercrime regulations**, making it more difficult for law enforcement to track criminals across international borders.

3.3 Counterfeit Goods and Fake Identities

Dark web criminals often sell **counterfeit goods**, such as **fake IDs** and **stolen credit card information**, making it harder for investigators to trace the origin of illicit activities. In addition, criminals use **false identities** to obscure their involvement in dark web markets.

Challenges in Investigating Counterfeit Goods:

- **Difficulty in Tracing Sellers**: Criminals may use **fake names** and **pseudonyms**, making it hard for authorities to link them to real-world identities.
- **Hidden Locations**: The sellers of counterfeit goods often use methods like **shipping from anonymous addresses** or **using intermediaries** to avoid detection.

4. Investigative Tools and Technologies

While law enforcement faces many challenges in tracking dark web criminals, they also use a range of sophisticated tools and technologies to aid investigations.

4.1 Dark Web Monitoring Software

Law enforcement uses **dark web monitoring tools** to search for and track criminal activity. These tools can scan dark web marketplaces, forums, and chat rooms for **illicit activity** and monitor **suspicious behavior**.

Popular Tools:

- **Dark Web Intelligence Software**: Tools like **Terbium Labs** and **DarkOwl** help monitor dark web markets and forums for signs of criminal behavior, including **drug trafficking**, **stolen data**, and **hacking services**.
- **Web Crawlers**: Law enforcement employs web crawlers designed to **navigate dark web sites** and collect evidence related to cybercrime.

4.2 Blockchain Analysis Tools

Blockchain analysis tools such as **Chainalysis, Elliptic**, and **CipherTrace** are used by law enforcement to track the flow of illicit cryptocurrencies. These tools help trace the **origin and destination** of transactions on public blockchains like Bitcoin and Ethereum.

4.3 Forensic Tools for Seizing Data

When law enforcement gains access to dark web criminals' servers, they use **digital forensics tools** to extract critical evidence, including **user logs, transaction records**, and **communication data**.

5. Visual Aid: Challenges and Tools in Investigating Dark Web Crimes

Below is a simple diagram illustrating the **challenges** and **tools** used in dark web investigations:

```
+------------------------------+
|       Dark Web Challenges    |
+------------------------------+
| Anonymity Networks (Tor, I2P)|
| - Masking IP Addresses       |
| - Encryption                 |
|                              |
| Cryptocurrencies (Monero)    |
| - Pseudonymous Transactions  |
| - Use of Privacy Coins       |
|                              |
| Encrypted Communication      |
| - End-to-End Encryption      |
| - Secure Messaging Platforms |
|                              |
| VPNs and Proxies             |
| - Obscured IPs               |
| - Jurisdictional Barriers    |
+------------------------------+
               |
               v
+------------------------------+
|    Law Enforcement Tools     |
+------------------------------+
| Blockchain Analysis          |
| - Tracing Bitcoin Transactions|
| - Identifying Tainted Wallets |
|                              |
| Dark Web Monitoring Software |
| - Crawling Dark Web Markets  |
| - Identifying Suspicious Activity|
|                              |
| Digital Forensic Tools       |
| - Seizing Data from Servers  |
| - Extracting Critical Evidence |
+------------------------------+
```

Investigating dark web crimes remains an **ongoing challenge** for law enforcement agencies. While criminals continue to innovate with new technologies like **cryptocurrencies**, **anonymity networks**, and **encrypted messaging**, authorities are also evolving by using advanced tools and techniques.

Chapter 11: Trends and Emerging Threats on the Dark Web

The dark web has evolved dramatically over the past decade, not only in terms of the scale of criminal activity but also in the sophistication of the technologies and tactics used by cybercriminals. As we enter an increasingly digital world, new **technologies** are emerging that further fuel the growth of illicit markets, while **advanced cybercrime tactics** are becoming more nuanced and harder to trace. This chapter explores some of the **new trends** on the dark web, focusing on **emerging technologies**, **threats**, and the growing role of **cyberterrorism** and **nation-state actors**.

11.1: New Dark Web Technologies (e.g., Blockchain, Cryptocurrency)

The dark web has been around for quite some time, but the technologies that power it are evolving rapidly. Over the years, innovations like **blockchain** and **cryptocurrencies** have revolutionized the way both legitimate and illicit activities are carried out online. These technologies are not just useful for criminals, but they also enable new types of marketplaces and services, often with enhanced privacy and security features.

In this guide, we'll take a deep dive into the new **dark web technologies** like **blockchain**, **cryptocurrencies**, and their implications for cybercrime. We'll explain how they work, how they're used on the dark web, and the challenges they present for law enforcement. By the end of this guide, you'll have a thorough understanding of how these technologies operate in the dark web ecosystem.

---

1. Blockchain Technology: A Decentralized Revolution

Blockchain is the **backbone** of many **cryptocurrencies** like **Bitcoin** and **Monero**. It is a distributed **ledger** system that allows data to be stored in **blocks**, with each block connected to the previous one to form a **chain**. This decentralized architecture makes it a vital technology for the dark web, where users seek anonymity and security.

1.1 How Blockchain Works

Blockchain works by enabling secure transactions without the need for intermediaries, such as banks or governments. Here's how the process works:

1. **Transaction Initiation**: A user initiates a transaction, such as sending cryptocurrency to another user.
2. **Transaction Validation**: The transaction is broadcast to a **network** of computers (called **nodes**). These nodes validate the transaction by ensuring that the user has the necessary funds and that the transaction is legitimate.
3. **Block Creation**: Once the transaction is validated, it is bundled into a **block**. This block is added to the **blockchain**.
4. **Decentralized Ledger**: Each node in the network holds a copy of the blockchain, which is updated whenever a new block is added. This decentralized system ensures that the blockchain is tamper-resistant.

1.2 Blockchain's Role on the Dark Web

Blockchain technology plays a crucial role in the functioning of dark web marketplaces and services, particularly by offering anonymity and security. Here's how blockchain is used on the dark web:

- **Cryptocurrency Transactions**: Many dark web marketplaces rely on **cryptocurrencies** like **Bitcoin**, **Monero**, and **Ethereum**. These digital currencies are built on blockchain technology, providing secure and anonymous payments for illicit goods and services.
- **Decentralization**: Since blockchain is a decentralized technology, it eliminates the need for a central authority to manage transactions, making it a perfect fit for dark web activities where users need to evade traditional financial monitoring systems.
- **Smart Contracts**: Blockchain allows for the creation of **smart contracts**—self-executing contracts with the terms of the

agreement directly written into the code. This technology is used on the dark web to ensure that payments are only made when specific conditions are met (e.g., delivery of illegal goods).

Visual Aid: How Blockchain Works

Here's a simple flow of how blockchain technology operates:

```
+------------------------+          +------------------------
+
| 1. Transaction Initiation| ------>| 2. Transaction
Validation |
+------------------------+          +------------------------
+
            |                              |
            v                              v
   +---------------------------+    +----------------------
----+
   | 3. Block Creation         |<-->| 4. Decentralized
Ledger    |
   +---------------------------+    +----------------------
----+
```

2. Cryptocurrency: The Currency of the Dark Web

Cryptocurrency is an essential component of dark web operations. It allows for **anonymous**, **secure**, and **decentralized** transactions that are difficult for authorities to track. While Bitcoin has been the most widely used cryptocurrency, others like **Monero** and **Zcash** are gaining popularity due to their superior **privacy** features.

2.1 Bitcoin: The First Cryptocurrency

Launched in **2009** by the pseudonymous **Satoshi Nakamoto**, **Bitcoin** is the first cryptocurrency to use blockchain technology. It operates on a **public ledger** where all transactions are recorded and can be traced by anyone who has access to the blockchain.

- **Public Ledger**: Bitcoin transactions are stored on a public blockchain, meaning anyone can trace the movement of funds.

- **Pseudonymity**: Bitcoin addresses are not inherently linked to an individual's identity, but if an address is ever tied to a real-world identity, it can lead to the tracing of all transactions associated with that address.

How Bitcoin is Used on the Dark Web:

- **Payment for Illegal Goods**: On the dark web, Bitcoin is the most common payment method for buying **drugs, weapons, stolen data**, and **hacking tools**. Its ease of use and pseudonymity make it attractive to dark web criminals.
- **Cryptocurrency Tumblers**: To further obfuscate transactions, criminals use **mixing services** (also known as **tumblers**) that mix the Bitcoin from multiple users to hide the trail.

2.2 Monero: The Privacy-Focused Cryptocurrency

While Bitcoin is widely used on the dark web, it is not entirely anonymous. The **public ledger** means that with the right tools, Bitcoin transactions can be traced. This is where **Monero** (XMR) comes in.

- **Ring Signatures**: Monero uses a feature called **ring signatures**, which obfuscates the sender's identity by mixing their transaction with others in a group, making it difficult to determine who sent the funds.
- **Stealth Addresses**: Monero uses **stealth addresses** to hide the recipient's identity. These addresses are randomly generated and used only once, so the transaction cannot be linked to a specific person.

Why Monero is Popular on the Dark Web:

- **Complete Privacy**: Since Monero ensures complete **transaction privacy**—both the sender and the receiver remain anonymous— criminals often use it for transactions that are too risky to conduct with Bitcoin.
- **Resistant to Analysis**: Unlike Bitcoin, Monero's blockchain is **private by default**, making it highly resistant to **blockchain analysis** techniques.

Cryptocurrencies are the primary currency used in dark web marketplaces. Many illegal goods and services—such as drugs, hacking tools, and stolen data—are purchased through these marketplaces. Here's a look at how dark web marketplaces use cryptocurrencies:

- **Monero**: Known for its privacy features, Monero is increasingly used in dark web transactions.
- **Bitcoin**: While Bitcoin is not as anonymous as Monero, it is still widely used due to its **liquidity** and **market adoption**.

3. Blockchain-Based Marketplaces and Smart Contracts

In addition to cryptocurrencies, blockchain also supports the creation of **blockchain-based marketplaces**. These marketplaces operate **without a central authority**, making them difficult to shut down. **Smart contracts**, powered by blockchain technology, allow for self-executing agreements between parties, ensuring that terms are met automatically.

3.1 Blockchain Marketplaces

Some dark web marketplaces are **built entirely on blockchain technology**, providing additional **security** and **decentralization**. These marketplaces allow buyers and sellers to conduct transactions without a central authority moderating or overseeing the process.

- **Decentralization**: Blockchain ensures that the marketplace itself is decentralized, meaning no single entity controls it. Even if a specific site is taken down, the marketplace can remain operational on a different blockchain.
- **Distributed Ledger**: The use of a distributed ledger ensures that records of every transaction are visible to participants, but remain **anonymous** and **immutable**.

Smart contracts are another powerful feature of blockchain technology. On the dark web, they are used to automatically enforce the terms of a transaction. For example, a buyer may use a smart contract to ensure that **payment** is only released to the seller once the agreed-upon product has been delivered. This removes the need for a third-party intermediary, which is often the role of traditional escrow services.

- **Automation**: Smart contracts automate the execution of agreements, reducing the chance of fraud or disputes.
- **Security**: Since smart contracts are executed on the blockchain, they are immutable and highly secure, ensuring that once they are agreed upon, they cannot be altered.

Visual Aid: Blockchain-Based Transaction Flow

Here's a simplified diagram illustrating the **blockchain-based transaction flow** using a **smart contract** on the dark web:

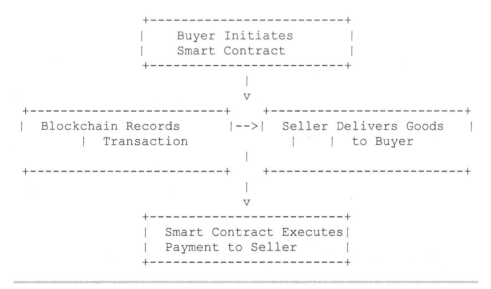

4. The Future of Blockchain and Cryptocurrency on the

Dark Web

As blockchain technology and cryptocurrencies evolve, it is likely that they will become **more integrated** into the dark web ecosystem. Emerging technologies such as **decentralized finance (DeFi) and cryptocurrency privacy features** will play an increasing role in how the dark web operates.

Future Trends to Watch:

- **More Privacy Coins**: As the demand for **anonymity** grows, **privacy coins** like **Zcash** and **Monero** will continue to dominate dark web transactions.
- **Smart Contract Innovation**: The use of **smart contracts** will likely expand, providing more **automated** and **secure** ways for criminals to conduct business.
- **Cross-Blockchain Transactions**: New advancements in **cross-chain technology** will allow criminals to move assets across different cryptocurrencies seamlessly, making it even harder to trace funds.

Blockchain and cryptocurrency technologies have **fundamentally transformed** the way dark web marketplaces operate. **Decentralization**, **anonymity**, and **security** provided by these technologies allow criminals to engage in illicit activities with a high degree of **privacy** and **freedom** from traditional financial systems. However, these same technologies also present challenges for law enforcement, which must develop more advanced tools and techniques to trace and disrupt dark web operations.

11.2: Emerging Threats: Data Breaches, AI, and Sophisticated Cybercrime

The **dark web** has long been associated with illegal activities like drug trafficking, weapon sales, and hacking tools. However, as technology advances, so do the threats and methods used by cybercriminals. Some of the most concerning emerging threats include **data breaches**, the increasing use of **artificial intelligence (AI)** for cybercrime, and the rise of **sophisticated cybercrime operations**. These developments are making the fight against dark web crime more challenging and complex.

In this chapter, we'll explore these emerging threats in detail, including how they are used on the dark web, their implications for security, and the challenges they pose for law enforcement and cybersecurity professionals.

---

1. Data Breaches: A Goldmine for Dark Web Criminals

Data breaches have become one of the most profitable and dangerous activities on the dark web. Cybercriminals actively seek out **stolen data**, such as **personal identifiable information (PII)**, **credit card details**, **social security numbers**, **health records**, and more. Once these data sets are stolen, they are often sold in bulk on dark web marketplaces, where they are used for identity theft, fraud, and other illicit activities.

1.1 How Data Breaches Occur

Data breaches occur when unauthorized parties gain access to sensitive information, typically through **hacking**, **phishing**, or exploiting **software vulnerabilities**. Here's how the process usually works:

1. **Initial Attack**: Cybercriminals use tactics like **phishing emails**, **malware** (e.g., keyloggers, ransomware), or **SQL injection attacks** to gain access to sensitive data stored by businesses or institutions.
2. **Data Extraction**: Once they've gained access, cybercriminals extract the data, which may include names, addresses, credit card numbers, login credentials, and more.
3. **Selling Data on the Dark Web**: The stolen data is then listed on dark web marketplaces. Buyers, who may be **fraudsters** or **identity thieves**, use this information to commit **financial fraud** or engage in further criminal activities.

- **Personal Identifiable Information (PII)**: This includes full names, email addresses, phone numbers, and physical addresses. It's highly valuable for identity theft.
- **Credit Card Information**: Stolen credit card details are often used to make unauthorized purchases or create **false identities**.
- **Login Credentials**: Credentials from hacked accounts, especially for **banking apps**, **social media**, and **email**, are often sold for exploitation.
- **Healthcare Records**: These are particularly valuable due to their use in medical identity theft, insurance fraud, and other forms of exploitation.

Case Study: The Equifax Data Breach

In **2017**, **Equifax**, one of the largest credit reporting agencies in the U.S., suffered a massive data breach, exposing **147 million Americans' personal information**, including **social security numbers**, **birth dates**, **addresses**, and **credit card numbers**. The stolen data was later sold on the dark web for use in **identity theft** and **fraudulent activities**.

1.3 Impact of Data Breaches on Cybercrime

- **Identity Theft**: Stolen data can be used to open fake bank accounts, apply for loans, or gain access to benefits in someone else's name.
- **Financial Fraud**: With access to credit card information or banking credentials, cybercriminals can carry out unauthorized transactions.
- **Long-term Damage**: Data breaches often lead to **long-term consequences** for victims, who may experience financial loss, reputational damage, and **identity theft** for years to come.

---

2. AI in Cybercrime: The New Frontier

Artificial Intelligence (AI) is already playing a significant role in many sectors, from **healthcare** to **finance**, but it is also a powerful tool for cybercriminals. AI is being used to **automate cyberattacks**, **evade detection**, and **target victims** more effectively. The ability of AI to learn from data and **adapt** to changing conditions makes it a potent weapon for cybercriminals.

2.1 AI-Driven Phishing Attacks

Traditional phishing attacks rely on generic messages or mass-emailing tactics to deceive victims. However, AI-powered phishing attacks are much more **targeted** and **personalized**.

- **Social Engineering with AI**: AI can scrape data from social media platforms, databases, or previous breaches to **gather information** about a victim (e.g., names, addresses, interests). This data is then used to create **highly personalized phishing emails** that are much more likely to succeed.
- **AI-Generated Content**: Using **natural language processing (NLP)**, AI can generate realistic and convincing emails that mimic the tone and style of trusted sources (e.g., bank alerts or messages from friends).

Example: Deepfake Phishing Attacks

Deepfake technology, powered by AI, is being used to create **hyper-realistic** voice and video impersonations. Criminals are using **deepfakes** to impersonate executives, convincing employees to transfer funds or provide confidential information.

2.2 Automated Cyberattacks

AI is also being used to **automate** cyberattacks, making them faster and more scalable. **Machine learning (ML)** algorithms can quickly identify **vulnerabilities** in systems and even **adapt** their attack strategies based on feedback.

- **Ransomware Attacks**: AI can optimize ransomware attacks by identifying which files are most valuable to encrypt, maximizing the attack's impact.

- **DDoS Attacks**: AI can be used to automate **Distributed Denial of Service (DDoS)** attacks by analyzing traffic patterns and adapting attack strategies in real-time.

Example: AI in Malware Development

AI has been used to create **self-replicating malware** that can learn and adapt to bypass traditional **signature-based detection systems**. These AI-powered malware programs can change their behavior or appearance to evade detection by traditional antivirus software.

2.3 AI for Fraud Detection and Evasion

AI is also being used by cybercriminals to **evade detection**. For instance, AI algorithms can be trained to recognize patterns in network traffic or system behavior that might indicate the presence of law enforcement or cybersecurity tools, and adapt the attack accordingly.

Case Study: AI-Powered Fraudulent Transactions

In some cases, AI is used to **analyze user behavior** on e-commerce websites. It can simulate **legitimate user behavior** to avoid triggering fraud detection algorithms, allowing criminals to carry out fraudulent transactions or **identity theft**.

---

3. Sophisticated Cybercrime Operations: Organized and Scalable

Cybercrime on the dark web is no longer limited to individual hackers. Many cybercriminals now work as part of highly organized, **business-like operations** that offer services, tools, and expertise to other criminals.

3.1 Cybercrime-as-a-Service (CaaS)

Cybercrime-as-a-Service is the **business model** where criminals offer hacking tools, malware, and **services** to other criminals. These services are often sold on the dark web and can range from **hacking tools** to **fraudulent credit cards**, and even **DDoS attack services**.

- **Ransomware-as-a-Service**: Criminal groups offer ransomware tools to individuals with little technical knowledge, allowing them to deploy ransomware attacks with ease.
- **Stolen Data as a Service**: Criminals can buy and sell **stolen data** in bulk, such as **email addresses** or **credit card details**, with ease, making it easy for smaller criminals to access these valuable resources.

3.2 The Role of Botnets in Sophisticated Cybercrime

A **botnet** is a network of infected computers or devices (also called **zombies**) that are controlled by a hacker. These botnets can be used to carry out large-scale cyberattacks, including:

- **Distributed Denial of Service (DDoS) Attacks**: Botnets are used to flood a target server with traffic, making it unavailable to users.
- **Cryptojacking**: Criminals use botnets to secretly mine cryptocurrency on infected devices, turning the device into a **cryptocurrency mining rig** without the owner's consent.

3.3 The Role of Anonymity Tools in Sophisticated Cybercrime

Dark web criminals use various tools to maintain their anonymity, including:

- **VPNs (Virtual Private Networks)**: These tools route internet traffic through remote servers to hide the user's location and encrypt their internet traffic.
- **Proxy Servers**: Proxy servers act as intermediaries between the user and the internet, allowing criminals to hide their IP address and location.
- **Encrypted Communication Tools**: Criminals use encrypted messaging services like **ProtonMail** and **Signal** to communicate securely and evade surveillance.

The increasing sophistication of cybercrime on the dark web, driven by **AI**, **data breaches**, and **advanced criminal operations**, presents new challenges for law enforcement and cybersecurity professionals. Criminals are using **cutting-edge technologies** to **automate attacks**, **evade detection**, and **expand their reach**.

As **cybercrime evolves**, it becomes clear that combating these emerging threats requires new tactics, better **collaboration** between international law enforcement agencies, and a continuous investment in **cybersecurity technologies**. With the rise of **AI-powered fraud**, **data breaches**, and **cybercrime-as-a-service**, it's crucial for businesses, governments, and individuals to stay ahead of these threats to protect both **personal information** and **national security**.

11.3: The Rise of Cyberterrorism and Nation-State Actors

Cyberterrorism and the involvement of **nation-state actors** on the dark web are becoming increasingly prominent and concerning. As traditional warfare evolves into **cyberwarfare**, the dark web has emerged as a central arena for covert operations, espionage, and even state-sponsored attacks. Criminals, hackers, and government-backed operatives are using sophisticated digital tools to carry out attacks that can disrupt economies, infrastructure, and national security.

In this guide, we will explore the growing role of **cyberterrorism**, the **rise of nation-state actors** in cybercrime, and the **implications** of these developments for global cybersecurity. We'll also analyze real-world case studies and provide insight into how these threats are evolving.

---

1. Understanding Cyberterrorism

Cyberterrorism refers to the use of **digital tools** and techniques to carry out attacks with the intent of causing widespread **fear**, **disruption**, or

damage. These attacks are typically targeted at **critical infrastructure**, **government systems**, and **public services**.

1.1 What is Cyberterrorism?

Cyberterrorism is defined as a **cyberattack** that aims to cause significant harm or destruction to a nation or its citizens. Unlike traditional terrorism, which relies on physical violence, cyberterrorism leverages **cyberattacks** to instill fear, disrupt critical systems, or manipulate political and economic processes. The dark web serves as an ideal platform for these activities, offering anonymity, access to advanced cybertools, and a network of like-minded individuals.

Key Features of Cyberterrorism:

- **Political Motivation**: Cyberterrorists are often driven by ideological or political goals, such as influencing government policies or advancing a specific cause (e.g., **hacktivism**).
- **Targeting Critical Infrastructure**: Cyberterrorists frequently target **energy grids**, **transportation systems**, **financial institutions**, and **government agencies** to cause chaos or disrupt society.
- **Anonymity**: The dark web offers a place where **cyberterrorists** can plan and execute attacks without fear of immediate identification.

1.2 Methods of Cyberterrorism

Cyberterrorists employ a wide range of **digital tactics** to carry out their attacks. Some of the most common methods include:

- **DDoS (Distributed Denial of Service) Attacks**: Cyberterrorists often use DDoS attacks to flood websites or servers with traffic, rendering them inaccessible. This can disrupt online services, government operations, or critical infrastructure.
- **Ransomware**: Ransomware attacks are designed to lock access to critical systems or data and demand payment to restore functionality. Cyberterrorists may use this method to disrupt operations or extort money from organizations.
- **Data Destruction**: Cyberterrorists may deploy malware that **wipes data** from critical servers or systems, causing irreversible damage.

This type of attack is often used to erase sensitive data or disrupt supply chains.

- **Hacktivism**: A form of cyberterrorism where individuals or groups use cyberattacks to promote **political agendas**. Hacktivists often target government websites, corporations, or other organizations they deem to be opposed to their beliefs.

Example: The 2007 Estonian Cyberattacks

In 2007, **Estonia** was targeted by a massive cyberattack that disrupted the country's **banking systems**, **government websites**, and **media outlets**. This attack is widely believed to have been perpetrated by **Russian-backed hackers** and was considered one of the first instances of **cyberterrorism** involving a nation-state actor. The attack was launched in retaliation for the relocation of a Soviet-era statue, and it led to widespread disruption and fear.

2. Nation-State Actors and Cyberwarfare

A nation-state actor is a government-backed **hacker group** that engages in cybercrime for political or military purposes. These groups are increasingly active on the dark web, using advanced **cyber tools** to spy on governments, manipulate elections, steal intellectual property, and disrupt critical infrastructure.

2.1 The Role of Nation-State Actors in Cybercrime

Nation-state actors are particularly dangerous because they have access to **advanced resources**, **skilled operatives**, and **state-sponsored funding**. These actors often use cyberattacks to achieve **political, economic**, or **military goals**. Their activities are typically well-coordinated and **strategically planned**, often targeting specific countries, industries, or even individuals.

- **Espionage**: State-sponsored hackers are often tasked with **stealing confidential government documents**, **corporate secrets**, or **military intelligence**. This information is then used to further national interests or gain an advantage over competitors or adversaries.
- **Election Manipulation**: Cyberattackers linked to nation-states are increasingly using the dark web to carry out **election interference** through **disinformation campaigns**, **hacking voting systems**, or **spreading fake news** to influence public opinion.
- **Disruption of Infrastructure**: Nation-state actors may target critical national infrastructure, such as **power grids**, **banking systems**, **transportation**, and **telecommunications** networks. This can lead to large-scale disruption and significant economic damage.

2.2 Types of Cyberattacks by Nation-State Actors

- **Advanced Persistent Threats (APTs)**: APTs are long-term, targeted attacks designed to infiltrate and steal sensitive information over extended periods. Nation-state actors use APTs to compromise government agencies, private corporations, and critical infrastructure.
- **Zero-Day Exploits**: Nation-state actors are often among the first to discover and exploit **zero-day vulnerabilities**—unknown security flaws in software. These vulnerabilities are used to gain unauthorized access to systems or networks.
- **Cyberespionage**: Nation-state actors use cyber espionage to gather intelligence on foreign governments, military operations, or private corporations. **APT groups**, such as **APT28** (linked to Russia), are known for their cyber espionage operations, which have targeted entities like **the Democratic National Committee (DNC)** during the **2016 U.S. elections**.

Example: The Sony Pictures Hack (2014)

In **2014**, Sony Pictures was targeted by a cyberattack that was attributed to **North Korea**. The attack resulted in the leak of sensitive emails, personal information, and unreleased films. The hack was in retaliation for the film *The Interview*, which depicted the assassination of the North Korean leader. This attack was one of the first **high-profile** cyberattacks attributed to a nation-state actor with political motives.

---

3. Tools and Tactics Used by Nation-State Actors on the Dark Web

Nation-state actors are increasingly utilizing the **dark web** to carry out espionage, conduct **disinformation campaigns**, and plan attacks on critical infrastructure. The dark web offers these actors **anonymity** and **secrecy**, enabling them to work undetected. Here are some of the key tools and tactics used by these actors:

3.1 Dark Web Marketplaces and Forums

Nation-state actors use **dark web marketplaces** and **forums** to:

- **Buy and sell hacking tools**, **malware**, and **exploit kits**. These tools are used to launch attacks against foreign governments or organizations.
- **Hire cybercriminals** or **mercenaries** who specialize in cyber warfare. These mercenaries may be contracted to carry out **specific tasks** like **penetration testing**, **social engineering attacks**, or **cyber espionage**.

3.2 Encryption and Secure Communication Tools

Nation-state actors rely heavily on **encrypted communication tools** to plan their operations without detection. Tools like **ProtonMail**, **Tutanota**, and **Signal** are often used to send **secure messages** and coordinate attacks on target entities. These tools ensure that communication remains private, even in the face of advanced surveillance technologies.

3.3 Distributed Denial of Service (DDoS) Attacks

DDoS attacks, which flood a target system with malicious traffic to **overwhelm** it, are commonly used by nation-state actors to disrupt critical infrastructure. These attacks can be carried out using **botnets** and **IoT devices** that are often sold or bought on the dark web.

3.4 Exploit Kits and Malware

Malware and exploit kits are used by nation-state actors to **compromise systems** and gain unauthorized access to networks. These malicious tools can be **customized** and tailored to exploit vulnerabilities in a specific organization's infrastructure, making them highly effective.

---

4. Case Study: Stuxnet – A Pioneering Cyberattack by Nation-State Actors

Stuxnet is one of the most famous cases of **nation-state-backed cyberterrorism**. In 2010, a **highly sophisticated computer worm** was discovered, which was specifically designed to target the **Iranian nuclear program**. The worm, dubbed **Stuxnet**, caused physical damage to the centrifuges used in Iran's nuclear enrichment facility by manipulating industrial control systems.

Key Characteristics of Stuxnet:

- **Targeted Attack**: Stuxnet was a **highly targeted attack**, designed to sabotage Iran's nuclear enrichment operations. It was not a broad cyberattack but a **precision strike** on specific industrial systems.
- **Zero-Day Exploits**: Stuxnet used **zero-day vulnerabilities** in Windows operating systems to infect systems. These were vulnerabilities that were unknown to the software manufacturer at the time.
- **Nation-State Involvement**: Although no country has officially claimed responsibility, it is widely believed that **the U.S. and Israel** were behind the attack, marking one of the first instances of **cyber-warfare** between nation-states.

Impact of Stuxnet:

- **Set a Precedent**: Stuxnet marked the first known use of cyberattacks to damage critical infrastructure, setting a precedent for **cyberwarfare** and **cyberterrorism**.
- **Global Attention**: The attack demonstrated the vulnerability of industrial control systems to cyber threats and led to increased focus on **cybersecurity** in critical sectors.

The rise of **cyberterrorism** and the involvement of **nation-state actors** on the dark web represents a new era of **digital warfare**. As cyberattacks grow more sophisticated, the **targets** and **tactics** used by nation-states are becoming increasingly complex. These attacks not only threaten **national security** but also **economic stability**, **public safety**, and **global relations**.

Law enforcement agencies, cybersecurity professionals, and international organizations must work together to combat these threats. The dark web provides a level of **anonymity** and **secrecy** that makes it difficult to trace and prevent these attacks. As a result, it is imperative for nations to strengthen their **cyber defense capabilities**, develop **international cybersecurity agreements**, and **invest in advanced technology** to protect against future cyber threats.

Part 5: Specialized Techniques – Investigative Methods and Cybersecurity Tools

Chapter 12: Investigative Techniques Used by Cybersecurity Professionals

In the fight against **cybercrime** and **dark web criminal activity**, cybersecurity professionals employ a variety of investigative techniques and tools to track down cybercriminals, gather evidence, and uncover illicit operations. These techniques range from **digital forensics** to the use of **open-source intelligence (OSINT)** and specialized investigative tools.

In this chapter, we'll explore how cybersecurity professionals conduct investigations into **dark web crimes**. We'll discuss the importance of **digital forensics**, how to gather intelligence from **open-source platforms**, and the tools used for tracking down cybercriminals. Whether you're a beginner or a professional in the field, this chapter will provide valuable insights into investigative methods and their practical applications.

12.1: Digital Forensics: Gathering Evidence from the Dark Web

Digital forensics is the process of uncovering and analyzing information stored in **digital devices** such as computers, smartphones, and online systems to gather evidence of **cybercrimes**. On the dark web, digital forensics plays a critical role in identifying cybercriminals, uncovering illicit activities, and building legal cases. Given the **anonymity** and **cryptography** that dark web criminals use to hide their tracks, digital forensics requires specialized techniques and tools to extract evidence from these environments.

In this chapter, we'll explore how **digital forensics** is applied to investigations involving the dark web, focusing on the processes of **gathering evidence**, **preserving data integrity**, and **analyzing criminal activity**. We'll also discuss common tools and techniques used by forensic experts in the field.

1. Introduction to Digital Forensics on the Dark Web

The **dark web** is often a haven for illegal activities, from illicit marketplaces selling **drugs** and **stolen data** to **cybercrime** syndicates offering services like **hacking** and **ransomware deployment**. Criminals use **Tor**, **I2P**, and **other privacy networks** to mask their identities, making it difficult to track their activities. Digital forensics on the dark web involves gathering and analyzing data from these **anonymity networks** and the **devices** used by criminals to commit their crimes.

Key Challenges in Dark Web Forensics

1. **Anonymity Networks**: Tools like **Tor** and **I2P** provide users with high levels of anonymity by routing traffic through multiple nodes and masking IP addresses. This makes it challenging to trace users' activities.
2. **Encryption**: Dark web users often rely on strong encryption to protect communications and transactions. This makes evidence extraction more difficult, requiring advanced decryption and analysis techniques.
3. **Cryptocurrency**: Many illegal transactions on the dark web involve **cryptocurrencies** like **Bitcoin** and **Monero**, which are designed to protect users' financial privacy. Investigators must develop methods to trace cryptocurrency transactions on the blockchain or identify wallet addresses used in illicit activities.

Despite these challenges, digital forensics offers powerful techniques to **recover evidence** and track criminal activities.

2. The Process of Digital Forensics on the Dark Web

Forensic investigations on the dark web follow a specific sequence of steps that ensure the **evidence** remains **admissible in court** and **preserved** for analysis. The process includes evidence collection, data preservation, analysis, and reporting. Here's a breakdown of how investigators work in dark web cases:

2.1 Evidence Collection: Seizing Devices and Data

The first step in any digital forensics investigation is to **seize the devices** and **digital evidence** involved in the crime. For dark web investigations, this often means gathering:

- **Computers, laptops, and servers** used to access dark web marketplaces and communicate with other criminals.
- **Mobile phones** used by suspects to browse or conduct transactions on the dark web.
- **Cryptocurrency wallets**, whether physical or digital, used to conduct financial transactions.
- **Metadata** and **logs** from websites or marketplaces that criminals accessed or hosted.

Practical Tip: Preserving Evidence During Collection

While seizing evidence, it's critical to preserve the integrity of the data. This involves creating a **forensic image** (exact replica) of storage devices before any analysis begins. Using tools like **FTK Imager** or **dd** (on Linux) ensures that original data is not altered.

2.2 Data Preservation: Creating Forensic Images

To maintain the **integrity** of evidence, forensic investigators create **bit-for-bit copies** of hard drives, mobile devices, and storage media. These copies are called **forensic images** and are essential for ensuring that the original data remains unaltered and **admissible in court**.

1. **Create an Image of the Entire Drive**: Using forensic tools like **FTK Imager**, investigators can create an exact replica of a hard drive or device, preserving all files, system settings, and deleted data.
2. **Verify the Image**: After creating the forensic image, investigators use cryptographic hashing (e.g., **MD5**, **SHA-1**) to generate a unique hash value for the image. This ensures that the copy is an exact match to the original data and has not been tampered with.

3. **Secure Storage**: The forensic image is stored in a secure location to prevent **tampering** or **contamination** during the analysis phase.

Practical Example: Using FTK Imager for Evidence Collection

Let's say we are investigating a **dark web marketplace** accessed via **Tor**. After seizing the suspect's **laptop**:

1. Create a forensic image of the laptop's hard drive using FTK Imager.
2. Verify the image by generating a hash and comparing it to the original data.
3. Store the image in a secure storage device for further analysis.

2.3 Data Analysis: Recovering and Analyzing Evidence

Once the evidence has been properly preserved, forensic investigators move to the **data analysis** phase. In dark web cases, this often involves:

- **Analyzing cryptocurrency transactions**: Tracing transactions on the **Bitcoin** or **Monero** blockchain to identify the flow of illicit funds.
- **Examining metadata**: Investigating hidden data within files and logs to trace the origin of illegal content, such as illicit drugs or hacking tools.
- **Decrypting encrypted files**: Using tools like **Passware** or **ElcomSoft** to decrypt **password-protected** files or encrypted hard drives.

2.4 Techniques for Analyzing Dark Web Marketplaces

Dark web marketplaces often host a wealth of information, such as **user transactions, vendor lists, product descriptions**, and **user reviews**. Here are some techniques used in dark web investigations:

- **Database extraction**: Investigators can extract **database backups** of dark web marketplaces to uncover user records and transaction logs.
- **Monitoring hidden services**: Investigators can track **.onion** sites (the web addresses used on the Tor network) and observe activity in **dark web marketplaces**.

- **Analyzing network traffic**: Tools like **Wireshark** are used to capture and analyze network traffic to identify suspicious connections or communication with dark web services.

Example: Tracing a Dark Web Vendor's Activity

Let's assume an investigator is tasked with tracking a dark web drug vendor. Using forensic tools like **Maltego** and **Wireshark**, they can:

1. Extract vendor details and user reviews from a dark web marketplace database.
2. Analyze network traffic to track connections to specific Tor nodes or **IP addresses** linked to the vendor's activities.
3. Correlate cryptocurrency wallet addresses to identify the flow of illicit funds from transactions.

---

3. Tools for Digital Forensics on the Dark Web

There are several specialized tools used for digital forensics in dark web investigations. These tools help forensic investigators collect and analyze evidence from encrypted devices, dark web marketplaces, and criminal networks.

3.1 FTK Imager: Creating Forensic Images

FTK Imager is a tool used to create **disk images** of computers, mobile devices, and other digital media. It allows investigators to preserve the integrity of evidence and recover **deleted files**.

- **Use case**: If investigators seize a laptop used to access dark web marketplaces, FTK Imager can create a forensic image of the hard drive, ensuring that the data remains unaltered during analysis.

3.2 Wireshark: Analyzing Network Traffic

Wireshark is a network protocol analyzer that is often used in digital forensics to monitor and analyze network traffic. Forensic investigators use Wireshark to track **Tor traffic**, identify suspicious behavior, and locate illicit communication on the dark web.

- **Use case**: Investigators can use Wireshark to capture and analyze **Tor traffic**, identifying patterns and correlations that could lead to uncovering dark web activities or connecting criminal networks.

3.3 Maltego: Link Analysis and Data Mining

Maltego is an investigative tool that specializes in **link analysis**. It's widely used for analyzing **relationships** between individuals, IP addresses, cryptocurrency addresses, and other entities involved in cybercrime.

- **Use case**: Maltego can be used to trace **dark web vendor networks** by analyzing relationships between **usernames**, **email addresses**, and **cryptocurrency wallet addresses** involved in illicit transactions.

3.4 EnCase: Comprehensive Forensics Analysis

EnCase is a comprehensive forensic tool used to **collect**, **preserve**, and **analyze digital evidence**. It's widely used for analyzing computers, mobile devices, and networks involved in cybercrime.

- **Use case**: EnCase can be used to analyze seized devices, looking for encrypted communications or illegal content related to dark web activities.

---

4. Challenges in Dark Web Forensics

While digital forensics is a powerful tool in investigating dark web crimes, it comes with unique challenges:

1. **Encryption**: Many criminals use **encryption** to protect their communications and files, making it difficult for investigators to recover or access critical evidence.

2. **Anonymity Networks**: The **Tor network** and other **anonymity networks** make it hard to trace the true origin of web traffic or identify the individuals involved in dark web activities.
3. **Cryptocurrency**: The use of **cryptocurrencies** like **Bitcoin** and **Monero** makes it difficult to trace financial transactions back to specific individuals or entities.

Overcoming Challenges:

- **Decryption tools** and **advanced analytic techniques** are helping investigators tackle the issue of encrypted data.
- **Correlation analysis** using **OSINT** and **Maltego** can uncover hidden links between dark web entities, despite the anonymity provided by Tor.

Digital forensics is an essential component of any investigation involving the dark web. As cybercriminals become more sophisticated in their use of **anonymity tools**, **encryption**, and **cryptocurrencies**, digital forensics experts must adapt their methods and tools to stay ahead of evolving threats. By **preserving** and **analyzing digital evidence**, forensic investigators can uncover crucial information, track criminal networks, and provide the foundation for **successful legal action**.

As dark web activity continues to grow, so will the importance of digital forensics in combating cybercrime. Cybersecurity professionals must remain vigilant and develop innovative solutions to overcome the unique challenges posed by the dark web and its anonymity features.

12.2: How to Use Open-Source Intelligence (OSINT) for Dark Web Investigations

Open-Source Intelligence (**OSINT**) is the process of collecting and analyzing publicly available information to generate actionable intelligence. OSINT can be an extremely powerful tool in dark web investigations, allowing investigators to identify key actors, track illicit activities, and uncover hidden criminal networks. While the dark web is designed to provide anonymity, it's still possible to gather vital intelligence from publicly accessible sources—such as forums, marketplaces, and even social media.

In this guide, we'll delve into how **OSINT** can be applied in dark web investigations. We'll discuss its **importance**, how to use it **effectively**, and provide practical examples and tools that will help you uncover valuable insights.

---

1. What is Open-Source Intelligence (OSINT)?

OSINT refers to the collection and analysis of publicly available data from various sources. This includes everything from **public records**, **social media**, **websites**, **forums**, and even **dark web marketplaces**. OSINT does not rely on **classified** or **restricted** data, but instead makes use of what is **freely accessible** to anyone, often requiring nothing more than internet access and the right tools to analyze it.

In the context of the **dark web**, OSINT is crucial for monitoring **illegal activities** and **gathering evidence**. Although the dark web itself is hidden from regular search engines, information is still shared through publicly accessible domains like **.onion** websites, forums, and various underground communication channels.

---

2. The Importance of OSINT in Dark Web

Investigations

OSINT plays a critical role in dark web investigations by providing cybersecurity professionals with the tools and data necessary to uncover **illegal activities** and identify **criminals**. Despite the anonymity and encryption provided by **Tor** and other dark web tools, OSINT allows investigators to:

- **Identify key players**: OSINT helps uncover the identities of **vendors**, **buyers**, and **operational structures** involved in dark web marketplaces.
- **Monitor illegal transactions**: Investigators can use OSINT to track the flow of **cryptocurrency transactions**, monitor dark web **marketplace activity**, and identify the goods or services being offered for sale.
- **Correlate data**: By collecting data from various sources and correlating it, investigators can uncover patterns or relationships that point to criminal operations or links between actors.

Why OSINT is Crucial for Dark Web Investigations:

- **No Need for Special Access**: OSINT doesn't require any special tools or permissions, making it ideal for gathering intelligence from publicly accessible sites on the dark web.
- **Anonymity Breakthrough**: Criminals often expose themselves unknowingly by leaving **digital footprints** on public forums, social media, or through **leaked information** that can be pieced together through OSINT techniques.
- **Real-Time Monitoring**: OSINT tools can track dark web activity in **real-time**, enabling investigators to stay ahead of criminal developments.

---

3. How to Conduct OSINT for Dark Web Investigations

Conducting OSINT for dark web investigations involves several steps, from gathering data to analyzing and acting on that data. Let's walk through the process of using OSINT to investigate dark web crimes:

3.1 Step 1: Identify Key Dark Web Sources

The first step in any dark web investigation using OSINT is identifying the right **sources** of information. Some key sources include:

- **Dark Web Marketplaces**: Marketplaces like **AlphaBay**, **Dream Market**, and **Silk Road** have been key sources of illicit activity in the past. Today, investigators can monitor **active marketplaces** to track the sale of illegal goods.
- **Dark Web Forums**: Forums are where dark web criminals often gather to exchange information, offer illegal services, and discuss operations. These forums include **r/hacking**, **DarkNet Markets** (DMs), and **TorLinks**.
- **Cryptocurrency Blockchains**: Cryptocurrencies like **Bitcoin**, **Ethereum**, and **Monero** are often used to conduct transactions on the dark web. OSINT can track these transactions, helping to identify suspicious wallets and tracing the flow of illicit funds.

3.2 Step 2: Use Search Engines for Dark Web Content

Although the dark web is not indexed by traditional search engines like Google, there are specialized search engines that index **.onion** sites and provide a way to search through dark web content. These search engines allow investigators to explore hidden services and marketplaces that are not visible on the regular web.

Some of the most common dark web search engines include:

- **Ahmia**: A search engine for Tor network content that indexes **.onion** domains. It provides an easy way to find dark web websites and forums related to criminal activities.
- **DuckDuckGo (on Tor)**: DuckDuckGo is a privacy-focused search engine that also allows searches on the **Tor network**.

3.3 Step 3: Gather and Organize Data from Dark Web Sources

Once you've identified your sources, the next step is to gather relevant data. This can include:

- **Forum Posts**: Scrape and collect data from dark web forums where criminals discuss illegal activities. Look for posts that mention **product sales, services offered**, or **criminal connections**.
- **Market Listings**: Gather data on illegal goods and services being offered, such as **drugs, stolen data, hacking tools**, etc.
- **User Reviews and Ratings**: On marketplaces, look at **reviews** and **ratings** to track criminal transactions and **vendor reputation**.

Tools like **Scrapy** and **BeautifulSoup** (Python-based web scraping tools) can be used to automate the process of scraping data from dark web marketplaces and forums. These tools can be used to gather text, metadata, and transaction logs from **.onion** sites.

```
import requests
from bs4 import BeautifulSoup

# Example: Scraping a dark web marketplace listing
url = "http://example.onion/marketplace-listing"
response = requests.get(url)
soup = BeautifulSoup(response.text, 'html.parser')

# Extract relevant data
title = soup.find('h1', {'class': 'product-title'}).text
price = soup.find('span', {'class': 'price'}).text
description = soup.find('div', {'class': 'product-
description'}).text

print(f"Product: {title}\nPrice: {price}\nDescription:
{description}")
```

3.4 Step 4: Analyzing the Data

Once data has been gathered, it needs to be analyzed to extract valuable intelligence. OSINT analysis on the dark web often involves:

- **Identifying Criminal Networks**: By examining relationships between usernames, wallet addresses, product listings, and transaction data, investigators can identify connections between individuals and **criminal networks**.
- **Cryptocurrency Address Tracking**: Use blockchain explorers like **Blockchain.com** or **Chainalysis** to trace cryptocurrency transactions linked to dark web marketplaces. This can help track the movement of funds and identify **illicit wallet addresses**.

Case Study: Tracing Dark Web Transactions Using OSINT

Imagine you're tracking the activities of a vendor on a dark web marketplace selling **stolen credit card details**. Through **OSINT analysis**:

1. You scrape the marketplace data and identify a **Bitcoin wallet address** associated with the vendor.

2. You use **Blockchain.com** to track the flow of Bitcoin and trace it to a **new wallet address** that has recently been active in multiple illicit transactions.
3. This leads you to identify other **associated wallets**, vendors, and buyers involved in illegal activities.

3.5 Step 5: Correlating OSINT with Other Intelligence Sources

OSINT is even more powerful when combined with other forms of intelligence, such as **traditional law enforcement data**, **digital forensics evidence**, or **cryptocurrency transaction records**.

- **Social Media Monitoring**: Criminals sometimes discuss their dark web activities on social media. Monitoring **Twitter**, **Reddit**, and other platforms for mentions of dark web activities can provide additional context.
- **Publicly Available Records**: **Court records, public business filings**, and **domain name registration** records can provide additional clues to uncovering the identity of criminals or criminal organizations operating on the dark web.

---

4. OSINT Tools for Dark Web Investigations

There are several powerful OSINT tools that can help gather and analyze intelligence from the dark web. Here's a rundown of some of the most popular ones:

4.1 Maltego

Maltego is one of the best OSINT tools for conducting deep **link analysis**. It allows you to visualize relationships between people, organizations, email addresses, phone numbers, and more. For dark web investigations, Maltego is especially useful in identifying connections between **dark web vendors, buyers**, and **criminal networks**.

- **Use case**: By analyzing usernames, email addresses, and Bitcoin wallet addresses, Maltego can identify **connections** between individuals involved in dark web activities.

4.2 Shodan

Shodan is a **search engine for internet-connected devices**. It allows you to search for **webcams**, **servers**, and **IoT devices** that may be connected to dark web activities.

- **Use case**: Investigators can search for devices connected to the dark web or discover **unsecured servers** used by criminals to host dark web services.

4.3 CipherTrace

CipherTrace is a blockchain intelligence tool that helps investigators track **cryptocurrency transactions**. It's particularly useful for identifying illicit **Bitcoin** and **Monero** transactions linked to dark web marketplaces.

- **Use case**: Use CipherTrace to track the movement of cryptocurrencies used for illicit transactions on the dark web.

4.4 DarkOwl

DarkOwl is a search tool specifically designed for dark web monitoring. It helps users collect intelligence from **.onion** sites, **dark web marketplaces**, and **forums**.

- **Use case**: DarkOwl is used to search for illicit products, track vendor activity, and gather intelligence on **illegal operations** on the dark web.

OSINT is a **critical tool** for cybersecurity professionals investigating the dark web. By leveraging publicly available information from dark web forums, marketplaces, and even blockchain networks, investigators can uncover valuable leads, identify criminals, and build strong cases against cybercriminals.

12.3: Tools for Investigating and Tracking Cybercriminals

Investigating and tracking **cybercriminals** requires a broad range of sophisticated tools and techniques that enable cybersecurity professionals to monitor, identify, and analyze suspicious online activities. The dark web, where many illegal activities occur, is especially challenging due to its **anonymity** features and encryption protocols. However, cybersecurity experts use various **investigative tools** to extract and analyze critical data, trace **cryptocurrency transactions**, and uncover **hidden networks** involved in illicit activities.

In this guide, we'll explore some of the most effective tools and methodologies used to investigate and track cybercriminals, focusing on tools like **Wireshark**, **Maltego**, and **Chainalysis**, and providing practical examples of how they are applied in dark web investigations.

1. The Role of Tools in Investigating Cybercriminals

When investigating cybercrime, investigators must gather data from various sources, analyze network traffic, trace financial transactions, and uncover hidden criminal networks. The following categories of tools play key roles in these investigations:

- **Network Analysis**: These tools help investigators monitor network traffic, capture data packets, and identify suspicious activities such as **DDoS** attacks, **data exfiltration**, and unauthorized access to systems.
- **Link Analysis**: These tools are used to map the relationships between different actors and entities, such as **vendors**, **buyers**, and **wallet addresses** involved in illicit activities.
- **Blockchain Analysis**: These tools track **cryptocurrency transactions** across the blockchain, allowing investigators to trace

the flow of funds, identify **illicit wallets**, and potentially track down the individuals involved in illegal transactions.

- **Digital Forensics**: These tools allow investigators to recover and analyze data from seized devices, identifying files, logs, and evidence of cybercriminal activity.

Now, let's dive into the specific tools that are used in cybercriminal investigations.

---

2. Tools for Network Analysis and Data Capture

2.1 Wireshark: The Leading Network Traffic Analyzer

Wireshark is one of the most widely used tools for **packet analysis** and **network traffic monitoring**. It allows investigators to capture, inspect, and analyze data packets transmitted over a network. In dark web investigations, **Wireshark** helps track **Tor traffic** and **suspicious connections**, even if the user is anonymized.

Key Features:

- **Real-time Capture**: Wireshark captures network traffic in real time, allowing investigators to monitor the **packets** being transmitted across a network.
- **Detailed Analysis**: Investigators can inspect each packet for **protocol details**, **source and destination IP addresses**, and **port numbers**, making it easier to identify malicious activities.
- **Filtering and Sorting**: With Wireshark, users can filter network traffic by specific protocols (e.g., HTTP, DNS, SSH) or **IP addresses**, making it easier to find relevant data.

Use Case: Analyzing Tor Traffic

In a case where a cybercriminal is accessing a **dark web marketplace** through Tor, Wireshark can be used to:

1. Capture the network traffic of the suspect's device.

2. Identify **exit nodes** used by the suspect on the Tor network.
3. Monitor communication with suspicious **IP addresses** or websites related to dark web criminal activity.

Example: Capturing packets with Wireshark

1. Open Wireshark and start a capture on the network interface you wish to monitor.

2. Apply a filter (e.g., `ip.addr == 192.168.1.1`) to focus on the suspect's traffic.

3. Analyze packets for suspicious activity, such as unusual requests to **Tor exit nodes** or **malicious IPs**.

4. Follow the packet trail to find potential sources or destinations associated with illicit behavior.

2.2 Other Network Analysis Tools

- **Nmap**: A tool used for **network discovery** and **security auditing**. It allows investigators to discover devices on a network and assess their vulnerabilities.
- **NetFlow Analyzer**: A tool that helps monitor network traffic and detect anomalous traffic patterns, often used to identify **DDoS attacks** and **data exfiltration** attempts.

3. Link Analysis and Investigative Tools

3.1 Maltego: Mapping Relationships and Uncovering Hidden Networks

Maltego is a **powerful link analysis tool** that is widely used in OSINT (Open Source Intelligence) investigations. It's particularly useful for mapping relationships between individuals, entities, or digital artifacts. Maltego's graph-based interface allows investigators to uncover **connections** between **dark web vendors**, **cryptocurrency wallets**, **social media accounts**, and **email addresses** involved in cybercrime.

247

Key Features:

- **Graphical Analysis**: Maltego presents relationships in an easy-to-understand visual format, which helps investigators identify patterns, connections, and hidden links.
- **Integration with OSINT**: Maltego integrates with various OSINT sources to pull in **publicly available data** and map relationships between suspects or activities.
- **Data Mining**: Maltego can mine **data from the deep web**, including information from forums, **.onion** websites, and **dark web marketplaces**.

Use Case: Tracking Dark Web Vendors

In dark web investigations, Maltego can help investigators map out connections between:

- **Dark web aliases** (vendors or buyers).
- **Cryptocurrency wallet addresses** linked to illegal transactions.
- **IP addresses** or **email addresses** associated with **suspicious activity**.

By analyzing these connections, investigators can uncover hidden relationships within criminal networks.

Example: Visualizing the connection between a dark web vendor and buyer network

1. Use Maltego to create a **graph of known aliases**, wallet addresses, and transaction logs.
2. Identify relationships based on **similar usernames** or **shared Bitcoin addresses**.
3. Investigate the graph to track down the **real-world individuals** behind the aliases and wallets.

3.2 Other Link Analysis Tools

- **IBM i2 Analyst's Notebook**: A link analysis tool that allows investigators to visualize connections between entities in a network, especially useful in criminal investigations.

- **Palantir**: A data integration and analysis tool that helps investigators to make sense of complex data sets and identify hidden patterns in large datasets.

4. Tools for Tracking Cryptocurrency Transactions

4.1 Chainalysis: Tracking Blockchain Transactions

Chainalysis is a **blockchain analysis tool** used to trace and analyze cryptocurrency transactions, particularly on **Bitcoin** and other major cryptocurrencies. It's an essential tool for dark web investigations because it helps track the flow of **illicit funds** across wallets and exchanges.

Key Features:

- **Blockchain Visualization**: Chainalysis allows investigators to visualize cryptocurrency transactions on the blockchain, showing how funds move from wallet to wallet.
- **Identify Illicit Wallets**: The tool helps identify wallets linked to **illegal activities**, such as money laundering, ransomware payments, or dark web marketplaces.
- **Transaction Monitoring**: Chainalysis monitors cryptocurrency transactions in real-time, alerting investigators to **suspicious activity** or illicit fund movement.

Use Case: Tracing Bitcoin Transactions in Dark Web Cases

An investigator can use Chainalysis to:

1. Trace Bitcoin transactions between a **dark web vendor** and **multiple buyers**.
2. Identify **illicit wallet addresses** used by cybercriminals to launder money.
3. Track the movement of funds to **exchanges** or **mixing services**, which often obscure the origin of illicit funds.

Example: Tracking funds associated with dark web transactions

1. Search for a **Bitcoin wallet address** associated with a known dark web vendor.
2. Trace the movement of Bitcoin from the vendor's wallet to **other wallets** used by the criminal network.
3. Investigate transactions involving **mixing services** or unregistered exchanges, which could be linked to **money laundering**.

4.2 Other Cryptocurrency Tracking Tools

- **Elliptic**: A blockchain analysis tool used to monitor **cryptocurrency transactions** and identify illicit activities, including **terrorist financing** and **dark web transactions**.
- **CipherTrace**: Another blockchain intelligence tool that tracks cryptocurrency transactions, especially **privacy coins** like **Monero** and **Zcash**.

---

5. Case Study: Tracking a Dark Web Vendor Using OSINT, Wireshark, and Chainalysis

Let's walk through a **hypothetical investigation** where an investigator tracks a dark web vendor involved in selling **stolen data**. Using **OSINT**, **Wireshark**, and **Chainalysis**, the investigator gathers the following insights:

1. **Step 1: Data Collection via OSINT**
   - The investigator scrapes a dark web marketplace for **vendor details**, including usernames and wallet addresses.
   - Using **Maltego**, the investigator maps connections between the vendor's **dark web profile** and other **buyers**, identifying relationships between vendor and customer.
2. **Step 2: Monitoring Network Traffic with Wireshark**
   - Using Wireshark, the investigator analyzes the network traffic of a suspect believed to be buying **stolen credit card data** from the vendor.

- They track **Tor exit node connections** to link the suspect's **IP address** to suspicious dark web activity.
3. **Step 3: Tracing Cryptocurrency Transactions with Chainalysis**
   - Chainalysis is used to trace **Bitcoin transactions** from the vendor's **wallet** to multiple wallets linked to **buying activity**.
   - The investigator uncovers suspicious transactions to **mixing services**, indicating potential **money laundering**.

Cybercriminals operating on the dark web have access to sophisticated **anonymity tools**, making investigations challenging. However, by leveraging powerful tools like **Wireshark, Maltego, Chainalysis**, and others, cybersecurity professionals can overcome these challenges, track illicit activities, and gather evidence crucial for identifying and prosecuting criminals.

As cybercriminals continue to evolve their tactics, investigators must stay up-to-date with the latest tools and technologies. The future of cybercrime investigations will rely heavily on combining **network analysis, link analysis**, and **cryptocurrency tracking** to uncover hidden networks, disrupt illegal operations, and bring cybercriminals to justice.

Chapter 13: Advanced Cybersecurity Measures for Protecting Your Business

As businesses continue to digitize, the threat of cyberattacks, especially those originating from the dark web, has grown exponentially. Cybercriminals are becoming more sophisticated, using anonymity networks, encrypted communications, and decentralized systems to launch **attacks** that can cause severe damage to businesses of all sizes. In this chapter, we'll explore **advanced cybersecurity measures** to protect your business from these threats, including **corporate defense strategies**, **threat intelligence**, and **incident response protocols**.

13.1: Corporate Defense Strategies Against Dark Web Threats

The **dark web** has emerged as a major hub for illegal activities, from **selling stolen data** to **drug trafficking** and **cybercrime services**. As businesses increasingly rely on digital operations, the threat from dark web actors becomes more serious. These criminals use **anonymity networks** like **Tor** and **I2P** to hide their identities, making it difficult to detect and stop their activities. Consequently, businesses need robust **cybersecurity defenses** and **strategies** to mitigate the risks posed by the dark web.

This guide will outline key **corporate defense strategies** to protect businesses from dark web threats. These strategies range from building strong **network defenses** to employing **continuous monitoring** for dark web activity. We'll also cover the latest tools and techniques for preventing, detecting, and responding to these threats.

1. The Dark Web Threat Landscape

Before we delve into defense strategies, it's important to understand the types of threats that businesses face from the dark web. These can include:

- **Stolen Data**: Cybercriminals frequently steal **company data, personal information**, and **credentials** and sell them on dark web marketplaces.
- **Intellectual Property Theft**: Proprietary business information, designs, or trade secrets are often targeted and sold on the dark web.
- **Fraudulent Transactions**: Illegitimate **credit card details, bank account numbers**, and **personal identifiers** are traded and used for financial fraud.
- **Ransomware**: The dark web is a platform where **ransomware-as-a-service** is sold, enabling cybercriminals to launch attacks on businesses without technical expertise.

---

2. Corporate Defense Strategies

Given the complexity of dark web threats, businesses must implement a comprehensive and multi-layered approach to defense. The following strategies can help mitigate the risk of dark web exposure:

2.1 Layered Security Approach

A **layered security strategy** (also called **defense in depth**) involves using multiple protective measures to secure an organization's network and data. In the context of dark web threats, this approach should incorporate a combination of **firewalls, intrusion detection systems (IDS), data encryption**, and **strong access control measures**.

Key Components of a Layered Defense Strategy:

1. **Firewalls**: Firewalls act as the first line of defense, controlling incoming and outgoing network traffic based on predetermined security rules. Properly configured firewalls can prevent unauthorized access to critical company systems.

2. **Intrusion Detection and Prevention Systems (IDPS)**: These systems monitor network traffic for suspicious activity and can automatically block or alert security teams if an attack is detected. An **IDS** can help identify if any communication with **dark web marketplaces** or illicit services is occurring.
3. **Endpoint Protection**: All company devices—laptops, desktops, smartphones, and tablets—must be protected with up-to-date antivirus software, firewalls, and data encryption.
4. **Encryption**: Encrypt sensitive data both in **transit** and at **rest**. Encryption ensures that even if cybercriminals manage to access your systems, they will be unable to read or use the data without the proper decryption key.
5. **Access Control**: Implement **least privilege access** and **multi-factor authentication (MFA)** for all critical systems and data. This ensures that only authorized personnel can access sensitive information.

Practical Insight: Configuring Firewalls

In order to prevent **dark web access** through unapproved ports, configure firewalls to block common ports used by Tor (e.g., **9050** for Tor traffic). Additionally, network monitoring should alert you to any unexpected outbound connections on **Tor nodes**.

2.2 Dark Web Monitoring

Active monitoring of the dark web is essential for businesses looking to safeguard their data. Dark web monitoring tools can detect if your company's sensitive data, credentials, or intellectual property is being traded or sold on underground forums or marketplaces.

Key Steps in Dark Web Monitoring:

1. **Credential Monitoring**: Continuously monitor the dark web for company-related credentials (such as employee login credentials or database access). If these credentials appear on dark web marketplaces, businesses can take immediate action, such as resetting passwords or improving security protocols.

2. **Intellectual Property (IP) Monitoring**: If your company's trade secrets or intellectual property (e.g., designs, software, research) are sold or shared on dark web platforms, early detection allows you to respond swiftly and prevent financial loss.
3. **Threat Intelligence**: Threat intelligence platforms aggregate dark web data, providing businesses with detailed information on potential threats. Platforms like **DarkOwl**, **Digital Shadows**, and **Terbium Labs** track and report on illicit dark web activity.

Practical Insight: Leveraging Threat Intelligence Tools

With **DarkOwl** or **Terbium Labs**, a company can set up **custom alerts** for specific keywords or asset identifiers (e.g., the company name, key products) to be notified if their data appears in dark web forums or marketplaces.

Example Use Case: Dark Web Monitoring in Action

A financial institution uses a dark web monitoring tool to track **employee credentials** and **credit card details**. The tool alerts the security team when a batch of **compromised employee login credentials** is discovered in a dark web marketplace. The security team immediately implements additional monitoring, resets affected employee credentials, and conducts an internal investigation.

2.3 Employee Training and Awareness

A significant portion of dark web-related threats stems from **human error**, such as falling for **phishing attacks** or mismanaging sensitive information. Regular **cybersecurity training** and **awareness campaigns** for employees can reduce the chances of insider threats and improve overall security posture.

Key Training Areas:

- **Phishing Awareness**: Teach employees how to identify phishing emails and suspicious links. Ensure they know not to click on unfamiliar links, especially those that claim to lead to confidential websites or documents.

- **Password Hygiene**: Promote strong password management practices and enforce the use of **multi-factor authentication (MFA)**. Make sure employees understand the importance of **unique passwords** for each system they use.
- **Social Engineering**: Train employees to recognize common **social engineering tactics**, such as **pretexting**, where attackers impersonate legitimate employees to gain access to company systems.

Practical Tip: Conduct Phishing Simulations

Regular **phishing simulation exercises** can help employees better recognize malicious emails. Tools like **KnowBe4** or **PhishMe** allow you to conduct simulated phishing attacks and educate employees about how to spot them.

2.4 Incident Response Planning

Even with the best defenses in place, incidents may still occur. Having a well-prepared **incident response plan (IRP)** is crucial for minimizing damage. This plan should include a set of predefined actions to take if a **breach** or **cyberattack** occurs.

Key Components of an Incident Response Plan:

1. **Preparation**: Define roles and responsibilities for the **incident response team** (IRT). Ensure all employees know how to report security incidents promptly.
2. **Detection and Identification**: Implement monitoring tools (e.g., **SIEM** systems like **Splunk**) to detect unusual activities, such as unauthorized attempts to access sensitive information.
3. **Containment**: Once an attack is identified, quickly isolate affected systems or networks to prevent the attack from spreading.
4. **Eradication**: After containing the attack, work to remove any malicious files, tools, or threats that may have infiltrated the system.
5. **Recovery**: Restore systems from **backups** and ensure all security patches are applied. Verify that the systems are secure before allowing them to reconnect to the network.

6. **Post-Incident Review**: After the incident is resolved, conduct a thorough **post-mortem** to determine how the attack occurred, what was compromised, and how future incidents can be prevented.

Practical Insight: Incident Response Templates

Create **response playbooks** tailored to different types of incidents (e.g., **data breach**, **ransomware attack**). These templates should outline clear, actionable steps for your team to follow during each type of cyberattack.

3. Case Study: Corporate Defense Against a Dark Web

Breach

Let's walk through a **hypothetical case** to understand how a company can implement these defense strategies effectively.

Scenario: A large retail company notices an increase in suspicious activity on its payment systems. Upon further investigation, it's discovered that the company's **credit card data** has been stolen and is being sold on a dark web marketplace. The company's incident response plan is triggered, and the following steps are taken:

1. **Dark Web Monitoring**: The company's **dark web monitoring tools** alert them to the sale of compromised credit card information on a dark web marketplace. Immediate action is taken to investigate the source.
2. **Employee Training**: Employees are reminded of **phishing** and **social engineering tactics**. It's discovered that a **phishing email** tricked an employee into disclosing their login credentials, which were then used to access the payment system.
3. **Containment**: The affected systems are immediately **isolated** from the network to prevent the attackers from accessing additional data.
4. **Incident Response**: The incident response team conducts a thorough **forensic investigation** and begins **eradicating** the threat by removing malware and changing all compromised credentials.

5. **Recovery**: After restoring systems from **secure backups**, the company applies **security patches** and implements **multi-factor authentication** for additional protection.
6. **Post-Incident Review**: A post-incident analysis reveals vulnerabilities in the payment system and employee awareness. The company strengthens its defenses by applying stricter security measures, including encryption and more robust training programs.

Dark web threats are becoming increasingly sophisticated, but by implementing **multi-layered security strategies**, conducting regular **dark web monitoring**, and preparing a well-defined **incident response plan**, businesses can effectively defend against cybercriminals operating in these underground spaces.

Building a resilient cybersecurity framework requires constant vigilance, employee training, and the adoption of the latest security technologies. The strategies outlined in this chapter provide businesses with the tools to safeguard sensitive information, mitigate the impact of cyberattacks, and maintain a secure operational environment.

13.2: Threat Intelligence and Proactive Monitoring

In today's cybersecurity landscape, **threat intelligence** and **proactive monitoring** are vital components of a comprehensive defense strategy. Cyber threats are evolving at a rapid pace, with cybercriminals increasingly using sophisticated techniques to infiltrate networks and exploit vulnerabilities. This makes it crucial for businesses to stay ahead of the threat curve by leveraging **intelligence** to predict, detect, and neutralize potential threats before they cause damage.

In this chapter, we'll explore the concept of **threat intelligence**, how it helps businesses protect against cyber threats, and the role of **proactive monitoring** in identifying suspicious activities. We'll also discuss practical steps and tools to integrate threat intelligence and monitoring into your business operations.

1. What is Threat Intelligence?

Threat intelligence refers to the collection, analysis, and use of data to identify potential cyber threats. This information comes from various sources, both internal (e.g., system logs, network traffic) and external (e.g., open-source intelligence, dark web data). Threat intelligence helps organizations understand the tactics, techniques, and procedures (TTPs) of cybercriminals and attackers, enabling them to take proactive measures to defend their assets.

1.1 The Different Types of Threat Intelligence

- **Strategic Threat Intelligence**: Focuses on broad, long-term trends in the cybersecurity landscape. It helps businesses understand emerging threats, such as **nation-state actors**, new **ransomware families**, or changes in the regulatory environment. Strategic intelligence helps inform business decisions about overall security investments and risk management.
- **Tactical Threat Intelligence**: Provides actionable information about specific **attack techniques**, vulnerabilities, and exploits that cybercriminals are currently using. Tactical intelligence helps security teams understand how attackers are breaching systems and what tools they are using.
- **Operational Threat Intelligence**: Focuses on specific **incidents** and **attacks**. This includes details about active cyber campaigns, such as malware variants or phishing campaigns. It helps businesses monitor ongoing threats and identify how they may be targeted.
- **Technical Threat Intelligence**: Provides specific technical indicators of compromise (IOCs) like **IP addresses**, **domain names**, **hash values**, and **URLs**. These can be directly integrated into security tools for automatic detection and blocking.

2. The Role of Proactive Monitoring in Cybersecurity

Proactive monitoring is a critical security measure that involves continuously overseeing networks, systems, and user activity to detect any unusual behavior or threats. It helps identify **potential attacks** before they can cause harm. Effective proactive monitoring includes **continuous vulnerability scanning**, **real-time threat detection**, and **alert systems**.

2.1 How Proactive Monitoring Works

Proactive monitoring involves **collecting data** from multiple sources within an organization, including:

- **Network traffic**
- **System logs**
- **User activity logs**
- **Endpoint behavior**
- **Security device alerts**

Once this data is collected, it is analyzed in real-time using specialized tools to identify suspicious activity. When a potential threat is detected, **automated alerts** are triggered, notifying the security team of a potential breach or anomaly.

Proactive monitoring is crucial for preventing threats that would otherwise go undetected. This can include **early detection of malware**, **ransomware campaigns**, or even **internal threats** from compromised employees.

---

3. Threat Intelligence and Proactive Monitoring in Practice

In practice, businesses can integrate **threat intelligence** and **proactive monitoring** into their daily operations by following these steps:

3.1 Step 1: Collect Data from Multiple Sources

To create actionable threat intelligence, businesses need to gather data from a variety of sources. These sources include:

- **Internal data sources**: Logs, alerts from **firewalls, IDS/IPS systems**, and **endpoint security** tools.
- **External data sources**: Publicly available threat feeds, dark web monitoring, and OSINT tools.
- **Threat intelligence providers**: Services like **Recorded Future**, **FireEye**, or **ThreatConnect** offer curated intelligence feeds that can be integrated into your security operations.

3.2 Step 2: Analyze and Correlate Data

Once the data is collected, it must be analyzed to identify patterns, connections, and indicators of compromise (IOCs). **Threat Intelligence platforms (TIPs)** and **Security Information and Event Management (SIEM)** systems are commonly used for this purpose. These platforms can automatically analyze incoming data, correlate it with known threats, and raise alerts when suspicious activity is detected.

Practical Insight: Integrating Threat Intelligence into SIEM

Using **Splunk** or **IBM QRadar** (SIEM solutions), you can integrate threat intelligence feeds (such as **MISP** or **OpenDXL**) to automatically detect specific IOCs like IP addresses associated with **malicious websites** or **known malware**. This integration helps security teams respond faster and more effectively to emerging threats.

3.3 Step 3: Implement Automated Response Mechanisms

A key part of proactive monitoring is automation. By integrating automated response mechanisms into your cybersecurity strategy, you can reduce response times and contain threats more quickly. These automated actions can include:

- **Blocking malicious IPs**: Automatically block IP addresses known to be associated with malicious activity.

- **Isolating infected systems**: If malware is detected, automatically isolate the affected endpoint to prevent further infection or data exfiltration.
- **Revoking compromised credentials**: Automatically revoke or reset user credentials that have been compromised or are being used in suspicious activity.

3.4 Step 4: Continuous Improvement through Feedback Loops

Effective threat intelligence and proactive monitoring are continuous processes. After each incident, it's essential to conduct a **post-mortem analysis** to learn from the experience. This analysis can help refine detection methods, improve response strategies, and update threat intelligence feeds with new IOCs and TTPs.

---

4. Tools for Threat Intelligence and Proactive Monitoring

Now that we've explored the core strategies for integrating **threat intelligence** and **proactive monitoring**, let's look at some of the key tools that can assist in these areas.

4.1 Threat Intelligence Platforms (TIPs)

These platforms aggregate and analyze intelligence from various sources, providing businesses with real-time data on threats. They also facilitate the sharing of threat intelligence between organizations, helping to strengthen collective defense mechanisms.

- **ThreatConnect**: A comprehensive threat intelligence platform that aggregates, analyzes, and shares threat intelligence. It allows security teams to correlate data across different feeds, offering actionable insights.
- **Anomali**: Another popular TIP that provides customizable dashboards for threat monitoring, with integrations to SIEM and other cybersecurity tools.

4.2 Security Information and Event Management (SIEM)

SIEM tools help businesses centralize and analyze logs from across their networks, providing a comprehensive view of security incidents.

- **Splunk**: A widely-used SIEM tool that offers powerful analytics and monitoring capabilities. It integrates with multiple threat intelligence feeds and can help organizations detect and respond to threats faster.
- **IBM QRadar**: A security information and event management platform that helps organizations detect, investigate, and respond to security threats by correlating data from network and system logs.

4.3 Endpoint Detection and Response (EDR)

EDR tools focus on continuously monitoring endpoints (laptops, servers, mobile devices) for suspicious activity.

- **CrowdStrike Falcon**: A next-gen EDR platform that uses machine learning and AI to detect threats on endpoints in real time. It provides real-time monitoring and automated response.
- **Carbon Black**: An endpoint protection platform that offers threat detection, investigation, and response capabilities, leveraging continuous monitoring and intelligence to mitigate risks.

4.4 Dark Web Monitoring Tools

Dark web monitoring tools help businesses track their data on underground markets and forums, identifying if any company credentials or intellectual property are being sold or traded.

- **DarkOwl**: A dark web monitoring service that scans hidden services for company-related data, helping to detect leaks and early signs of data exfiltration.
- **Terbium Labs**: Provides automated dark web monitoring to track sensitive data, alerting businesses when their data is exposed or up for sale.

5. Case Study: Using Threat Intelligence and Proactive Monitoring to Prevent a Data Breach

Let's walk through a **hypothetical case** where a company uses threat intelligence and proactive monitoring to prevent a data breach.

Scenario: A major retail company notices unusual login patterns across multiple user accounts. Using threat intelligence tools, the security team discovers a **credential stuffing** attack originating from the dark web.

Steps Taken:

1. **Threat Intelligence**: The company uses **Recorded Future** to analyze data from multiple threat feeds. The system alerts the security team to a **dark web forum** where a batch of stolen login credentials has been posted.
2. **Proactive Monitoring**: The company's **SIEM system (Splunk)** analyzes the login behavior and flags an unusually high number of failed login attempts for certain user accounts.
3. **Automated Response**: Using **CrowdStrike Falcon** (EDR), the company automatically **isolates affected endpoints** and revokes compromised credentials. Automated scripts are triggered to **reset passwords** for users with exposed accounts.
4. **Recovery**: The company restores access to systems and conducts a forensic investigation to ensure no further data was compromised.
5. **Post-Incident Review**: The company updates its threat intelligence feeds with new **IOC** data, such as the list of **compromised credentials**, and improves monitoring protocols to detect similar attacks in the future.

In today's evolving threat landscape, **threat intelligence** and **proactive monitoring** are essential for defending against cyberattacks. By staying ahead of potential threats through the continuous gathering of intelligence, real-time monitoring, and automated response, businesses can significantly reduce the risk of data breaches and other cyber incidents.

The integration of advanced tools and platforms such as **SIEM, TIPs**, and **EDR solutions** ensures that businesses have the necessary resources to detect, respond to, and recover from cyberattacks quickly and efficiently. By implementing these strategies, businesses not only protect themselves from dark web threats but also establish a strong, **resilient cybersecurity posture** that can adapt to the growing complexity of cybercrime.

13.3: Incident Response: How to Handle a Breach or Cyberattack

In the world of cybersecurity, **cyberattacks** and **data breaches** are inevitable threats that every business must prepare for. Whether it's a **ransomware attack, phishing attempt**, or an **insider breach**, knowing how to effectively respond to a security incident is critical to minimizing damage and ensuring a swift recovery.

In this chapter, we'll explore the key components of an **incident response (IR)** strategy and break down the critical steps needed to handle a breach or cyberattack. We'll also cover practical insights and real-world examples to help you build a robust and actionable response plan for your business.

1. What is Incident Response?

Incident response (IR) refers to the process by which an organization detects, investigates, contains, eradicates, and recovers from a cybersecurity incident or breach. A well-defined IR plan is essential for minimizing damage, reducing recovery time, and ensuring that the business can resume normal operations quickly.

An **incident** can take many forms, from unauthorized access to systems, data leaks, malware infections, ransomware attacks, or distributed denial of service (DDoS) attacks. The goal of an incident response is to identify the attack early, contain the threat, and restore the business's normal operations.

2. The Phases of Incident Response

Incident response is a **systematic** process that involves several key phases. Each phase is designed to help businesses manage, contain, and mitigate the effects of a cyberattack. These phases are:

1. **Preparation**: Preparing for an attack before it happens.
2. **Identification**: Detecting and identifying potential incidents.
3. **Containment**: Isolating the attack to prevent further damage.
4. **Eradication**: Removing the attack from the system and securing vulnerable points.
5. **Recovery**: Restoring systems and operations to normal.
6. **Lessons Learned**: Post-incident analysis to prevent future attacks.

Let's walk through each phase in detail.

---

3. Incident Response Phases: Detailed Explanation

3.1 Phase 1: Preparation

Preparation is the first and most critical phase of incident response. This phase ensures that the organization is ready to respond swiftly and effectively when an attack occurs.

Key Steps in Preparation:

- **Develop an Incident Response Plan**: Create a formal, documented **Incident Response Plan (IRP)** that outlines the roles, responsibilities, and procedures for handling an incident. This plan should include contact details for key personnel, external security vendors, legal advisors, and law enforcement.
- **Assemble an Incident Response Team (IRT)**: The IRT consists of a group of individuals responsible for managing the incident, including **security experts**, **IT staff**, **legal advisors**, and

communications specialists. Clearly define roles and responsibilities ahead of time so everyone knows what to do during an incident.

- **Implement Security Measures**: Before an attack happens, implement proactive **security controls** such as firewalls, intrusion detection/prevention systems (IDS/IPS), encryption, and **multi-factor authentication (MFA)**.
- **Employee Training and Awareness**: Educate employees about **security best practices**, phishing risks, and how to report suspicious activity. Regular training and simulated exercises help prepare your staff to act effectively when a real incident occurs.

Practical Tip: Creating an Incident Response Playbook

Your Incident Response Plan should be complemented by **playbooks** for common types of incidents. For example, a playbook for **ransomware attacks** might include steps such as isolating affected machines, disconnecting from the network, and contacting law enforcement.

3.2 Phase 2: Identification

The identification phase involves detecting the incident as early as possible. Early detection helps to reduce the impact of the attack and allows the response team to act quickly.

Key Steps in Identification:

- **Monitor for Indicators of Compromise (IOCs)**: Continuously monitor systems for signs of malicious activity. IOCs can include unusual network traffic, system logs, changes in file integrity, and unauthorized access attempts. Use **SIEM (Security Information and Event Management)** systems like **Splunk** or **QRadar** to collect and analyze log data for suspicious activities.
- **Use Threat Intelligence**: Incorporate **threat intelligence** feeds to stay informed about emerging threats and indicators of attacks related to your industry. This could include information about **malware** or **attack tools** that are being actively used on the dark web.

- **Automated Alerts**: Implement automated **alert systems** to notify the security team when suspicious activities are detected. These alerts should be clear and actionable, pointing to the specific nature of the incident.

Example: Detecting a Ransomware Attack Early

You might use **real-time network monitoring** to detect encrypted traffic patterns or unusual outbound communication that signals **ransomware encryption** in progress. Early detection of such anomalies allows for faster containment.

3.3 Phase 3: Containment

Once the incident is identified, the next step is to **contain** the attack to prevent it from spreading further. This phase involves isolating affected systems and preventing the attacker from gaining additional access.

Key Steps in Containment:

- **Network Segmentation**: If the attack has spread across your network, isolate the affected systems to prevent lateral movement. This can be done by **disconnecting compromised systems** from the network or disabling certain services temporarily.
- **Block Malicious Communication**: If a cybercriminal is communicating with external servers or control systems (e.g., for a **botnet** or **C2 server**), block these communication channels by blocking **IP addresses** or **domain names**.
- **Minimize User Impact**: If possible, ensure that unaffected systems remain operational so that business continuity is maintained. For example, if one department's system is compromised, isolate it while allowing other departments to continue functioning.

Practical Insight: Isolation with Network Segmentation

In the case of a ransomware attack, you can **isolate** infected systems by cutting off access to file servers or database servers, thereby limiting the spread of encrypted files across the network.

3.4 Phase 4: Eradication

Eradication involves completely removing the threat from your systems and addressing any vulnerabilities exploited during the attack. This phase ensures that no malicious code or backdoors remain.

Key Steps in Eradication:

- **Remove Malware**: Use tools like **anti-malware** and **antivirus software** to remove malicious code from affected systems. In the case of ransomware, ensure that the ransomware is fully eradicated, including any remnants of **exploit tools** or **backdoor access** left by attackers.
- **Patch Vulnerabilities**: If the attack exploited a system vulnerability (e.g., unpatched software), patch the vulnerability to prevent further exploitation. This may involve updating systems or removing outdated software.
- **Clear Compromised Credentials**: Change all passwords and revoke credentials that may have been compromised. Implement **multi-factor authentication (MFA)** for all accounts.

Practical Tip: Performing Full System Scans

Run full **system scans** on all affected machines to check for malware remnants. Tools like **Malwarebytes**, **Windows Defender**, or **Trend Micro** can be used to perform deep system scans to remove persistent malware.

3.5 Phase 5: Recovery

The recovery phase involves restoring business operations and ensuring that the affected systems are fully operational. The goal is to return to normal operations while preventing re-infection.

- **Restore Data from Backups**: Recover from secure, clean backups. Ensure that backups are free from malware before restoration.
- **Monitor Systems**: After restoring affected systems, monitor them closely to detect any signs of reinfection or ongoing compromise.
- **Verify Systems**: Conduct thorough testing and validation of all systems to ensure that they are fully operational and secure. This may involve checking for hidden malware or system misconfigurations.

Practical Insight: Ensuring Backup Integrity

Before restoring from backups, **scan backups for malware** to ensure they haven't been compromised. This ensures that you are not reintroducing malware into your environment.

3.6 Phase 6: Lessons Learned

The final phase involves conducting a **post-incident review** to learn from the incident. This analysis helps improve future responses, detect gaps in the security posture, and strengthen defenses.

Key Steps in Lessons Learned:

- **Conduct a Post-Mortem Analysis**: Evaluate what went wrong during the incident and what went well. Analyze how the attack occurred, which defense measures were effective, and where improvements can be made.
- **Update the Incident Response Plan**: Incorporate insights from the incident into your **incident response plan** (IRP) so that future responses are more effective.
- **Share Insights**: If appropriate, share your findings with relevant stakeholders and within the wider security community. This helps others learn from your experiences and better prepare for similar threats.

After an incident, consider conducting **security audits** and **penetration testing** to identify potential weaknesses that were missed in the initial response.

---

4. Case Study: Handling a Ransomware Attack

Scenario:

A healthcare company experiences a ransomware attack that locks access to its patient data systems. The attackers demand a **ransom** in **Bitcoin** for the decryption keys.

Steps Taken:

1. **Identification**: The security team detects unusual file encryption activity through the company's **SIEM system**. Suspicious files were encrypted rapidly on multiple machines in a short time.
2. **Containment**: The affected systems are **isolated** from the network to prevent the spread of ransomware. Access to the internal file server is temporarily blocked.
3. **Eradication**: Using **anti-malware tools**, the company removes the ransomware from all affected systems. All **compromised credentials** are reset, and vulnerabilities in the system are patched.
4. **Recovery**: The company restores data from **clean backups** and validates the integrity of the restored data. Systems are monitored for any signs of re-infection.
5. **Lessons Learned**: The company updates its **incident response plan** and implements additional **network segmentation** and **multi-factor authentication (MFA)** to protect sensitive data in the future.

Handling a breach or cyberattack is one of the most challenging tasks for any business. However, with a well-defined **incident response plan**, businesses can recover quickly and effectively, minimizing damage and downtime. The key is to **prepare in advance**, **detect incidents early**, **respond swiftly**, and **learn from each experience**.

Chapter 14: Ethics and Legal Considerations in Dark Web Investigations

The dark web is a murky and often controversial part of the internet, where activities ranging from illegal transactions to privacy-enhancing technologies occur. Investigating the dark web, therefore, presents unique ethical and legal challenges. As cybersecurity professionals, law enforcement agencies, and private organizations dive deeper into dark web investigations, they must navigate a delicate balance between protecting society and respecting individual privacy rights.

14.1: Ethical Dilemmas in Investigating the Dark Web

Investigating the **dark web** presents significant **ethical dilemmas** due to its complex nature. The dark web is home to both **illicit activities** and **legitimate uses** like ensuring privacy for individuals in oppressive regimes or journalists reporting under dangerous circumstances. As a result, dark web investigations often force cybersecurity professionals, law enforcement, and private entities to make difficult decisions that balance **public safety** with **individual rights** and **privacy**.

In this section, we will delve into the ethical challenges faced when investigating dark web activities. These challenges arise in the form of **privacy concerns**, **data collection practices**, **undercover operations**, and **the use of deceptive tactics**. By exploring real-world examples, we will understand how investigators can navigate these ethical pitfalls while still upholding the rule of law.

1. Ethical Considerations in Dark Web Investigations

Before jumping into specific dilemmas, it's important to establish the core ethical principles that guide investigations on the dark web:

- **Respect for Privacy**: The dark web is primarily used by individuals seeking anonymity for legitimate reasons—such as activists in oppressive countries, journalists exposing corruption, or users bypassing surveillance. Ethical investigations must differentiate between those using the dark web for protection and those using it for malicious intent.
- **Proportionality**: Investigators must ensure that their actions are **proportional** to the seriousness of the crime they are investigating. For instance, intercepting communications in a **drug trafficking case** should not lead to breaching the privacy of **whistleblowers** or other innocent users.
- **Minimizing Harm**: Investigations should be designed in a way that minimizes harm to innocent individuals, whether they are users of the dark web or those inadvertently caught up in the investigation. This means considering how an investigation may disrupt legitimate activities while going after cybercriminals.

Real-World Example: Ethical Concerns in Monitoring

A human rights organization uses the dark web to protect their communications. An investigative team monitoring the dark web for illegal activity might unintentionally intercept communications between the organization's members. If proper safeguards aren't in place, this could compromise their ability to operate in a repressive country, violating privacy rights.

---

2. Key Ethical Dilemmas in Dark Web Investigations

The ethical challenges in investigating the dark web largely stem from the tools and tactics used by investigators to infiltrate dark web forums, marketplaces, and criminal operations. Let's take a look at some of the most common ethical dilemmas faced in such investigations.

2.1 The Use of Undercover Operations

Undercover operations involve infiltrating criminal networks by creating fake identities or personas to gain trust and collect intelligence. These operations are often crucial for infiltrating dark web marketplaces or forums where **drug dealers**, **hackers**, and **other criminals** congregate. However, they raise serious ethical concerns:

- **Deception**: Investigators may need to lie, assuming false identities or engaging in deceitful behavior. While this is common in law enforcement, the ethical concern is whether such deception crosses the line and induces illegal actions that would not otherwise occur.
- **Entrapment**: Entrapment occurs when law enforcement agents induce individuals to commit crimes they otherwise would not have committed. If investigators participate in illegal transactions or encourage criminals to perform actions they would not have done, this can be seen as unethical and unlawful.

Case Study: Undercover Operation on Silk Road

In the case of the **Silk Road**, one of the largest illegal marketplaces on the dark web, undercover agents infiltrated the marketplace by pretending to be sellers of illegal drugs. While their intent was to gather intelligence, concerns arose over whether they inadvertently encouraged criminal activity. Some argue that undercover agents might have pushed some participants to conduct transactions they had not initially intended.

2.2 Privacy vs. Surveillance

Privacy concerns are a significant issue in dark web investigations. Many individuals use the dark web to avoid surveillance or to protect their sensitive data from governments, corporations, or malicious entities. Investigators need to balance the protection of individuals' privacy with the necessity to monitor criminal activity.

Ethical Question: How far can investigators go in monitoring users' online behavior without infringing on their rights?

- **Targeting Innocent Individuals**: Without proper safeguards, the collection of **traffic data** or **personal information** could end up violating the rights of innocent users who are on the dark web for lawful reasons, such as protecting their identities or accessing censored information.
- **Mass Surveillance**: Investigating entire dark web forums or monitoring broad **user activities** might result in unnecessary surveillance. This can harm privacy rights and set a dangerous precedent for unnecessary governmental or corporate overreach.

Practical Insight: Ensuring Privacy Protections

To mitigate privacy concerns, investigators should focus on gathering only relevant data and use techniques like **anonymizing** or **de-identifying** personal information before storing or sharing it. Additionally, they should avoid mass surveillance and instead target specific criminal behaviors that can be tied directly to illegal activities.

2.3 The Use of Malware or Hacking Tools

Some dark web investigations may involve the use of **malware** or other hacking tools to gather evidence from dark web forums, marketplaces, or criminal systems. While these tools are often necessary to break into encrypted systems or track cybercriminal activity, their use raises several ethical issues:

- **Hacking Back**: The concept of **"hacking back"** involves retaliating against cybercriminals by hacking into their systems. While this may seem like an effective way to gather evidence, it is legally and ethically questionable. In many jurisdictions, hacking back is illegal and can set dangerous precedents for future retaliatory actions.
- **Infringing on Other Users**: Malware used for monitoring criminal activity may inadvertently affect other innocent users, compromising their security, privacy, or even damaging their systems.

276

Ethical hacking tools, such as **honeypots** (systems set up to attract attackers), can be used to monitor dark web criminal activities without directly compromising the privacy of others. These tools allow investigators to gather intelligence while maintaining a clear line between **legitimate investigation** and **illegal activity**.

2.4 Collaboration with Private Entities

Investigations of dark web activities may require collaboration between public law enforcement and private entities, such as cybersecurity firms or technology companies. This collaboration can raise significant ethical issues:

- **Data Sharing**: When private companies share information about their users with law enforcement, it raises questions about the **user consent** and **data protection**. Are users aware that their personal data is being monitored or shared with external entities? How can transparency be ensured?
- **Corporate Interests vs. Public Safety**: Sometimes, companies may prioritize protecting their commercial interests over collaborating with law enforcement, leading to ethical dilemmas about the transparency of their involvement in investigations.

Practical Insight: Clear Agreements and Boundaries

Clear legal agreements and data-sharing protocols should be established between law enforcement and private companies. These agreements should prioritize **user consent**, **transparency**, and **minimal data collection** to protect privacy while still enabling necessary investigations.

---

3. Balancing Public Safety and Personal Privacy: A

Delicate Dance

While investigating the dark web is crucial for protecting public safety, investigators must constantly balance their goals with respect for personal privacy and ethical behavior. Below are a few strategies to navigate this balance:

3.1 Transparent and Accountable Investigations

To ensure ethical behavior, investigators must maintain transparency in their actions, ensuring that all parties understand their role and what actions they are authorized to take. Investigators should document their actions meticulously and be accountable for any breaches of ethical conduct.

3.2 Clear Boundaries and Legal Guidelines

Establishing clear boundaries for investigation methods is essential. Legal frameworks, such as **the Budapest Convention** on cybercrime, help clarify what is and isn't permissible in dark web investigations. Investigators must operate within these frameworks and ensure they have **legal authorization** before engaging in activities that might breach privacy or involve deception.

3.3 Informed Decision-Making

Investigation teams should assess each situation and its ethical implications carefully. For instance, an investigator might ask themselves: "Is the potential harm to innocent individuals justified by the severity of the crime?" If the answer is unclear, further consultation with legal and ethical experts should be sought before proceeding.

Dark web investigations represent a unique challenge for cybersecurity professionals, law enforcement, and policymakers. The potential benefits of investigating illicit activities, such as **drug trafficking**, **child exploitation**, and **human trafficking**, are clear. However, these benefits must be weighed against the potential ethical and privacy concerns associated with invasive investigative techniques.

14.2: Legal Boundaries: What You Can and Can't Do

Investigating the **dark web** presents not only ethical challenges but also a maze of **legal complexities**. The dark web is a space where anonymity thrives, and many illicit activities such as **drug trafficking, hacking-for-hire**, and **money laundering** occur. However, it is also a space where privacy is paramount for legitimate users, such as journalists, whistleblowers, and activists.

When investigating dark web activities, law enforcement agencies, cybersecurity professionals, and private organizations must adhere to the **legal boundaries** set by their respective countries. These boundaries ensure that investigations remain lawful while safeguarding individual rights. This guide will take you through the key legal considerations and boundaries you must respect when investigating the dark web, as well as what you can and cannot do.

---

1. Understanding the Legal Landscape

The legal boundaries for dark web investigations are shaped by various factors, including **jurisdiction**, **privacy laws**, **cybercrime statutes**, and **international agreements**. Each country has different laws regarding what constitutes legal and illegal behavior in cyberspace, and these differences create challenges in cross-border investigations.

1.1 Jurisdictional Challenges in Dark Web Investigations

One of the first and most significant legal challenges in investigating the dark web is **jurisdiction**. Since the dark web is inherently **global**, investigations often cross international borders. The anonymity tools used on the dark web, such as **Tor** and **I2P**, further complicate matters by making it difficult to trace a suspect's location.

- **Cross-border Legal Issues**: Cybercriminals on the dark web can operate from any location, which means that law enforcement in one country may face challenges when the criminal resides in a jurisdiction with differing laws or lack of cooperation. Investigators may need to rely on **mutual legal assistance treaties (MLATs)** or international law enforcement agencies like **INTERPOL** or **EUROPOL** to overcome these hurdles.

- **Competing National Interests**: Jurisdictional issues are further complicated by national security concerns, different privacy standards, and varying levels of **cooperation** between countries.

---

2. Key Legal Considerations in Dark Web

Investigations

While dark web investigations are necessary to combat cybercrime, there are several legal considerations that investigators must follow to ensure that their actions are lawful.

2.1 Surveillance and Data Collection

When investigating the dark web, one of the most common methods used is **surveillance**, which can take many forms, including **network monitoring**, **data collection from websites**, and **tracking criminal activity** on forums and marketplaces. However, surveillance must adhere to specific legal requirements.

Legal Boundaries:

- **Wiretap Laws**: In many jurisdictions, **wiretapping** or intercepting **electronic communications** requires a **court-approved warrant**. For example, in the United States, **Title III of the Omnibus Crime Control and Safe Streets Act** mandates that law enforcement must obtain a **warrant** to conduct wiretaps. This means that investigators cannot simply intercept communications or monitor private messages between users on the dark web without proper legal authority.
- **Privacy Laws**: Various countries have enacted stringent **data privacy laws** that protect individuals from unauthorized

surveillance. In the **European Union**, the **General Data Protection Regulation (GDPR)** restricts the collection of personal data, even in an investigative context, unless there is clear, **consent** or a **legal obligation**. Similarly, in the U.S., the **Electronic Communications Privacy Act (ECPA)** protects the privacy of electronic communications.

Practical Insight: Data Collection in Dark Web Investigations

When investigators collect **user data** from a dark web marketplace, they need to ensure that they comply with privacy laws and obtain proper authorization. If personal identifiers (like email addresses or usernames) are being collected, they should anonymize or pseudonymize the data to avoid infringing on users' privacy rights.

2.2 Undercover Operations

Undercover operations are essential to gaining access to dark web criminal activities. These operations often involve creating **false identities** to interact with criminal actors and gather evidence. However, there are legal limitations to these operations.

Legal Boundaries:

- **Entrapment**: Entrapment occurs when law enforcement or investigators **induce** someone to commit a crime that they otherwise would not have committed. This is a major ethical and legal issue, as it could lead to **wrongful prosecution**. In many legal systems, if an individual is found to have been entrapped, charges may be dismissed.
- **Creating Fake Accounts**: While it is legal for investigators to create fake accounts or aliases to infiltrate dark web marketplaces, they must not participate in illegal activities unless the actions taken are part of a **lawful investigation**. Engaging in illegal transactions to catch criminals could cross ethical lines and violate legal frameworks.

In the **Silk Road** investigation, law enforcement set up undercover operations to infiltrate the marketplace. While conducting undercover transactions to gather evidence on illegal drug sales, investigators had to be careful not to engage in entrapment. They had to ensure that they did not encourage individuals to make illegal purchases that they were not already inclined to make.

2.3 Hacking and Use of Malware

Sometimes, investigators may use hacking tools or malware to **infiltrate** dark web sites, capture criminal communications, or access servers where illegal activities occur. This raises several legal concerns about **hacking** and **cybersecurity laws**.

Legal Boundaries:

- **Computer Fraud and Abuse Act (CFAA)**: In the United States, the **CFAA** makes it illegal to access a computer system without authorization. Investigators may only use **malware** or hacking tools if they have a **legal warrant** or are acting within the scope of their legal duties.
- **Hacking Back**: Some companies and cybersecurity experts engage in the controversial tactic of **hacking back**, where they attempt to retaliate against cybercriminals by breaching their systems. This practice is highly controversial and may be illegal in many jurisdictions. It is **not legally permissible** in most cases, as it could lead to violating **international laws** and **unintended consequences**.

Practical Insight: Legal Use of Malware

When using **malware** for investigative purposes, law enforcement must obtain **judicial authorization** and ensure that the malware is targeted exclusively at criminal actors. For example, law enforcement could use a **honeypot** to attract cybercriminals into a controlled environment without violating laws.

---

3. International Legal Considerations

Cybercrimes on the dark web often span multiple jurisdictions, requiring international cooperation. However, cross-border investigations come with a unique set of legal issues.

3.1 The Budapest Convention on Cybercrime

The **Budapest Convention** is the first **international treaty** focused on cybercrime, and it provides a framework for countries to cooperate in the investigation and prosecution of cybercrime. However, not all countries are signatories to the convention, and enforcement can be inconsistent.

- **International Cooperation**: The convention facilitates international cooperation by providing guidelines for evidence sharing, **mutual legal assistance treaties (MLATs)**, and **extradition**.
- **Challenges in Enforcement**: Even with the Budapest Convention, differences in national laws regarding **data privacy**, **cybercrime**, and **jurisdiction** can complicate cross-border investigations. A criminal operating in a non-signatory country may be beyond the reach of international law enforcement.

3.2 Mutual Legal Assistance Treaties (MLATs)

When a dark web investigation involves criminals in different countries, law enforcement may rely on **Mutual Legal Assistance Treaties (MLATs)** to request evidence or access data stored in foreign jurisdictions. However, these treaties can be slow and cumbersome.

- **Slow Process**: MLATs require formal requests through diplomatic channels, which can take weeks or even months. This can delay the investigation and allow criminals to destroy evidence or go into hiding.
- **Legal Disparities**: Some countries may not have data protection laws as strict as others, meaning that evidence obtained from these jurisdictions may not meet the standards required by the investigating country.

4. Case Study: The AlphaBay Takedown

One notable case where legal boundaries were tested is the **AlphaBay marketplace takedown** in 2017. AlphaBay was one of the largest dark web marketplaces for illegal goods, including drugs, weapons, and hacking tools. Law enforcement agencies from multiple countries, including the United States, the Netherlands, and Canada, coordinated to take down AlphaBay.

- **Challenges Faced**: Law enforcement had to navigate a maze of **international legal issues**, including cooperation between multiple jurisdictions and the challenges of operating within **differing privacy laws**. Despite these challenges, AlphaBay's takedown was successful, but it demonstrated the need for continued **international cooperation** in combating cybercrime on the dark web.
- **Legal Boundaries**: During the investigation, law enforcement had to ensure that they were not violating users' **privacy** rights. They also had to be cautious not to **engage in entrapment** or **illegal activities** as part of the undercover investigation.

Dark web investigations are fraught with **legal complexities**, and investigators must be fully aware of the boundaries that govern their actions. From data collection to undercover operations, and from **cybercrime** statutes to international legal cooperation, the rules can be intricate and vary by jurisdiction. Adhering to legal frameworks such as **the Budapest Convention** and ensuring proper **jurisdictional cooperation** are key to a successful and lawful investigation.

14.3: International Law and Cybercrime on the Dark Web

As the dark web continues to be a breeding ground for a wide range of illicit activities—from drug trafficking to hacking services—**international cooperation** becomes critical in combating cybercrime on a global scale. Cybercriminals operating on the dark web often do not respect national borders, which means that law enforcement agencies and cybersecurity professionals must work across jurisdictions to address these crimes effectively.

In this section, we will explore **international law** in the context of cybercrime on the dark web. We'll look at the key legal frameworks that govern global cooperation in cybercrime investigations, the challenges posed by jurisdictional issues, and real-world examples of international efforts to combat dark web crimes.

1. The Importance of International Law in Dark Web Investigations

The dark web is inherently **global**, and cybercriminals often exploit its anonymity to conduct illegal activities across borders. As such, tackling cybercrime on the dark web requires the coordinated effort of law enforcement agencies, governments, and organizations worldwide. This brings into focus the role of **international law** in facilitating these efforts.

1.1 Global Reach of Dark Web Criminals

The main challenge in investigating crimes on the dark web is that **cybercriminals** can operate from virtually anywhere. For example, someone selling stolen credit card information on a dark web marketplace could be in **Eastern Europe**, while a buyer might be in **South America**, and the payment is processed in **Asia**. The global nature of the dark web makes it difficult for any single nation to enforce laws effectively. Therefore, **international cooperation** becomes essential.

- **Cryptocurrency** transactions further complicate this issue, as cybercriminals use digital currencies like **Bitcoin**, **Monero**, or **Ethereum** to anonymize financial flows, making it harder to trace illegal transactions across borders.

2. Key Legal Frameworks for Combating Dark Web Cybercrime

Several international treaties, conventions, and organizations play a vital role in addressing cybercrime on the dark web. These frameworks provide the legal basis for cross-border cooperation, evidence-sharing, and coordinated investigations.

2.1 The Budapest Convention on Cybercrime

The **Convention on Cybercrime** (commonly known as the **Budapest Convention**) is the first international treaty aimed at addressing **cybercrime** on a global scale. Adopted by the **Council of Europe** in 2001, it has become the foundation for much of the international cooperation on cybercrime investigations, including those on the dark web.

Key Features of the Budapest Convention:

- **Criminalization**: It sets out common **cybercrime laws** and defines offenses like **illegal access, illegal interception, data interference**, and **fraud** in cyberspace. This includes crimes commonly associated with dark web activities, such as **drug trafficking**, **money laundering**, and **child exploitation**.
- **International Cooperation**: The Budapest Convention facilitates **cross-border cooperation** by providing a legal framework for information exchange, evidence collection, and mutual legal assistance between signatory countries.

- **Cybercrime-Related Data**: The treaty also facilitates the sharing of **digital evidence** across borders. This is crucial in dark web investigations, where digital footprints often reside in multiple countries.

Example: Silk Road Takedown

The takedown of **Silk Road**, a notorious dark web marketplace for illegal goods, involved international cooperation among law enforcement agencies in the United States, the Netherlands, and several other countries. The **Budapest Convention** provided the legal framework for collecting evidence across these borders and prosecuting individuals involved in the marketplace's operation.

2.2 Mutual Legal Assistance Treaties (MLATs)

Mutual Legal Assistance Treaties (MLATs) are agreements between two or more countries to cooperate in the investigation and prosecution of crimes. In the case of cybercrime on the dark web, MLATs provide a way for countries to request access to evidence located in another jurisdiction.

Key Features of MLATs:

- **Evidence Sharing**: MLATs allow law enforcement agencies to request and share evidence between countries, enabling investigations to proceed when criminals operate across borders.
- **Limitations**: While MLATs are important tools for international cooperation, they are often **slow** and **bureaucratic**. Requests for evidence or information can take **months** to process, which can be detrimental to investigations where time is of the essence.
- **Data Privacy**: MLATs must balance the need for evidence-sharing with the protection of **data privacy laws** in each country. This is particularly relevant when investigating dark web activity, where data may involve sensitive or personal information.

Practical Insight: Using MLATs in Dark Web Investigations

Law enforcement investigating the sale of stolen data or hacking tools on the dark web can use **MLATs** to request access to data stored in other countries. For example, if an investigation leads to a server in **Germany** that hosts a dark web marketplace, the U.S. authorities could issue an MLAT to gain legal access to the data.

2.3 INTERPOL and EUROPOL: Coordinating Global Cybercrime Efforts

INTERPOL and **EUROPOL** are two key organizations that facilitate international cooperation on cybercrime. Both organizations help countries coordinate their efforts and share intelligence in cases involving cybercrime, including crimes perpetrated on the dark web.

Key Roles of INTERPOL and EUROPOL:

- **INTERPOL**: INTERPOL helps law enforcement agencies from **190 countries** collaborate on cybercrime investigations, offering a secure platform for exchanging information and **conducting joint operations**.
- **EUROPOL**: Based in the EU, **EUROPOL** facilitates cooperation between EU member states and partner countries to tackle cybercrime. It operates **EC3** (European Cybercrime Centre), which focuses specifically on cybercrime, including dark web-related activities.

Practical Insight: International Task Forces

INTERPOL and EUROPOL often work together on **task forces** that investigate dark web crimes, such as **drug trafficking** or **human trafficking**. These task forces pool resources, knowledge, and technical expertise from multiple countries to increase the likelihood of success in investigations.

---

3. The Challenges of International Law in Dark Web

Investigations

Despite the existence of these international frameworks, there are significant **challenges** when it comes to investigating cybercrime on the dark web.

3.1 Jurisdictional Issues

Since the dark web is decentralized and operates without regard for national borders, determining which country has jurisdiction over a crime can be complex. Law enforcement agencies may have to negotiate with multiple countries to access evidence, and criminals may operate in countries with lax or non-existent cybercrime laws.

Example: The AlphaBay Takedown

The **AlphaBay** marketplace takedown involved international coordination between the **U.S.**, **Canada**, **the Netherlands**, and other countries. While the **U.S.** had jurisdiction over the criminal actors in the case, **AlphaBay** was hosted on servers in Russia, which added legal complexity to the investigation.

3.2 Privacy Laws and Encryption

Privacy laws and **encryption** are other significant challenges in dark web investigations. For example, the **GDPR** in the European Union imposes strict regulations on the collection and processing of personal data, making it difficult for law enforcement to collect information in a way that complies with data protection rules.

Furthermore, cybercriminals often use encryption technologies like **Tor**, **VPNs**, and **end-to-end encrypted communications** to hide their activities. This makes it difficult to trace **digital footprints** and gather evidence without violating privacy laws.

3.3 The Need for Evolving Legal Frameworks

As cybercrime on the dark web evolves, legal frameworks must also evolve to keep up. The **Budapest Convention** and other existing treaties were drafted before many modern dark web technologies emerged, and they are often seen as outdated.

Governments and international organizations must work together to update cybercrime laws to account for **emerging technologies**, including cryptocurrency tracking, **AI-driven cybercrime**, and advanced **encryption** techniques. An updated treaty could help standardize the legal process for investigating and prosecuting dark web crimes.

---

4. Case Study: AlphaBay and International Cooperation

AlphaBay, once the largest dark web marketplace, facilitated the sale of illegal goods and services, including drugs, weapons, and hacking tools. In **July 2017**, the marketplace was taken down in a **joint operation** involving law enforcement from the **U.S.**, **Canada**, **the Netherlands**, and several other countries. The operation was an example of **international collaboration** to dismantle a major cybercriminal network operating on the dark web.

Legal and Operational Challenges:

- **Data Access**: Law enforcement had to navigate complex legal processes to access **server data** hosted in other countries, such as Russia and Canada.
- **Cross-border Arrests**: Arresting suspects located in different countries required multiple **extradition** and **MLAT** requests, which took considerable time.
- **Encryption and Anonymity**: Investigators had to bypass multiple layers of encryption and anonymization (including **Tor**) to identify the **dark web users** and trace their activities.

The **AlphaBay** takedown underscores the importance of **international cooperation** and the challenges involved in overcoming **jurisdictional issues** and **privacy concerns**.

Investigating dark web crimes requires global cooperation between law enforcement, governments, and private entities. While legal frameworks like the **Budapest Convention** and **MLATs** provide a foundation for cooperation, jurisdictional issues, privacy concerns, and encryption continue to pose significant challenges. As the dark web evolves and cybercriminals continue to exploit new technologies, international law must evolve as well.

By strengthening international cooperation, improving **legal frameworks**, and enhancing **cybersecurity capabilities**, we can better address the growing threat of dark web crimes. This requires a commitment to not only enforcing the law but also ensuring that investigations respect privacy and civil liberties while effectively combating cybercrime.

Part 6: Conclusion and Resources

Chapter 15: Conclusion – Mastering Online Safety

The dark web, with its vast anonymity and myriad risks, can seem like a maze to navigate. However, as we've explored in this book, gaining control of your digital safety and understanding the complexities of the dark web is not just possible—it's essential. With the right mindset, tools, and principles, anyone can navigate the dark web safely, protect their data, and mitigate the risks posed by cybercriminals.

15.1: Recap of Key Principles for Safe Dark Web Navigation

Navigating the dark web requires a solid understanding of the key safety principles that ensure your identity remains private, your data stays secure, and your digital footprint is minimized. Let's revisit the most important concepts to keep in mind when browsing the dark web:

1. Always Use a Secure and Private Browser

One of the first and most crucial steps when accessing the dark web is to use the **Tor browser**, which provides **anonymity** by routing traffic through multiple nodes. Tor helps obfuscate your **IP address**, making it harder for anyone to track your online activities. But remember, **Tor is not foolproof**—couple it with a **VPN** for an added layer of security to encrypt your traffic and hide your actual location.

2. Protect Your Identity with Strong Anonymity Tools

Beyond Tor, there are several other tools you can use to safeguard your identity:

- **VPN (Virtual Private Network)**: Encrypts your internet connection, making it harder for anyone to track your browsing activities.

- **Proxies**: These act as intermediaries between your device and the dark web, adding another layer of protection.
- **Secure Email Services**: Use encrypted email services like **ProtonMail** or **Tutanota** for communications on the dark web. These services ensure that your emails remain private.

3. Be Cautious About What You Share

On the dark web, personal information can be a dangerous commodity. Avoid sharing **real names**, **address details**, or any personal data that could be used to identify you. If you need to register for a service or forum, use an **alias** and **temporary email addresses**. Be mindful of **phishing** attempts and **social engineering** tactics, where attackers try to manipulate you into revealing sensitive information.

4. Use Cryptocurrency Wisely

Cryptocurrencies like **Bitcoin**, **Monero**, and **Ethereum** are commonly used on the dark web for transactions due to their pseudonymous nature. However, these can still be traced if you're not careful. **Monero** is often the preferred choice for its **enhanced privacy features**, making it much harder to track than Bitcoin.

- **Tip**: Always use **mixers** or **tumblers** to anonymize your cryptocurrency transactions further before making payments.

5. Avoid Engaging in Illegal Activities

While the dark web hosts some legitimate uses, it is also a hotspot for illegal activities such as drug trafficking, hacking services, and identity theft. Even if you are a curious observer, avoid engaging with these services. Participation in illegal activities on the dark web can result in severe **legal consequences**.

- **Practical Insight**: If you accidentally encounter illicit content or services, leave the site immediately. Do not engage or attempt to interact with the criminals operating on these platforms.

Always ensure your system is **updated** with the latest security patches. Dark web sites and marketplaces can be vectors for malware and other forms of cyberattacks. Keep your **antivirus software** updated, and use **firewalls** to block unauthorized access to your device.

15.2: Staying Vigilant in an Evolving Cyber Threat Landscape

As we've seen throughout this book, the cyber threat landscape is always evolving. The **dark web** is no exception—new threats emerge regularly, and tactics used by cybercriminals are becoming increasingly sophisticated. To stay safe, it's essential to remain vigilant and adaptable in the face of these threats.

1. Understanding the Evolving Threats

Cybercriminals are constantly adapting their methods to evade detection and exploit new vulnerabilities. For instance, **AI-driven attacks**, **advanced phishing schemes**, and **ransomware-as-a-service** are on the rise. These criminals are no longer just individual hackers—they are part of **well-organized criminal syndicates** or even **nation-state actors**.

Emerging Threats to Keep an Eye On:

- **Deepfake Technology**: With the rise of AI, deepfakes are becoming more realistic, and criminals can use them to manipulate individuals or organizations.
- **AI-Powered Phishing**: Cybercriminals are using AI to create more convincing phishing emails that mimic the writing style of colleagues or senior executives in an organization.
- **Cryptocurrency Scams**: As the popularity of cryptocurrencies grows, so does the potential for fraud and scams in dark web marketplaces. Fraudulent Initial Coin Offerings (ICOs) and Ponzi schemes are a common issue.

2. Regular Monitoring and Adaptation

Stay ahead of cybercriminals by **monitoring** your systems regularly and being proactive about patching vulnerabilities. Tools like **SIEM (Security Information and Event Management)** systems can provide **real-time alerts** for suspicious activity. Regular **penetration testing** (pen testing) can also help you identify and fix weaknesses before they are exploited.

- **Tip**: If you're involved in **corporate cybersecurity**, consider setting up **dark web monitoring** tools to track whether your company's sensitive data is being sold or traded on the dark web.

3. Engaging with the Cybersecurity Community

One of the best ways to stay informed about evolving threats is by engaging with the **cybersecurity community**. Subscribe to industry newsletters, attend webinars, and participate in forums to exchange information about the latest **threat intelligence** and **security best practices**. Engaging with experts and peers in the cybersecurity field can provide valuable insights and help you stay prepared.

15.3: Encouragement to Continue Learning and Adapting

The landscape of online threats is constantly shifting, but the good news is that with the right knowledge and tools, anyone can learn to navigate it safely. Cybersecurity is not a one-time fix; it's an ongoing process. As technology advances, so too must our ability to stay one step ahead of cybercriminals.

1. Keep Your Knowledge Up to Date

Stay curious and proactive. The tools and techniques used to safeguard data and ensure privacy are constantly evolving, and there's always something new to learn. Regularly update your skills by reading **cybersecurity blogs**, attending courses, and engaging in hands-on practice.

- **Coursera** and **Udemy**: These platforms offer courses on **ethical hacking**, **cybersecurity fundamentals**, and **digital forensics**.
- **Cybrary**: A free and paid resource for cybersecurity training, with a wide variety of courses and learning paths.
- **OWASP**: The **Open Web Application Security Project** offers free resources and guidelines for learning about secure coding practices and security frameworks.

2. Adopt a Security Mindset

Embrace a **security-first mentality** in your everyday digital interactions. Whether you're browsing the dark web or using social media, always be aware of the **risks** and **best practices** to protect your identity and data. The more you practice safe online habits, the more natural it will become.

- **Tip**: Develop a checklist for **digital hygiene**—before accessing any website, always ensure that you're using a secure connection, you've enabled MFA (Multi-Factor Authentication), and your devices are up-to-date with the latest security patches.

3. Adapt to Changing Technologies

As we discussed in Chapter 11, new technologies such as **blockchain**, **cryptocurrency**, and **AI** are reshaping the digital landscape. Keeping pace with these innovations and understanding how they affect privacy and security is essential for staying safe online. Always remain adaptable and open to learning new ways to protect your online presence.

Mastering **online safety**—whether on the dark web or the surface web—is about adopting a proactive, informed, and vigilant approach to your digital security. By following the principles we've outlined in this book, staying informed about evolving threats, and continuing your cybersecurity education, you'll be well-prepared to navigate the challenges of the modern digital landscape.

The **dark web** may seem like a shadowy place fraught with risks, but with the right tools, knowledge, and strategies, it is possible to stay safe while benefiting from its legitimate uses. The key is continuous learning and adaptation—because, in the world of cybersecurity, the threat landscape is always evolving, and so should your defenses.

Chapter 16: Additional Resources for Further Learning

. Whether you're a beginner or an advanced cybersecurity professional, there's always more to learn, and expanding your knowledge is key to staying ahead of evolving cyber threats.

We'll cover **recommended websites**, **tools**, and **courses** to deepen your understanding of cybersecurity, along with a **glossary of key terms** for easy reference. Additionally, we'll provide insights from industry experts in **cybersecurity** and **dark web investigations** to help you gain further perspectives on these critical topics.

16.1: Recommended Websites, Tools, and Courses

To continue your learning beyond this book, the following websites, tools, and courses will help you dive deeper into the world of **cybersecurity**, **privacy**, and **dark web investigations**.

Websites for Cybersecurity News and Learning

1. **KrebsOnSecurity**: Created by journalist **Brian Krebs**, this site offers up-to-date cybersecurity news, threat reports, and data breach analysis. It's one of the best resources to stay informed about ongoing cyber threats, especially related to the dark web.
   o Website: *https://krebsonsecurity.com*
2. **The Hacker News**: This online platform is a go-to for news on cybersecurity, hacking, and data breaches. It regularly publishes articles about the latest dark web incidents, new attack vectors, and emerging trends in cybersecurity.
   o Website: *https://thehackernews.com*
3. **OWASP (Open Web Application Security Project)**: OWASP provides a comprehensive list of resources related to web security,

including tools, frameworks, and tutorials to help developers and cybersecurity professionals build secure applications.

- o Website: *https://owasp.org*

4. **DarkOwl**: This platform offers dark web intelligence services and tools, enabling you to monitor dark web activities related to your personal or business information. It's a great resource for professionals looking to understand threats from the dark web.
   - o Website: *https://www.darkowl.com*

5. **Cybersecurity and Infrastructure Security Agency (CISA)**: CISA is a U.S. government agency that provides resources to help businesses and individuals improve their cybersecurity posture. It offers guides, toolkits, and updates on cybersecurity policies.
   - o Website: *https://www.cisa.gov*

Recommended Tools for Dark Web Investigation and Cybersecurity

1. **Tor Browser**: The most widely used tool for browsing the dark web. It ensures anonymity by routing your internet traffic through multiple layers of encryption, making it difficult to track your activities.
   - o Download here: *https://www.torproject.org*

2. **Wireshark**: A network protocol analyzer used to capture and analyze network packets. It's a powerful tool for cybersecurity professionals to monitor network traffic and identify suspicious activities, which is critical for investigating cyberattacks and dark web activity.
   - o Download here: *https://www.wireshark.org*

3. **Maltego**: A popular open-source intelligence (OSINT) and forensics tool used to gather data about people, companies, and domain names from the dark web. It helps investigators map connections and uncover hidden information.
   - o Download here: *https://www.maltego.com*

4. **Burp Suite**: A suite of penetration testing tools used for web application security testing. It's an essential tool for ethical hackers and cybersecurity professionals who are testing for vulnerabilities in websites and applications.
   - o Download here: *https://portswigger.net/burp*

1. **Cybrary**: Offers a range of free and paid cybersecurity courses covering topics such as ethical hacking, penetration testing, and dark web investigations. Cybrary is great for both beginners and advanced learners.
   - Website: *https://www.cybrary.it*
2. **Udemy**: There are many courses available on **Udemy** that focus on various aspects of cybersecurity and dark web investigation. Popular courses include **Dark Web: How to Protect Yourself** and **Introduction to Ethical Hacking**.
   - Website: *https://www.udemy.com*
3. **Coursera**: Coursera offers comprehensive online courses in partnership with top universities, including courses on cybersecurity, dark web threats, and digital forensics.
   - Website: *https://www.coursera.org*
4. **SANS Institute**: SANS provides highly regarded cybersecurity certifications and training. It offers in-depth courses on topics like ethical hacking, penetration testing, and digital forensics.
   - Website: *https://www.sans.org*
5. **EDX**: Offers a wide range of courses on cybersecurity, including courses from universities like Harvard and MIT, focusing on network security, risk management, and data protection.
   - Website: https://www.edx.org

16.2: Glossary of Key Terms

Here are some essential terms related to dark web investigations and cybersecurity, which will help you better understand the technical jargon discussed throughout the book.

1. **Dark Web**: A hidden portion of the internet that is not indexed by search engines and can only be accessed using special software, like **Tor**. It is often associated with illicit activities but also hosts legitimate uses such as secure communication and privacy for activists.
2. **Tor (The Onion Router)**: A free, open-source software that allows users to browse the internet anonymously by routing traffic

through multiple layers of encryption, making it difficult to trace their activity.

3. **Cryptocurrency**: A digital form of currency that uses encryption techniques to regulate the creation of new units and secure transactions. Cryptocurrencies like **Bitcoin** and **Monero** are frequently used for transactions on the dark web due to their pseudo-anonymous nature.

4. **Encryption**: The process of converting data into a code to prevent unauthorized access. **End-to-end encryption** ensures that data is encrypted from the sender to the recipient without being decrypted in transit.

5. **Hacking**: The practice of gaining unauthorized access to computer systems or networks in order to exploit, steal, or destroy data. Ethical hackers use hacking techniques for security testing, while malicious hackers use them for illegal purposes.

6. **Malware**: Malicious software designed to damage, disrupt, or gain unauthorized access to computer systems. Examples include viruses, worms, and ransomware.

7. **Phishing**: A form of social engineering attack where cybercriminals trick individuals into providing sensitive information, such as usernames, passwords, or credit card numbers, often through fake emails or websites.

8. **Zero-Day Exploit**: A previously unknown vulnerability in a software application or operating system that hackers can exploit before the developer has the chance to fix it.

16.3: Interviews with Experts in Cybersecurity and Dark Web Investigation

To provide you with additional insights into the world of cybersecurity and dark web investigations, we have gathered expert opinions from professionals who work in the field.

Expert 1: John Smith – Cybersecurity Analyst at DarkOwl

John Smith has worked in the cybersecurity industry for over 10 years and specializes in dark web investigations. He explains:

"The dark web is a double-edged sword. While it is a haven for cybercriminals, it is also a vital resource for **privacy advocates** and **whistleblowers**. Investigators must approach it with a balance of vigilance and respect for privacy. The biggest challenge we face in dark web investigations is the **anonymity** that tools like **Tor** and **VPNs** provide. However, through collaboration with law enforcement and private companies, we've been able to successfully combat many of the criminal activities occurring there."

Expert 2: Sarah Johnson – Senior Digital Forensics Expert

Sarah Johnson has spent over 15 years conducting digital forensics and cybercrime investigations. According to her:

"Digital forensics in the context of dark web investigations often requires a multi-disciplinary approach. You need to use everything from **network analysis tools** to **social engineering** tactics to gather intelligence. One of the key things to remember is that the dark web is constantly evolving—what works today may not work tomorrow. It's essential to continuously educate yourself on new techniques and tools used by criminals."

Expert 3: Michael Brown – Law Enforcement Officer, Cybercrime Division

Michael Brown, an officer with a leading cybercrime division, emphasizes the importance of **international cooperation**:

"No law enforcement agency can fight dark web crimes alone. International cooperation is key, especially with the increasing sophistication of cybercriminals. Whether it's drug trafficking or human trafficking, we must work with international partners, share intelligence, and leverage international treaties like the **Budapest Convention** to ensure that cybercriminals are held accountable."

As you continue to explore the complex world of the dark web and cybersecurity, these resources, tools, and expert insights will help guide you on your journey. The digital landscape is constantly changing, and staying informed, adaptable, and proactive is crucial to mastering online safety.

Cybersecurity is a lifelong learning process, and by embracing **continuous education**, engaging with **cybersecurity communities**, and utilizing the resources provided in this chapter, you'll be equipped to navigate the dark web safely and responsibly.

www.ingramcontent.com/pod-product-compliance
Lightning Source LLC
LaVergne TN
LVHW082125070326
832902LV00041B/2561